Jacob Eriksson is a lecturer in Post-war Recovery Studies in the Post-war Reconstruction and Development Unit (PRDU) at the University of York. He holds BA and MA degrees from the War Studies Department at King's College London, and a PhD from the School of Oriental and African Studies (SOAS).

'This work highlights Norway and Sweden, two smaller states, in one of the world's most intractable conflicts, the one between Israel and its neighbours. It is a story about how these states contributed to changes towards a more peaceful future. In particular, Eriksson's work brings forward the lesser-known contributions of Sweden, before and parallel to the process known as "Oslo". It demonstrates that smaller states can do things that are difficult for more powerful actors, but it also points to some of the limits in small state peace diplomacy.'

Peter Wallensteen, Professor of Peace and Conflict Research,
Uppsala University and University of Notre Dame

'Having spent the better part of a professional lifetime in the study of peace through international diplomacy, conflict prevention and conflict mediation, Eriksson's narrative of Sweden's endeavours in the Israeli-Palestinian context is insightful and intriguing. He skilfully highlights not only the possibilities, but also the limitations, of small-state mediation in international conflicts.'

Jan Eliasson, Deputy-Secretary General, The United Nations

SMALL-STATE MEDIATION IN INTERNATIONAL CONFLICTS

Diplomacy and Negotiation in Israel–Palestine

Jacob Eriksson

I.B. TAURIS
LONDON · NEW YORK

Published in 2015 by
I.B.Tauris & Co. Ltd
London • New York
www.ibtauris.com

Library of International Relations 76

ISBN: 978 1 78453 229 1
eISBN: 978 0 85773 911 7

A full CIP record for this book is available from the British Library
A full CIP record is available from the Library of Congress

Library of Congress Catalog Card Number: available

Typeset in Garamond Three by OKS Prepress Services, Chennai, India

For my parents, Bo and Annika, and Emily

CONTENTS

ACKNOWLEDGEMENTS

This book is the product of many years of research, beginning during my MA in the War Studies Department at King's College London. My interest in Sweden and the Israeli–Palestinian peace process then developed into a PhD at the School of Oriental and African Studies in London. These were some of the best years of my life to date, so there are many thanks due to those who were a part of them.

First and foremost, I would like to thank my parents, Bo and Annika, for everything they have given me, including the opportunity to pursue this research. Without their support, neither this book nor my doctorate would have been possible. My father's advice, constructive criticism of earlier drafts, and encouragement throughout the process has been invaluable.

Thanks to a grant from the University of London Central Research Fund I was able to undertake research in Israel, the West Bank, and the USA, in addition to my research in Sweden and the UK. I am deeply indebted to all of my interviewees who took the time to speak with me about their experiences in the peace process and share their analysis of these complex events. Sadly, two interviewees – Amnon Lipkin-Shahak and Ron Pundak – have since passed away. I feel immensely privileged to have met them and discussed their work.

Thank you to Steph, Sam and Reed, Adi and Alain in New York, and Xitij and the Rais in DC. I am eternally grateful to Marc, Yaniv and Ranit in Tel Aviv and Tomer, Merav and Itay in Jerusalem for their friendliness, generosity, and kindness. A big thank you also to Jared for showing me Ramallah for the first time, making subsequent trips that much easier.

Thank you to the archivists at the Swedish Labour Movement Archives and Library in Stockholm and the Liddell Hart Centre for Military Archives at King's College London for their assistance in procuring an awful lot of material, sometimes at short notice. I am also indebted to the Trustees of the Liddell Hart Centre for Military Archives for allowing me to quote from their collections.

Thank you to Professor Colin Shindler, my PhD supervisor, for his advice and guidance over the years, and to Professors Clive Jones and Neil Lochery for their comments as examiners of my doctoral thesis. Thank you also to Dr Ahron Bregman at King's for stimulating my interest in the subject in the first place, and encouraging me to pursue this specific research project. Thanks are also due to Maria Marsh, my editor at I.B.Tauris, for her comments on the manuscript and her help guiding me through the publishing process.

Finally, thank you to my wonderful partner Emily who has been so encouraging and supportive throughout it all. I look forward to our many trips to Israel and, hopefully one day, the state of Palestine to show you these places that I find so fascinating.

Jacob Eriksson
York

A NOTE ON SOURCES AND TRANSLATION

This book is based on a combination of primary sources – original interviews with key negotiators and officials, in addition to new archival research – and analysis of existing secondary sources.

Due to official secrecy restrictions, the archival material which informs this book is not from the official archives of the Ministry of Foreign Affairs, but the personal collection of former Swedish Foreign Minister Sten Andersson. It is a mixture of official documents, press releases, personal correspondence and press cuttings which cover roughly two decades of involvement in the Israeli–Palestinian peace process which Andersson, upon his death in 2006, bequeathed to the archives of the Swedish Social Democratic Party. As such, it is important to note that this is not an exhaustive and complete collection of Foreign Ministry documents from this period, but a selective one. There is no accounting for documents which Andersson himself may have chosen to omit from this collection.

As a result of this lack of official archival material, one of the key primary sources of information are the people themselves, the politicians and negotiators who took part in and shaped the events examined in this book. While most of their contributions are attributed, some contributions remain anonymised at their request. Every effort has been made to piece together an accurate picture of events from multiple sources. Personal recollections have been weighed against each other, against information from archival sources and existing secondary sources, in an attempt to find the most widely corroborated accounts of events. Where accounts differ, I have tried to make this clear and provide the differing perspectives as presented to me in my research. While a number of key figures were unfortunately not available for interview, despite the best efforts of the author, their views have been obtained as far as possible through other interviews and secondary sources.

The book contains numerous translations from Swedish to English – both from original interviews and from archival documents – all of which I have translated myself. Translation is a difficult business. I have tried to translate all expressions and phrases as accurately and faithfully as possible, balancing elements of content, tone, and expression. Swedish Prime Minister Olof Palme's classic statement, '*Politik är att vilja något*', is just one difficult example, rendered here as, 'Politics is to aspire to something'. I feel that this embodies the spirit of the phrase beyond the more direct rendition of 'Politics is to want something'. Others may well disagree and are welcome to, but this is my personal interpretation and understanding. Any errors of translation that appear here are thus mine alone.

INTRODUCTION

On Thursday 22 August 1929, Harry Charles Luke, the acting British high commissioner in Palestine, invited representatives of the Arab Muslim community and the Zionist Organisation to his home in Jerusalem. Tensions between the two peoples were running high following demonstrations by each party at the Western Wall of the Haram al-Sharif or Temple Mount, dual expressions of nationalism to illustrate ownership of this holy site and the wider validity of their claims to the land. Violence began to erupt, and Luke sought to organise a cease fire of sorts, a joint announcement to soothe tensions before the Muslim prayer services the following day. Though ostensibly a conversation between community leaders, Segev writes that 'it was conducted like any diplomatic conference of representatives of two national movements, a summit conference in a sandbox'.[1]

The events of that day have turned into a familiar pattern. The two sides characteristically blamed each other for the situation, arguments ensued about the content and language of a statement, and no agreement was reached.[2] On Friday, the two communities clashed in the Old City of Jerusalem, and the violence then spread to Hebron. According to the British authorities, 133 Jews were killed and 339 were injured; 116 Arabs were killed and 232 were injured, mainly at the hands of the British. Luke had felt that war was predestined, that there was no point in the dialogue between Jews and Arabs that he initiated, 'but at least Luke could tell himself, as everyone else did, that he had done his best'. Despite his failure, Segev asserts that 'Luke deserves to be remembered as the first peacemaker in the history of the Israeli–Palestinian conflict.'[3]

Like Luke, many others have tried and failed, their stories often a scrambled version of that first effort. UN mediator Gunnar Jarring and US Secretary of State William Rogers each unsuccessfully tried to broker agreements to implement UN Security Council Resolution 242 prior to the 1973 Arab–Israeli war. US President Jimmy Carter initially strove to reach an all-encompassing Arab–Israeli peace which included the Israeli–Palestinian conflict, but tempered his ambitions in the face of a difficult reality and settled for a separate Israeli–Egyptian accord. In recent decades when Palestinians have represented themselves at the negotiating table with Israel, there have been numerous sets of official and unofficial negotiations, conferences and high-level summits. Throughout this time, a number of different mediators have been involved, with few glimpses of success amidst a wider backdrop of overall failure.

This record suggests that unfavourable conflict characteristics are likely to defeat even the most skillful mediators.[4] If the parties are not ready to make compromises and move from a zero-sum to a cooperative win-win dynamic, then a mediator will struggle to produce an agreement. It is going too far, however, to suggest that the characteristics and tactics of a mediator are marginal in the outcome of mediation.[5] While it is true that the nature and context of the conflict are the most decisive variables in determining the outcome of mediation, the nature of the mediator and the mediation strategy pursued are nonetheless critical.

Jacob Bercovitch, a prominent conflict resolution scholar, identifies four main components of mediation: a mediator; at least two conflicting parties; a strategy of mediation; and the context of the conflict within which mediation occurs. The interaction between these elements determines the nature, quality, and effectiveness of any mediation process.[6] This is a complicated matrix of interests, political calculations, and value judgements which all parties feed into, and where all components matter. Fundamentally, a successful mediator must apply an appropriate strategy at a particular stage of the conflict, and their role must be predicated on a rigorous analysis of their suitability, capabilities, and what the context calls for.

This book pays particular attention to the nature of the mediator, but also the strategy pursued and the relevance of certain strategies to certain types of conflict. Although conventional wisdom suggests that a superpower like the United States should be the third party at the helm of negotiations, the fact is they have proved 'unfailingly inept at launching successful initiatives' in the realm of Israeli–Palestinian peace.[7] A number of significant breakthroughs and positive developments have taken place, but the United States has not been directly involved in any of them. This book shows that much more discrete mediators like Norway and Sweden have been at the heart of these efforts. Though bereft of coercive power, these two Scandinavian countries have made substantial contributions to the quest for peace. American negotiator Aaron Miller has referred to these nations as the 'guardian angels of the peace process', and Israeli academic and negotiator Ron Pundak similarly has acknowledged that 'if ever peace will be achieved, the contribution of these two countries is huge'.[8]

Small states are traditionally accepted as mediators due to their non-threatening political posture; they do not normally have the capability to directly threaten the security of the parties, or otherwise coerce them into an agreement. Instead, they tend to use tools of moral and intellectual persuasion to their advantage. Their position within the international system is often a criteria used to deem them suitable, often characterised by existing reputations for skilled diplomacy, regional expertise, or impartiality, based on a history of finely tuned diplomatic relationships. Norway and Sweden are prime examples of this.

In order to contribute effectively to the resolution of a conflict, a mediator must possess a high level of understanding about the fundamental nature and character of the dispute. They must 'know the file'; they must be knowledgeable about the conflict, its roots, its historical progression, the major issues at stake, and any cultural sensitivities of the parties. When former Swedish Prime Minister Olof Palme was appointed the UN Secretary General's special representative to Iran and Iraq in November 1980, he made reading of the Qur'an compulsory for his staff, together with other works on Islamic culture.[9]

A great respect for history, culture and religion was not just a manifestation of his personal attitude towards people and the mediation mission, but also a way to create trust and confidence in a mediator during the negotiations. These attributes are central to success, and can stem from a variety of different factors,[10] including both personal and institutional relationships. For small states, impartiality is often the key ingredient, and is characterised by a lack of vested interest in either side benefiting more than the other from an agreement.[11]

However, it is not always a defining characteristic. A mediator with an affinity for one side can potentially exercise a certain degree of influence over them and can be useful to the opposing party if it means the third party can convince them to make concessions.[12] Other characteristics, such as power, can make a third party attractive. In an asymmetric conflict like that between Israel and the Palestinians, a third party can be an important asset for the weaker party.[13] In other Arab–Israeli negotiations, Arab interest in improving relations with the United States made them a valuable mediator.[14] Disputants will submit to mediation only when they believe that the mediator can act fairly and recognise the importance of their interests.[15]

A mediation strategy is the approach or method adopted by a mediator, which primarily involves how they manage the interaction of the parties, and how they engage with the issues under negotiation.[16] Sheppard's categorisation of mediator behaviour is a model prevalent in conflict resolution literature, and involves three strategies: (a) communication-facilitation, (b) formulation, and (c) manipulation.[17]

First, there is the role of 'facilitator', where the mediator serves primarily as a channel of communication between the two parties. These duties range from arranging interactions between the parties, helping them gain trust and confidence in the goodwill of the other, to communicating messages between the two parties. In this case, the main challenge for the mediator is to develop a rapport between the two parties in order to create and maintain a dialogue that is productive and focused by clearly identifying issues and points of contention. It is important to encourage communication between the parties in order for them to be able to discuss all of their interests, and to develop a framework for a mutual understanding. There is, however, no substantive contribution to the negotiations themselves.

Second, similar to the role of facilitator but slightly more involved, is the role of 'formulator'. Here, the mediator performs the same roles as a facilitator, but exercises a greater degree of control over the meetings in terms of their pace, formality, protocol and procedures, and the physical environment they are set in. A formulator continues to develop the relationship between the parties, but can also make some substantive suggestions or proposals.[18]

Third, there is the role of the 'manipulator'. This role is much more involved in the actual detailed content of the dispute. Such a strategy allows the mediator to put forth suggestions or proposals for solutions, help change the parties' expectations, and take responsibility for concessions that could otherwise be unpopular with respective domestic audiences. It is a coercive strategy, in that the mediator often uses power and leverage to guide the negotiations by, for example, pressuring the parties to be flexible, rewarding concessions by promising resources, offering to verify compliance with any agreement, or threatening to withdraw from the process. Essentially, the mediator offers 'carrots' or 'sticks' to the parties; it can offer incentives to encourage co-operation and compliance, while also punishing intransigence and making clear what the cost of a non-agreement would be.

A comparative study of different mediation strategies and their effects on crisis outcomes by Beardsley *et al.* offers interesting results. Using a database of international crises that took place between 1918 and 2001 compiled by the International Crisis Behaviour project, Beardsley and his associates have statistically examined the use of these three strategies. They determine the predominant strategy used in different circumstances, and the outcome. For a reduction of tensions, a facilitative strategy was the most effective, followed by a formulative; a manipulative strategy proved to help only slightly. Facilitation also proved the best strategy to achieve a reduction in post-crisis tension, but in the case of protracted conflict this is naturally much more difficult to achieve. When pursuing a formal agreement, a manipulative strategy proved to be the most effective.[19]

Based on their results, they draw other conclusions that are highly relevant to this analysis. First, different strategies used with varying degrees of intensity seem to be required to yield results. Mediation is not as effective when only one style is used, therefore a balance of strategies should be undertaken in order to maximise the effectiveness of each in turn. Second, the most durable agreements are the ones reached with as little outside help as possible. An intrusive style can create a passive stance on behalf of the parties, when what they need the most is to both have a sense of ownership over any agreement.[20]

As a process of cultivating greater understanding between the parties, facilitation is sometimes separated from mediation and referred to as pre-negotiation.[21] The term 'pre-negotiation' is problematic in a sense, since this phase can in itself sometimes require negotiation and third-party mediation in a variety of forms, as the case studies examined in this book will demonstrate. While pre-negotiation and negotiation are theoretically distinguishable, it is not always easy to draw a line between them in practice.

This is evident in the practice of 'Track II diplomacy', a concept based on a distinction between two levels of interaction: one official, formal and public known as Track I, and another informal and clandestine known as Track II. Track II talks are discussions held by non-officials of conflicting parties who attempt to clarify outstanding disputes and to explore the options for resolving them under circumstances that are less sensitive than those associated with official negotiations.[22] In such unofficial and more informal settings, concerns, limits, priorities, and possible solutions can be creatively and honestly explored without commitment from either party, thereby preparing the ground for official negotiations.[23]

Though Track II talks are unofficial, the participants must have relations to officials in decision-making circles in order to communicate their impressions and conclusions, thereby making the task potentially politically significant. These 'mentors', or the high level political leaders who supervise the talks, must consider it a useful exercise and devote time and energy to its organisation or monitoring.[24] Should the talks produce valuable formulas or other useful results, these can then be fed into official negotiations. Using non-officials as the primary interlocutors helps ensure that secrecy is maintained, as their movements are subject to less scrutiny than government officials, and additionally provides an important cloak of deniability should the talks be exposed.

To exclude facilitation and Track II diplomacy from the classification of mediation would be to grossly underestimate its importance in the development of a peace process, and would be an injustice to the mediators who undertake it. Rather, one should acknowledge the efforts made by all actors in the intricate process of conflict resolution. Bercovitch comprehensively encapsulates all relevant components when he defines mediation as

> a process of conflict management, related to but distinct from the parties' own efforts, where the disputing parties or their representatives seek the assistance, or accept an offer of help, from an individual, group, state or organization to change, affect

> or influence their perceptions or behaviour, without resorting to physical force or invoking the authority of the law.[25]

The strength of this interpretation is that it acknowledges the wide variety of possible mediators and strategies that they can employ, while making no assumptions as to the goals or expected results of a mediation attempt. Crucially, not all instances of mediation or mediation strategies are geared towards completely resolving a conflict in one fell swoop, as this is often extremely demanding and unrealistic in intractable conflicts. Success can thus not necessarily be defined by whether or not an agreement is reached. Success and failure are 'construed rather than discovered', and rely on 'idiosyncratic values, interpretations and labelling, like many other concepts in the social sciences'.[26] Given the very subjective nature of the concept, success needs to be considered from a variety of angles, including but not limited to the objectives of the mediator, negotiators, and the parties.

In the realm of Scandinavian mediators, most emphasis has been placed on Norway rather than their easterly neighbour. While there is no doubt that the Norwegian contribution in the form of the Oslo Agreement was momentous, it did not take place in a vacuum. This book focuses on the contributions of Sweden as a small-state mediator in the Israeli–Palestinian conflict. Despite having repeatedly been involved in important aspects of the peace process over more than a decade, Sweden's role has not been authoritatively or comprehensively analysed by Swedish or international researchers. Studies by Bjereld and Carmesund[27] have examined Swedish policy toward Israel, Palestine, and the wider Middle East, but these have not focused on the Swedish role as a mediator.

Existing Swedish scholarship on the case studies examined here is extremely limited.[28] Though aspects of each have been scrutinised by a multitude of international scholars, this has not been from a Swedish perspective. Crucially, an examination of the change and continuity of aspects of Swedish mediation over time does not exist, nor does a comparative analysis between Sweden and other mediators. This book aims to fill in these gaps.

Just as a mediator must 'know the file', any analysis of conflict resolution requires an understanding of the conflict itself. The book thus begins by exploring the nature of the Israeli–Palestinian conflict. What type of conflict is it? What are the underlying issues in dispute? Why has it proved so difficult to resolve? It examines the historical narratives of each party and how these have become entrenched over time. It also considers the mutual and individual challenges that Israeli and Palestinian society still face, despite the considerable progress of the last 20-odd years, in order to fully reconfigure the conflict situation.

As the primary mediator studied in this book, the second chapter examines the historical development of Swedish foreign policy towards Israel and the Palestinians, and the effects of this policy on the Swedish capacity to act as a mediator in the conflict. Over the course of the twentieth century, attitudes towards the two conflicting parties have changed considerably, particularly within the traditionally dominant Social Democratic party. This chapter looks to dispel certain myths and misconceptions about Social Democratic foreign policy as being anti-Semitic or anti-Israeli by looking more holistically at its wider development and the values that underpinned it.

The third, fourth, and fifth chapters deal with individual case studies, including: the initiation of dialogue between the United States and the Palestine Liberation Organisation (PLO) in 1988; the process behind the 'Beilin–Abu Mazen Understandings' of 1995, also known as the 'Stockholm document'; and the 'Stockholm channel' of May 2000 that preceded the failed Camp David summit. The origin, progression, and result of each initiative is discussed and dissected. Were the correct strategies pursued to deal with the particularities of the Israeli–Palestinian conflict?

Each case is also considered in the wider context of the peace process and the events surrounding it. Swedish efforts are compared with those of different mediators who also operated during the periods in question, specifically the Oslo channel sponsored by Norway and the continuous but varied involvement of the United States. The book will consider the differences and similarities in the nature of these mediators and their strategies at various stages of the peace process, the successes and failures of their undertakings, the relationship between the different mediators and the links between the processes they set in motion. It shows how Norway and Sweden have, as individual states and as collaborative Social Democratic partners, effectively encouraged dialogue and negotiations between Israelis and Palestinians who decided to take concerted steps towards a peaceful resolution of their conflict.

This book does not purport to contain a magic formula for future mediators. Rather, it offers observations on the utility of small-state mediation in the Israeli–Palestinian conflict and beyond, its limitations, and the potential of multiparty mediation. It makes a number of suggestions based on the historical record, but also asks as many difficult questions as it answers. In doing so, it hopes to make at least a modest contribution to the wider study of the pursuit of peace, a goal that remains as elusive as ever.

CHAPTER 1

THE ISRAELI–PALESTINIAN CONFLICT: COMPETING NATIONAL NARRATIVES AND THE ETERNAL 'RASHOMON EFFECT'[1]

Arab and Jewish designs for the future of Palestine are diametrically opposed, and they were not at all interested in discussing compromises.
– Count Folke Bernadotte[2]

The passions aroused by Palestine have done so much to obscure the truth that the facts have become enveloped in a mist of sentiment, legend and propaganda, which acts as a smoke-screen of almost impenetrable density ... the most formidable obstacle to an understanding, and therefore to a solution, of the Palestine problem lies not so much in its inherent complexity as in the solid jungle of legend and propaganda which has grown up around it.
– George Antonius[3]

Do you know what astonished me most in the world? The inability of force to create anything. In the long run the sword is always beaten by the spirit.
– Napoleon Bonaparte[4]

The Israeli–Palestinian conflict is not just a conflict about land, nor is it a conflict purely about religion. While these are important parts of the dispute, this is a wider conflict about people, memory, politics, and self-determination. Israeli novelist Amos Oz expresses the problem quite well:

> It is not a struggle between good and evil, rather it is a tragedy in the ancient and most precise sense of the word: a clash between right and right, a clash between one very powerful, deep, and convincing claim, and another very different but no less convincing, no less powerful, no less humane claim.[5]

Such an understanding, however, is not widely shared among either side in the conflict. Lowenthal's assessment is perhaps more accurate:

> We confront one another armoured in identities whose likenesses we ignore or disown and whose differences we distort or invent to emphasise our own superior worth. Lauding our own legacies and excluding or discrediting those of others, we commit ourselves to endemic rivalry and conflict.[6]

This chapter outlines these two competing claims and identities, analysing how the parties frame and understand themselves, the 'other', and their conflict, focusing on a number of key themes such as victimhood, martyrology, and the construction of nationalism.

On 8 December 1987, four Palestinians were killed in a car crash with an Israeli vehicle at the Erez crossing between Israel and the Gaza Strip. In the eyes of many Palestinians, the incident was an act of deliberate vengeance for the murder of an Israeli in Gaza a few days before. Rioting ensued in the Jabaliya refugee camp, Palestinians clashed with the Israel Defence Forces (IDF), and the violence spread to other parts of the Gaza Strip and on to the West Bank. This was the trigger of the first Palestinian *intifada*, or 'uprising'. The fact that most other observers, international and Israeli, believed that the collision was merely an unfortunate accident was quickly rendered academic. The *intifada* swiftly gathered incredible momentum, feeding off the bitterness and resentment that had been building up among Palestinians for decades, and the results changed Palestinian society, their image among the international community, and their relationship with their Israeli occupiers forever.

The eruption of the second *intifada* also remains mired in a fog of competing perceptions. When Likud leader Ariel Sharon visited the

Temple Mount, or Haram al-Sharif, on 28 September 2000, accompanied by hundreds of Israeli bodyguards and police officers, it was primarily a campaign tactic for the upcoming Israeli elections. He sought to exhibit symbolic Israeli sovereignty over the Jewish holy sites in the Old City of Jerusalem, and his personal commitment to their retention in any future peace agreement. It was a political demonstration against Prime Minister Ehud Barak and his offer at Camp David a few months earlier to divide Jerusalem with the Palestinians. Barak has explained that Sharon 'wanted to show the extremists in Israel that he is faithful to the Temple Mount, as opposed to Barak who is willing to discuss [and] negotiate, and they of course exaggerated what we would be willing to negotiate'.[7]

Such a large Jewish presence at the third holiest site in Islam was perceived by the Palestinians as a deliberate provocation. The following day, Palestinian riots in and around the Old City led to violent clashes with Israeli police, leaving seven Palestinians dead, some 300 wounded, and 70 Israeli policemen injured. Over the next week, violence escalated drastically and spread throughout the West Bank and Gaza Strip.

The official position of the Israeli Ministry of Foreign Affairs is that Palestinian leader Yasser Arafat and the Palestinian Authority (PA) had given up on the peace process and made a strategic choice to return to violence. Israeli intelligence sources claim to have proof of a calculated beginning to the riots traced back to PA ministers and Arafat himself.[8] Palestinians viewed the *al-Aqsa intifada*, as it came to be known, as the natural product of a combination of factors: years of frustration with a peace process that was not delivering an end to the occupation; Sharon's inflammatory visit; and the repressive Israeli military reaction to Palestinian protests the following day.[9]

Coined by the film directed by Akira Kurosawa, the term 'Rashomon' commonly refers to the impact of subjectivity on memory. The plot revolves around four characters who provide wildly differing versions of the same events. Though not espoused as the definitive truth, the account of the woodcutter – an eyewitness not directly involved in the events – is implied to be the most accurate. As *Rashomon* illustrates, authoritative history is never straightforward, since the absolute truth behind events is hard to ascertain amid competing accounts. One can argue that objective, precise, and truthful history should be the ultimate goal of the historian, accurately describing exactly what happened and why. Whether or not this is possible is another matter.

In his work on *lieux de mémoire* ('sites of memory'), Nora makes a clear distinction between memory and history:

> Memory is life, borne by living societies founded in its name. It remains in permanent evolution, open to the dialectic of remembering and forgetting, unconscious of its successive deformations, vulnerable to manipulation and appropriation, susceptible to being long dormant and periodically revived. History, on the other hand, is the reconstruction, always problematic and incomplete, of what is no longer. Memory is a perpetually actual phenomenon, a bond tying us to the eternal present; history is a representation of the past. Memory, insofar as it is affective and magical, only accommodates those facts that suit it; it nourishes recollections that may be out of focus or telescopic, global or detached, particular or symbolic – responsive to each avenue of conveyance or phenomenal screen, to every censorship or projection. History, because it is an intellectual and secular production, calls for analysis and criticism.[10]

Halbwachs too draws a clear line between memory and history. Collective memory, he argues, is a social construction determining 'how members of society remember and interpret events, how the meaning of the past is constructed, and how it is modified over time'.[11] Individuals become socialised into a collective memory through collective social frameworks that are 'the instruments used by the collective memory to reconstruct an image of the past which is in accord, in each epoch, with the predominant thoughts of the society'.[12] In his seminal work *On Collective Memory*, Halbwachs posits that historians, using 'historical memory', tend to deviate from the accepted values of collective memory.[13] Nora further elaborates upon this distinction:

> Memory is blind to all but the group it binds – which is to say, as Maurice Halbwachs has said, that there are as many memories as there are groups, that memory is by nature multiple and yet specific; collective, plural, and yet individual. History, on the

> other hand, belongs to everyone and to no one, whence its claim to universal authority ... History's procurement, in the last century, of scientific methodology has only intensified the effort to establish critically a 'true' memory.[14]

Lowenthal similarly differentiates between the two, though using the concept of 'heritage' rather than memory: 'To serve as a collective symbol heritage must be widely accepted by insiders, yet inaccessible to outsiders. Its data are social, not scientific. Socially binding traditions must be accepted on faith, not by reasoning. Heritage thus defies empirical analysis; it features fantasy, invention, mystery, error.'[15]

Khalili argues that these distinctions are problematic and hyperbolic. To approach memory and history as 'popular' and 'intellectual' respectively 'ignores the mutual imbrication of these two categories of narratives and dehistoricises and sanctifies an object called memory'.[16] Zerubavel also observes this difficulty while adopting a more nuanced approach, acknowledging both the conflict and interdependence which exists between the two terms.[17] Litvak similarly criticises the 'rather crude positivist approach' of Halbwachs and Nora, pointing out that they disregard the impact of the society's collective memory on the historian. Historians are, after all, often actively engaged in shaping collective memory and national identity.[18]

Indeed, these two mutually dependent concepts, identity and collective memory, conjoin the past and the present and are readily adaptable to serve particular interests. Halbwachs contends that 'it is in society that people normally acquire ... recall, recognise and localise their memories', and that societal groups provide the means to reconstruct memory and adapt individuals to a way of thinking. In other words, identity is dependent upon the constant construction and reconstruction of one's memory in concert with the collective memory. Each group is free to evoke and 'choose from the past the period into which we wish to immerse ourselves ... If certain memories are inconvenient or burden us, we can always oppose them the sense of reality inseparable from our present life.'[19]

Gillis too reminds us that 'memories and identities are not fixed things, but representations or constructions of reality, subjective rather than objective phenomena ... we are constantly revising our memories to suit our current identities'.[20] Useful memories are confirmed by the collective and others can be neglected as deemed appropriate. Lowenthal observes that 'for all but amnesiacs, heritage distils the past into icons of identity, bonding us with precursors and progenitors, with our own earlier selves, and with our promised successors'.[21]

Zertal holds a similar view, describing collective memory as 'a social reality, a political, cultural product that takes shape within the system of social, political variables, and interests of a given community'.[22] Mead, a contemporary of Halbwachs', similarly put forth the notion of a 'symbolically reconstructed past', which entails 'redefining the meaning of past events in such a way that they have meaning in and utility for the present'.[23] Lassner and Troen express the nationalist application of this principle eloquently when they suggest that 'it is as though modern nation builders throw stones into the troubled waters of history and create with each toss perfectly concentric circles'.[24] On the basis of his earlier dichotomy, Lowenthal states that 'history co-opted by heritage exaggerates or denies accepted fact to assert a primacy, an ancestry, a continuity. It underwrites a founding myth meant to exclude others.'[25]

Collective memory and identity are the handmaidens of modern nationalism, codified and expressed in national narratives. Kacowicz refers to narrative as 'a fundamental way of organising human experience and explaining human behaviour, and as a tool for constructing models of reality'. They 'embody explanations, though they also mobilise the mythology of their times, mixing literary tropes, notions of morality, and causal reasoning in efforts both to justify and to explain events', thereby rationalising or legitimising the present.[26]

Both Israelis and Palestinians have over time developed an identity and a narrative that justifies and legitimises their respective claims to the land known as Palestine, while rejecting those of the other as artificial and illegitimate. Questions of territory, sovereignty, and security cannot be separated from religion, ideology, or culture, rendering the conflict immensely difficult to resolve. When national identities and claims of self-determination collide, they often result in an intractable identity-based conflict, where 'one group's sense of identity seems to deny the reality or legitimacy of the other group's identity'.[27] As Kelman explains, 'each perceives the very existence of the other – the other's status as a nation – to be a threat to its own existence and status as a nation ... *They* can acquire national identity and rights only at the expense of *our* identity and rights.'[28] Thus, any acknowledgement of the other weakens one's own claim.[29]

Such a situation where the existence of one denies the existence of the other is known as a zero-sum conflict, where there is victory or defeat, but no middle ground. It is difficult to overstate the significance of the zero-sum perception and its role in the perpetuation of conflict. 'Fulfillment of the other's national identity is experienced as equivalent to destruction of one's own identity'; this is symptomatic of what Kelman calls 'negative interdependence'.[30] What emerges is 'a suicidal cohabitation between two equally determined protagonists engaged in a merciless and hard zero-sum struggle for security and, indeed, for life'.[31] Each group believes that its destruction is inherent in the ideology of the other, and so success for one automatically means disaster for the other.

Consequently, a security dilemma exists where each party's efforts to increase its own security actively reduces the security of the other. In line with Wendt's classic constructivist work,[32] behaviour under a security dilemma is not only influenced by 'the participants' perception of that situation', but also by 'their expectations of each others' likely behaviour in that situation'.[33] Acrimonious interaction resulting from the basic incompatibility of the two identities and their maximalist claims has left important imprints upon social attitudes, and greatly influenced the development of Israeli and Palestinian national narratives.

Conversely, narratives significantly shape social attitudes and behaviour towards the other and can therefore prolong conflict. Bar-Tal and Salomon have identified four main themes within conflict narratives that are relevant in this regard.[34] First, the outbreak of the conflict is justified with reference to the existential importance of the conflicting goals. Those of the other are considered unjustified and unreasonable. Second, the acts, traits, or values of one's own group are always presented in a positive light. Third, while parties engage in self-justification, self-glorification, and self-praise, they simultaneously demonise, dehumanise and delegitimise their opponent. Responsibility for the conflict lies squarely at the feet of the other who, in the course of the conflict, acts in a cruel, immoral, and vicious manner. It is their intransigence and irrationality that stand as the most significant impediment to a resolution of the conflict.[35]

Fourth, as a corollary of the previous themes, one's own group is always presented as a victim. The conflict and all the suffering it elicits is seen as having been imposed on the righteous self by the evil adversary, whose ultimate goal is the destruction of one's own group. Such a self-perception has the effect of legitimising one's violent actions towards the other. Viewed in such immutable terms, cycles of retaliatory violence create a destructive self-fulfilling prophecy for both parties.

In the process of constructing their respective identities and narratives, both Israelis and Palestinians have employed such arguments and reasoning. Despite their best efforts to portray their historical experience as unique and unparalleled, the two in fact share many parallel experiences and have adopted similar strategies to address them.[36]

Justifications of statehood

The Jewish narrative is one of persecution and redemption following the return to the ancestral homeland of *Eretz Israel* (the Land of Israel) after 2,000 years of exile. Jewish claims to the land stem from passages of the first book of the Bible, Genesis, where God promised the land of modern day Palestine to Hebrew patriarch Abraham and his progeny, Isaac and Jacob.[37] This covenant is said to be unconditional, literal and everlasting. This purportedly unique relationship with God has created a sense of exclusiveness, a notion that the Israelites were chosen by the Almighty to prevail among all other people.

Moses, Joshua, King David and his son Solomon are all prominent figures in ancient Jewish foundational myth.[38] The Temple Mount within the Old City of Jerusalem is the site of two destroyed Jewish temples from that period, the second during the Roman War of 66–70 CE Of the Second Temple, only a segment of the Western Wall remains, and it is the holiest site of prayer in Judaism. It also serves as an important reminder of Jewish eviction and displacement at the hands of the Romans.

As a diaspora community, this mythological biblical history has long been of vital importance to the continued existence of Jewish identity. Their survival as a people has depended on the retention of these foundational myths, which have functioned as a metahistory of remembrance but also instilled the hope of future redemption. The biblical accounts of this period 'linking Israel the people and Israel the land to each other and to the one and only God of Israel has given every generation of Jews a sense of common identity and purpose'.[39]

As the most distinctive cultural feature of the people of Israel, Judaism has been at the centre of this process. Indeed, most of the main Jewish holidays are exercises in remembrance. Passover commemorates the Exodus from Egypt, and the last pronouncement of the ritual text (*haggadah*) read during the meal (*seder*) reads, 'Next year in Jerusalem', speaking clearly to the restoration of Jewish sovereignty there. A number of modern *haggadahs* published in the West conclude with the nineteenth century hymn '*Hatikvah*' ('The Hope'), the Israeli national anthem, which expresses a yearning for the full restoration of the ancestral homeland.[40] *Shavuot* venerates the day God gave the Torah to Moses and the Israelites at Mount Sinai. *Sukkot*, translated as 'booths' or 'tabernacles', was a thanksgiving for the fruit harvest, but also intended to remind later generations of the hardships of the 40 years of exile in Egypt.[41] *Purim* is a celebration of deliverance from mass murder of the Jewish exiles at the hands of Haman under the Persians, as recounted in the biblical Book of Esther. *Hanukkah*, meaning 'dedication', celebrates the rededication of the Second Temple from pagan to Jewish worship after the Maccabees defeated the Seleucids. Thus, the divine commandment to remember is a key foundation of the Jewish faith and Jewish life, and in accordance with the word of God, the ancestral Land of Israel is to be returned to the Jewish people.[42]

Zionism, the Jewish nationalist ideology that prevailed over others, began to develop in late nineteenth century Europe and articulated their claim to statehood in their ancient homeland. After a widespread series of pogroms against Jews in tsarist Russia in 1881, Leo Pinsker wrote an article entitled, *Auto-Emancipation: An Appeal to His People*. In it, he identifies 'the Jewish Question' as an eternal unsolved problem, the essence of which is that 'in the midst of the nations among whom the Jews reside, they form a distinctive element which cannot be assimilated, which cannot be readily digested by any nation'.[43] Jews 'are everywhere as guests, and are nowhere at home', a point made forcefully throughout:

> As for the Jew, not only is he not a native in his own home country, but he is also not a foreigner; he is, in very truth, the stranger *par excellence*. He is regarded as neither friend nor foe but an alien, of whom the only thing known is that he has no home.[44]

Life in the Diaspora had prevented the development of a distinctive Jewish national character. Many had assimilated, divesting their Jewish identity in favour of 'the alien traits' of their host nation, a practice that

Pinsker deplored. He bemoaned the lack of dignity, self-love, and national self-respect among the Jewish people, which, although explainable by Diaspora conditions, was nonetheless inexcusable and unacceptable.

> The Jews are aliens who can have no representatives, because they have no fatherland. Because they have none, because their home has no boundaries behind which they can entrench themselves, their misery also has no bounds ... We are a flock scattered over the whole face of the earth, without a shepherd to protect us and gather us together.[45]

Pinsker espoused the creation of a Jewish state equal to all the other nation states of the world. 'We must prove that the misfortunes of the Jews are due, above all, to their lack of desire for national independence; and that this desire must be aroused and maintained in time if they do not wish to be subjected forever to disgraceful existence – in a word, we must prove that *they must become a nation.*'[46]

This notion was expressed more famously 14 years later by Theodor Herzl in his seminal work *Der Judenstaat* (*The Jewish State*). Like Pinsker, Herzl envisioned a territorial solution in the form of a state as the only solution to the persecution suffered by Jews throughout history, which, given the growing tide of anti-Semitism in Europe, showed no signs of abating.

> The Jewish question persists wherever Jews live in appreciable numbers. Wherever it does not exist, it is brought in together with Jewish immigrants. We are naturally drawn into those places where we are not persecuted, and our appearance there gives rise to persecution. This is the case, and will inevitably be so, everywhere, even in highly civilised countries ... so long as the Jewish question is not solved on the political level.[47]

In contrast to Ahad Ha'am who advocated a more spiritual-cultural Jewish autonomy, Herzl called for the political sovereignty of a nation-state as an immediate rather than an eventual goal, to be attained through diplomatic negotiations with the Great Powers rather than an outgrowth of a broad, pre-existing national society and culture. Herzl's view of Jewish history and his conclusions reflected the intellectual influence of nationalist tendencies dominant in Europe at the time. Although this premise proved erroneous, with the latter eventually leading to the former, his contribution was extremely valuable to Zionist discourse. As Kornberg explains, 'Herzl's political maximalism captured the imagination of Jews, raised Zionism's standing in the Jewish world, and implanted Zionism in the European political arena.'[48]

The Balfour declaration of 2 November 1917, committed the British government to help the Zionists achieve 'a national home for the Jewish people' in Palestine. This policy remained in force throughout the British Mandate of Palestine and, as envisioned by Herzl, was important to the development of the *Yishuv*, the pre-state Jewish community in Palestine. Though the declaration pledged that 'nothing shall be done which may prejudice the civil and religious rights of existing non-Jewish communities in Palestine', it completely failed to acknowledge any political rights of the Palestinian Arab residents. In a memorandum dated 11 August 1919, Foreign Secretary Arthur James Balfour made his feelings clear: 'Zionism, be it right or wrong, good or bad, is rooted in age-long traditions, in present needs, in future hopes, of far greater import than the desires and prejudices of the 700,000 Arabs who now inhabit that ancient land.'[49]

Upon hearing of the first Zionist Congress in Basle in 1897, the mayor of Jerusalem and former deputy in the Ottoman parliament, Yusuf Zia al-Khalidi, exchanged letters with Herzl where the former expressed concern at the goals of the budding Zionist movement. He commended the Zionists and admitted that their ideals were theoretically 'natural, fine, and just': 'Who can contest the rights of the Jews to Palestine? God knows, historically it is indeed your country!' Still, he explained that Palestinian Arabs already resided on substantial parts of the land.[50] Nearly half a century later, Antonius similarly asserted that although the basis of the Jewish claims to Palestine were well-known, 'an historic connection is not necessarily synonymous with a title to possession, more particularly when it related to an inhabited country whose population claims, in addition to an ancient historic connexion of their own, the natural rights inherent in actual possession'.[51]

Palestinian Arabs have inhabited parts of Palestine for many centuries, and thus have very strong historical ties to the land. Muslims consider the prophet Muhammad and the Arab people descendants of Ishmael, Abraham's first-born son by his wife Sarah's handmaiden Hagar. Contrary to the Jewish position, the case is sometimes made that the covenant Abraham made with God applies to Ishmael rather than Isaac.

Some Palestinian scholars have argued for the existence of a relationship between the Canaanites, the ancient indigenous tribes from the eastern shore of the Arabian Gulf displaced by the Jews, and the Philistines, who together form the core of present-day Palestinian ancestry. Such contentions have been used to emphasise the eternal and permanent nature of the struggle with Israel and the Jews, today's manifestations being a mere continuation of a conflict that began three millennia ago.[52]

Yet compared to the Israeli narrative, the Palestinians have focused much less on their ancient ancestry since many do not necessarily see a need to establish themselves before the Israelites. The historical period that resonates most profoundly and has defined their identity for over 1,300 years is not the biblical era, but the rise of Islam and the Arab conquests of the seventh century.[53] The divine revelations received by Muhammad are the great watershed. Still, prominent Israelites such as Moses are revered as prophets, but Abu Sway argues that the story of Moses and the exodus 'show that assigning the land to the Children of Israel was as a community of believers and not as cultural Jews. It was submitting to God's will, and not specific genetic codes, that determined the relationship with the land.' Muslims too are a continuum of the followers of Moses, Abraham or Noah, and 'no specific religious group was ever granted the upper hand or sovereignty in the absolute sense'.[54]

Palestine is mentioned once in the Qur'an by the designation '*al-Ard al-Muqaddasah*', 'the Holy Land', and was perceived to be sacred land due to its history as the land of the prophets and the site of divine revelation. This term applied not only to Jerusalem, but also the surrounding area, from the Euphrates in the north to the Sinai desert in the south, and from the Mediterranean in the west to the deserts beyond the River Jordan in the east.[55]

Jerusalem has long been crucial to Palestinians because of its religious significance. Muslims believe that the prophet Muhammad went on a miraculous night journey (*al-Isra*) from Mecca to Jerusalem, as told in *sura* (chapter) 17 of the Qur'an. The 'Farthest Mosque', Masjid al-Aqsa, mentioned in this *sura* is widely believed to refer to the Haram al-Sharif

(Noble Sanctuary), the current site of the al-Aqsa mosque, the third holiest site in Islam, and the Dome of the Rock, the oldest extant Islamic structure in the world. The Western Wall is also held to be the place where Muhammad tethered his winged steed Buraq. From the Foundation Stone, today housed within the Dome of the Rock, Muhammad supposedly ascended to Heaven (*al-Miraj*), where he spoke to Allah and the earlier prophets before returning to Mecca to impart his story upon the people. For Palestinian Christians, Jerusalem is the site of the crucifixion and death of Jesus Christ. Within the Old City lies the Via Dolorosa lined with the Stations of the Cross, and the Church of the Holy Sepulchre where Jesus is believed to have been removed from his crucifix and laid to rest.

The Arab world contained a number of simultaneous and complementary conceptions of identity which were different to the European idea of the nation state that influenced the main Zionist ideologues. In the fourteenth century, Arab philosopher Abd al-Rahman Ibn Khaldun developed the cultural concept of *asabiyya*, which can be interpreted as 'a solidarity or identity group based on real or imagined blood or primordial ties, strengthened by actual or invented common ancestry'.[56] Denominations of this phenomenon include the terms *qawm*, or people, which refers to the people of the Arab Fertile Crescent and Arabia, *al-qawmiyya al-Arabiyya*, and *watani* or *wataniyya*, which emphasises loyalty to a particular local region.

Beyond ethnic or geographical identification, Islam has been a crucial aspect of collective identity and a driving force behind the conquest, expansion, and politics of the Arab dynasties. Indeed, this process brought about the concept of a worldwide Muslim community, *al-umma al-islamiyya*, which functioned on a social and moral order based on the Qur'an, written and disseminated in Arabic. On yet another level, village and clan solidarity are extremely important social units and create a 'strong, stable environment for the individual, a sense of rootedness and belonging'.[57] On the basis of these multiple associations, Ahmad Muhammad Jamal, a Saudi professor, contends that 'Arab familiarity with *asabiyya* was an authentic pattern of nationalism *long before* [emphasis added] the historical phenomenon related to this ideology took place in Europe or the Americas'.[58]

Whether these various identities actually constituted nationalism is, however, contentious.[59] Still, as Rouhana argues, whatever one's perspective on that debate, it does not change the fact that the Arabs of Palestine 'were a people and Palestine was their homeland'.[60] Strong, organised communities existed with political, economic, and social institutions. Familial lines tended to dominate certain localities and created a strong attachment to a particular city or village. This is reflected in the use of cities in family names, such as al-Maqdisi (Jerusalem), al-Nabulsi (Nablus), al-Ghazzawi (Gaza), al-Khalili (Hebron), and others.[61] Many prominent families also dominated certain professional offices, as it was customary for a son to follow in his father's footsteps.

Under the Ottoman Empire, a system of indirect rule existed whereby the provincial governor and the *qadi* (judge) were sent from Constantinople, while locals occupied all other important offices, such as that of *mufti* (the legal jurisconsult), *naqib al-ashraf* (head of the Prophet's descendants), secretariat of the Shari'a court, manager of the Haram al-Sharif area, deputy judges, and so on. In Jerusalem, for example, a member of the Husseini family has held the office of *mufti* and *naqib al-ashraf* since at least the eighteenth century, while the Khalidi have held the secretariat of the Sharia court.[62] Other prominent Jerusalem families included the Nashashibi and the Alami. These *ayan* (notables) were the principal leaders of the Palestinians, and functioned as an intermediary political structure closely linked to the rule of the Ottoman Empire, mediators between the local populace and the central government in all matter of grievances. Highly respected by the people, they provided a sense of cohesion and community to the area.

Hussein ibn Ali, the Grand Sharif of Mecca, led the 1916 Arab Revolt against the Ottomans under the banner of Arab nationalism, in co-ordination with the British. Hussein's vision of an independent Arab state was supported by the British, who promised to realise it after the defeat of the Ottomans. This pledge was formulated in the 'McMahon letter', a series of correspondence between Sir Henry McMahon, the British High Commissioner in Egypt, and Hussein outlining their agreement. But Arab independence did not come to fruition. The tenets of the secret Sykes–Picot agreement of 1916 – the British and French plan to divide up control of the Middle East – conflicted explicitly with the British promise to Hussein, and the mandate system devised following the conclusion of the war ensured that no united Arab state was created.

Although supported by Hajj Amin al-Husseini – who later became the *mufti* of Jerusalem and a central figure of the entire mandate period, a man heavily demonised by the Israelis for his close relations with Nazi Germany – the Arab Revolt and Arabism in general had only limited appeal in Palestine. Loyalty toward the Ottoman state existed simultaneously with a wider Arabism and a basic Palestinian identity. The close relationship between the Palestinian elite and the Ottoman authorities based on the provincial power structure made local patriotism more readily adoptable than wider Arab nationalism, particularly in Jerusalem.[63]

Glorious pasts, hero worship and martyrology

The biblical period has not just been used to justify Jewish claims, but importantly also to inspire the new Hebrew nation. A prominently secular movement, Zionism framed itself as a revolution against traditional orthodox religious Diaspora thinking, which considered their exile the result of unworthy actions of God's chosen people and violations of their covenant. Instead, Zionists focused on the proud memories of valiant Jewish behaviour in service of the ancient nation.[64] Pinsker lamented the state of Jewry, with reference to glories long since past:

> What a pitiful figure do we cut! We do not count as a nation among the other nations, and we have no voice in the council of the peoples, even in affairs which concern us. Our fatherland is the other man's country; our unity – dispersion, our solidarity – the general hostility to us, our weapon – humility, our defence – flight, our individuality – adaptability, our future – tomorrow. What a contemptible role for a people which once had its Maccabees![65]

Thus, despite being secular, Zionists were not prepared to compromise the declared biblical links between their forefathers and the Promised Land. Connections were made between the past and the present in terms of the continuity of the history of the Hebrew nation and an eternal bond to the land of Israel, rather than any relationship with the divine. The mythological stories of the Bible served as a kind of template for re-constituting an ancient nation, and selected episodes functioned as reminders of inspirational Israelite strength, heroism, and resilience in the face of adversity.

Following the Kishinev pogroms of 1903, poet Ya'acov Cahan penned the line, 'With blood and fire Judea fell; with blood and fire Judea will rise!' which became a widespread Zionist slogan representing the ethos of self-defence.[66] The nascent *Yishuv* and the state it evolved into were seen as the direct heirs of the mythological kingdom of David and Solomon.[67] Other useful religious symbols and motifs were secularised and imparted with national meaning.[68] These included, among many others, the victory of the Maccabees over the Seleucids alluded to by Pinsker, the bravery of the Bar Kochba rebellion against the Romans, and Joseph's conquest of Canaan. In twentieth century secular Zionist education, the biblical Book of Joshua, which recounts Joseph's conquest of Canaan, was extremely useful due to the parallels between the ancient Exile and the war with the Philistines, and modern Exile and the antagonistic relationship with the Palestinian Arabs. Possession of the homeland in the twentieth century was thus portrayed as an echo of an earlier generation of Israelites.[69]

Other legends were also introduced into public consciousness throughout the beginning of the twentieth century to strengthen national identity and resolve during the development phase of the *Yishuv*. A prominent example is the story of the battle of Masada in 73 AD, popularised by the publication in 1927 of a poem entitled 'Masada' by a Jewish Ukranian immigrant to Palestine, Yitzhak Lamdan. After the devastation of Jerusalem and the destruction of the Second Temple, the last remnants of Jewish resistance holed up in a fortress at Masada. 900 Jewish 'zealots' resiliently resisted the Roman army siege, but faced certain defeat. Rather than allow the Romans a military victory and to save themselves from the humiliation of surrender, the zealots took their own lives as their defences crumbled. The event was recorded only by Josephus' *The Jewish War*, written in Aramaic. It is not mentioned in the Talmud or any other sacred text, it was not commemorated in any way; as an object of collective memory, it was forgotten for almost 2,000 years.

As Schwartz, Zerubavel, and Barnett suggest, at the time of the poem's publication, Masada served as an allegory of the Zionist settlement project in Palestine. The image of the zealots trapped in the fortress produced a sense of identification for the Zionist settlers in Palestine for whom this was the only option, at a time when the prospects of emigration to another country was limited due to immigration quotas, and a return to the difficult circumstances of their Diaspora origin was rejected. Collective suicide is repeatedly used in Lamdan's poem as a metaphor for noncommitment and spiritual surrender in modern Palestine. Such imagery was particularly relevant in light of the escalating violence with the local Palestinian Arab population at the time, bolstering the collective ego and imbuing the situation with historical meaning that is still relevant today; 'like the besieged and outnumbered defenders of Masada, contemporary Israelis find themselves surrounded by hostile and numerically superior forces'. One certain line of the poem – 'Never again shall Masada fall!' – has become a common expression of national will, heroic national commitment, and a symbol of military courage.[70]

An event that had a similar resonance for Israeli national identity was the battle of Tel Hai and the death of Yosef Trumpeldor on 1 March 1920. An ardent Zionist, Jewish political activist, and military man, Trumpeldor was killed defending a remote Jewish settlement in the upper Galilee called Tel Hai from Arab forces. His last words, 'It is good to die for our country', quickly became engrained in the national psyche.[71] The death of Trumpeldor was one of the first 'new' Hebrew national myths and an example of the ethos of patriotic sacrifice. It is a concept that stems from the intense identification with societal values and norms and a sense of moral obligation toward the national collective, serving as a symbolic reaffirmation of a nation's transcendental value.[72]

Israelis remember Trumpeldor as a heroic martyr who demonstrated the importance of holding onto the 'homeland', and elevated the collective nation and the land over individuals. In Labour leader Berl Katznelson's memoriam to the fallen of Tel Hai he described them as 'men of toil and peace, who walked behind the ploughshare and risked their lives', for the 'usurped lands' of the people of Israel. He continued: 'May the people of Israel remember and be blessed in its seed and mourn the radiance of the lost ones and the delight of heroism and the sanctification of desire and the devotion that fell in the heavy battle.'[73] The intended longevity of this episode is clearly articulated in the 'History of the Haganah', which describes Tel Hai as 'a sublime and edifying folk legend' that 'will stay in the people's hearts for generations', and that future generations would 'draw upon it until the end of time'.[74]

For many Jewish nationalists, specifically the more militant right-wing elements, death and sacrifice lie at the heart of collective memory and the Zionist narrative.[75] As expressed by national Hebrew poet Chaim Nachman Bialik, 'In their death they commanded us to live'; the living community has a moral debt to the dead, which enhances the commitment to collective survival.[76] Consequently, in addition to creating bonds between the past and present aiding in the identification with previous generations, death also serves to embolden the living, enhance a sense of national victimhood, and creates an acute need for security to prevent further disaster.

An article published on the first anniversary of Tel Hai declared: 'With their blood they purchased and bequeathed to us the mountains of the Galilee.' Similarly, the 'History of the Haganah' says that 'a spot where Hebrew warriors spilt their blood will never be forsaken by its builders and defenders'.[77] This attitude towards death and resultant symbolic ownership of land has been a recurring theme in Israel, expressed by early twentieth century Labour Zionists and both the national-religious and more secular right wing segments.

On 23 August 1929, news of clashes between Arabs and Jews in Jerusalem and deaths on both sides elicited violent rioting by the Arabs of Hebron against the Jewish residents, 67 of whom were killed.[78] Jewish blood spilt on that land created an eternal bond that the Israeli national-religious settler community has never forgotten. In addition to the religious significance of Hebron as the burial place of Abraham, this history of bloodletting served as a mark of ownership and hence a justification for Israeli settlement in the area.[79]

> The national-religious martyrology is sustained in Hebron in all its complexity: death as a creator of meaning, as a basis and a catalyst of the project of revival and renewal; the eradication of the shame of the slaughtered ancestors who did not know how to defend themselves; revenge on murderers and enemies, whose names and faces change but who never die out ... Thus, in its replication of an ancient Jewish pattern of destruction and redemption, the cycle of catastrophe and revival, of wrongdoing and its redress, has revived and brought the dead victims into the community of their living redeemers.[80]

On 30 January 1980, Yehoshua Saloma, a student at the paramilitary (*hesder*) *yeshiva* in Kiryat Arba, was killed in the Hebron marketplace by a Palestinian. In response, settlers from Kiryat Arba took over five buildings in the old Jewish Quarter of Hebron. Rather than remove them, the government decided to strengthen the Jewish presence in Hebron by establishing a branch of the Kiryat Arba *yeshiva* there. Then-agricultural minister Ariel Sharon was an ardent advocate of this reaction, viewing it as 'an appropriate Zionist response to the murder'.[81]

The era of the Crusades is an historical period that truly resonates with the Palestinian people. Lost to the Crusaders in 1099, Jerusalem was recaptured in 1187 in a *jihad* (holy war) led by Salah al-Din (Saladin), ruler of Syria and Egypt. A history of Jerusalem from the 1490s by Mujir al-Din is described by Gerber as an 'unquestioned celebration of the deeds and exploits of Salah al-Din', a figure idolised for his heroism.[82]

For the Palestinian narrative, this history of repelling foreign invaders from Islamic lands is of great significance. The valour of Salah al-Din as a warrior-liberator and the expulsion of the Franks represent the important theme of triumph in the face of alien invasion and colonisation. Historical parallels between the Crusades and the Zionist venture have often been made in Palestinian society, with calls to emulate Salah al-Din and deliver the people from these re-incarnated infidel invaders.[83]

Such connections were widely employed at the beginning of the twentieth century when Zionist immigration was increasing during the second and third *aliyah* (literally translated as 'ascent', the term refers to Jewish immigration to *Eretz Israel*). The Israeli town of Afula was once an Arab locality called al-Fulah, purchased by Zionists from absentee Arab landlords in late 1910. Despite a campaign launched by local Arab notables, including the *qaimmaqam* (governor) of nearby Nazareth, Shukri al-Asali, and *fellahin* (farmers) to protest the sale with the Ottoman authorities, the sale went ahead. The land was namely the site of an old Crusader fortress recaptured by Salah al-Din in his campaign against the Franks in the twelfth century. To have reclaimed the place with Muslim blood only to sell it back to unbelievers eight centuries later was sacrilege that undermined Muslim hegemony over sacred land. This point was made forcefully by al-Asali, who wrote an open letter about the sale that emphasised such historical patriotic themes, and was published in numerous daily newspapers in Damascus, Haifa, and Beirut. Deeply critical of Zionism and accusing them of separatist nationalist objectives, al-Asali turned the case into a popular cause celebre, which demonstrated the fierce resistance which existed to Zionism. Unfortunately for the peasants of al-Fulah, rich Arab merchants who purchased the land felt no attachment to it and merely saw the sale as a tidy profit on an investment.[84]

With its origins in the time of Salah al-Din around the end of the twelfth century, the Nebi Musa festival is a pilgrimage to a shrine representing the tomb of Moses, located between Jerusalem and Jericho. For centuries, Muslims from all corners of Palestine, from Hebron and the wider south, Nablus and the rural hill areas, were brought together with Jerusalemites in what was effectively a proto-national holiday. Porath believes that 'the annual recurrence of this event, and the importance of the festival in the religion of Palestinian Muslims undoubtedly created a bond between the various parts of the country'.[85] Khalil al-Sakakini, a well-known intellectual, writer, and publisher wrote in his diary during the Mandate period that 'the Nebi Musa festival in Jerusalem is political, not religious'. People came from all over the country 'with their flags and weapons, as if they were going to war'.[86]

The inscription on the tomb at Nebi Musa reads:

> Ordered the building of this sacred place over the tomb of Moses ... the Sultan of Islam and the Muslims, master of the kings and sultans, conqueror of the cities, annihilator of the Franks and the Mongols, who rests castles from the hands of unbelievers.

Gerber suggests in his analysis that the pilgrimage began to commemorate the Crusades, as an anti-European manifestation and a counterweight to Christian celebrations, falling just a week before the Easter holiday in the Christian calendar. Muslims massed in Jerusalem in order to prevent the Christian pilgrims from overwhelming the city. The procession, observed by residents of Jerusalem from the surrounding hills, began at the Haram and left through the Lion's Gate, with an array of mock fights involving horse riding and swordplay, potentially a symbolic reconstruction of Crusade-era battles against enemies of Islam.[87] The 1920 Nebi Musa celebration became the scene of the first large-scale urban riots by Arabs against Jews, with shouts of

'Independence! Independence!' emanating from the crowd. The violence lasted for three days and left hundreds of Jews and Arabs wounded, with a few fatalities on each side.[88]

In November 1935, Sheikh Muhammad Izz al-Din al-Qassam, a Syrian-born Palestinian nationalist and religious figure in Haifa, left with several armed followers for the hills around Jenin, where they planned to attack the British and Jews. Following the murder of a Jewish policeman by his men, the British initiated a manhunt for al-Qassam and his followers, and he was killed in a gun battle. His last words, shouted as a response to calls for him to give himself up, were supposedly, 'Never, this is a *jihad* for God and country!'[89] He and his Jewish counterpart Trumpeldor each 'gave their national movement a heroic myth, a far more useful contribution than anything they had done in life'.[90]

In death, he became the first legendary hero of the Palestinian cause, portrayed as a warrior whose love for his God and his country made him willing to face martyrdom. This notion of the heroic martyr has been key to various Palestinian groups of different ideological persuasions who have emphasised resistance to Zionism. During the Arab revolt of 1936–9, groups of fighters inspired by al-Qassam referred to themselves as *Qassamiyun*. One such was Sheikh Farhan al-Sadi, a rebel leader captured, tried and executed by the British, who thus became a martyr in al-Qassam's image.[91] Other 'revolutionaries' who suffered a similar fate included Fouad Hijazi, Abu Ibrahim, and Muhammad Jamjoum, who became the subjects of popular songs of remembrance.[92]

In the 1960s, the Marxist Democratic Front for the Liberation of Palestine (DFLP) named their armed wing after al-Qassam, as have Hamas, the Palestinian Islamic fundamentalist organisation. In each case, they emphasise the characteristics of al-Qassam which suit their ideology, as an organiser of the working class and an Islamic preacher, respectively.[93] The crude homemade rockets that Palestinian militants fire at Israel from the Gaza Strip also bear his name.

For both secular and Islamist Palestinian armed resistance organisations, the death of a fighter or leader at the hands of the Israelis, and their subsequent commemoration, has and continues to function as a tool of recruitment and a rallying call for the cause. Images of martyrs stir feelings of militancy and revenge, inspire communal defiance, and 'weaves the community of the dead into the daily lives of the living.'[94]

Victimhood

While the fighting during the pre-state *Yishuv* years provided Jews with heroic models of self-sacrifice, death also enhanced a crucial sense of victimhood.

> Through the constitution of a martyrology specific to that community, namely, the community becoming a remembering collective that recollects and recounts itself through the unifying memory of catastrophes, suffering, and victimisation, binding its members together by instilling in them a sense of common mission and destiny, a shared sense of nationhood is created and the nation is crystallised.[95]

Nothing is more important to Jewish identity than the *Shoah* (Holocaust). The systematic Nazi genocide of six million European Jews decimated the world Jewish community. An ever-present shadow and a constant point of reference, Israeli society has always defined itself in relation to the Holocaust. Whether to highlight the virtues of 'new' Israeli Jews vis-à-vis their 'weaker' Diaspora counterparts who perished, as the state did throughout the 1950s, or to articulate the constant threat of anti-Semitism and destruction emanating from the Palestinians and the rest of the Arab world, the Holocaust was and remains a central recurring theme in Israeli society. As expressed in an editorial in Israeli daily *Maariv*,

> the Holocaust is the epicentre of our collective consciousness. Whoever does not understand that behind everything we do and do not do, as a people, hides the threatening and warning shadow of the Holocaust, will never understand our actions.[96]

Following a decade of nation-building in Israel that emphasised 'heroes and martyrs', such as those of the Warsaw ghetto uprising and other archetypes of the strong 'new' Israeli Jew, rather than the helpless victims, the trial of Adolf Eichmann in Jerusalem in April 1961 was a history lesson under a legal cloak. As Arendt observes in *Eichmann in Jerusalem*, 'it was history that, as far as the prosecution was concerned, stood at the centre of the trial. "It is not an individual that is in the dock at this historic trial, and not the Nazi regime alone, but anti-Semitism throughout history."'[97] It was an exercise in the formation of collective historical consciousness to emphasise to Israelis the horrors of the Holocaust, their status as victims of history, and the imperative to ensure that such a catastrophe should never befall the Jewish people again.[98]

Trevor-Roper similarly explained that the trial was a personal undertaking by Ben-Gurion to unite an increasingly fragmenting country through collective memory: 'the trial is not so much the punishment of a particularly odious criminal, as the exposure of a sacred experience in the history of Israel'. Ben-Gurion admitted as much himself when he said that Eichmann's fate did not interest him in the slightest, but that it was 'the spectacle' that was important.[99] 'It is necessary that our youth remember what happened to the Jewish people. We want them to know the most tragic facts in our history.'[100] In addition to being a collective experience of patriotism and national catharsis, it was also a message to the international community that the state of Israel represented world Jewry as a whole and that, given their tortuous history, an international obligation existed to ensure their future security.[101]

The period surrounding the Eichmann trial has also been described by Zertal as a landmark in mobilisation of the Holocaust, not just for internal political reasons but also in the context of the conflict with the Arabs. Indeed, there has not been a war involving Israel – and there has been at least one a decade since its establishment – that has not been perceived, defined, and conceptualised in terms of the Holocaust. It became part of the civil religion of Israelis. For the Zionist movement, it served as proof that only a state of their own would provide real security for the Jewish people, and that they must be ready to defend themselves militarily at all times. 'Ultimately, the trial sharpened the sense that Israelis, as Jews, stood alone in the world and could not rely on anyone.'[102] Whether facing the conventional army of an Arab state or irregular attacks by terrorist militant movements, Zertal observes that the rationale has always been the same: 'the dangers which Israel confronted and still confronts are Nazi in essence and scope, and any military threat or apparent threat to Israel means a new Holocaust'.[103]

During Eichmann's trial, Ben-Gurion expressed this notion in the following manner: '150 metres from the courtroom there is a border, and behind that border thousands of [Palestinian] Eichmanns lie in wait, proclaiming explicitly, "what Eichmann has not completed, we will."'[104] In an interview with a British newspaper, Ben-Gurion said, 'When I listen to the speeches of the Egyptian president on world Jewry controlling America and the West, it seems to me that Hitler is talking.'[105] Prior to the Six-Day War of 1967, when Arab leaders in Cairo and Damascus spoke of destroying Israel and liberating Palestine, Ben-Gurion told *Ha'aretz*, 'None of us can forget the Nazi Holocaust, and if some of the Arab leaders, with the leader of Egypt at their head, declare day and night that Israel must be destroyed ... we should not take these declarations lightly.'[106]

Indeed, Israeli politicians and press regularly expressed such feelings, and a significant portion of the population genuinely held existential anxieties. Many on the right wing compared Israel's situation to that of Czechoslovakia in 1938, and likened Prime Minister Levi Eshkol's approach to Neville Chamberlain's appeasement policy.[107] Bregman observes that,

> rightly or wrongly, most Israelis were convinced that the Arabs were bent on destroying their state and that they were fighting with their backs to the wall. For them there could be no retreat because there was no place to retreat to and in every war the individual soldier believed that he was fighting for the life of his family, his home, and his nation.[108]

As explained by a 'second generation' *kibbutz* child, 'if Nasser wins, we were all born in vain'.[109]

Prime Ministers Menachem Begin[110] and Benjamin Netanyahu[111] have both made clear analogies between the Nazi enemies of the past and the Arabs of the present and future. Such references have also often been used by right-wing maximalists to demonise Israeli leaders and politicians who support a negotiated peace with the Palestinians. Famously, former Prime Minister Yitzhak Rabin was depicted as an SS officer at a rally condemning the Oslo Agreement. Right-wing leaders compared him to Marshal Philippe Petain, the leader of the Vichy France government that collaborated with the Nazis, and Raful Eitan of Tsomet referred to the government as 'a bunch of *judenrat* quislings', further references to Jewish and other Nazi collaborators.[112] Uri Savir, Israeli negotiator of the Oslo Agreement, notes that 'Holocaust images were being used to spread anxiety, to imply that Oslo meant extermination. Rabin was depicted as a "traitor," murderer," "Nazi," and "illegal prime minister."'[113] Demonstrators outside Rabin's home warned that he and his wife Leah would suffer the same fate as Benito Mussolini and his mistress Clara Petacci, who were executed and hung up for public humiliation.[114]

Palestinians too see themselves as victims of European politics, whether in reference to British imperialism, the Zionist colonial movement, or the Western acceptance of the state of Israel to assuage collective guilt for the Holocaust. Former Palestinian head negotiator Saeb Erekat laments these aspects of history, remarking that 'it's shameful what you [Westerners] did to us, it's shameful'.[115]

Antonius argues that the actions of the British and French during the Mandate period hindered and suppressed the development of Arab nationalism as a whole.[116] With specific reference to Palestine, Khalidi argues that the British Mandate authorities were discriminatory against the Arab population, denying them the infrastructure, institutions, and administrative structures that were accorded the Jewish *Yishuv*, and thereby creating an ideological, material and structural imbalance which ultimately tipped the scales in favour of the Jews when the British abandoned the territory.[117] The Peel Commission Report of 1937 noted that government schools were 'seminaries of Arab nationalism' and were closely monitored by the British to prevent the spread of Palestinian nationalism, deemed to constitute 'subversive' thinking.[118]

Palestinian frustration was building in time with the increasing Jewish presence in Palestine through mass immigration, and serious intercommunal violence took place on multiple occasions in the 1920s and 1930s. Gerber acknowledges that there was a simultaneous struggle on two fronts, against both an ethnic adversary and a foreign occupier. A British General Staff intelligence report noted that these were 'the expressions of a deep-seated and widely spread popular [Palestinian] resentment at the present British policy' which allowed an alien community to take over their land.[119] When the Palestinian attitude towards the British changed from one of cooperation to confrontation during the Arab revolt of 1936–9, the rebellion was brutally repressed and its leaders were either killed or, like the *mufti* of Jerusalem, al-Husseini, eventually forced to flee the country. The effects of this leadership decimation continued to be felt a decade later when the Palestinians unsuccessfully fought for their political rights.[120]

Plans to partition Palestine into two states, one Jewish and one Arab, were rejected outright by the Arabs. The Palestinians were convinced that any Jewish state or national home with territorial sovereignty would not be possible without the forced displacement of their communities.[121] This was confirmed by the Peel Commission of 1937, which proposed giving around 20 per cent of the land to the Jews and 80 per cent to the Arabs when the Arabs were an absolute majority.[122] Significantly, it recommended the 'forced transfer' of Arabs from territory allotted to the Jews.[123] Ten years later, the UN partition plan of 1947 was based on the same principles but went even further, allotting around 55 per cent to the Jews and leaving the Arabs with only about 45 per cent of Mandatory Palestine, even though at the beginning of 1948 they constituted approximately 70 per cent of the population.[124] Although Arab rejection of these plans can be seen to reflect Abba Eban's famous observation that 'the Arabs never miss an opportunity to miss an opportunity', in principle it is not at all surprising given the Arab demographic majority in the land and the historic longevity of their presence there.

The most crucial element of the Palestinian narrative is the war of 1948 and the months of civil war that preceded it. The newly established state of Israel defeated the Arab armies and ended up in control of roughly 78 per cent of Mandatory Palestine. Known in Arabic as the *Nakba*, meaning 'disaster' or 'catastrophe', this wholesale dispossession represents the nadir of the Palestinian people, a cataclysmic event of unmitigated proportions that irreversibly changed their world forever. Approximately 750,000 Palestinians became refugees and fled to Egypt, Jordan, Lebanon, Syria, and Arab parts of Palestine.[125]

From the outset, the desire for restitution and revenge inspired by the *Nakba* was clear. On 2 August 1948, UN mediator Count Folke Bernadotte had lunch with Arif al-Arif, the Administrative Governor of the Ramallah area, who 'said that if they had no justice, they would educate their children for generations to carry on war against them [the Jews]'.[126] At a meeting during the Lausanne conference in 1949, overseen by the UN established Palestine Conciliation Commission, talks were held between the small Palestinian refugee delegation and Israeli representatives Eliyahu Sasson, the Jewish Agency's chief Arab affairs expert, and Walter Eytan. The Palestinians explained, with a poignant clarity of vision, that:

> the refugees, if they remain dispossessed and disinherited outside their home, are the closest thing to wild animals. They will be on the lookout for an opportunity to bounce back and destroy your security . . . Forever is a very long time for you to live without any feeling of security . . . If the refugees remain outside, they will be the greatest motivation for [a true Arab awakening] . . . and this awakening will be filled with hatred and a desire for vengeance.[127]

This experience of defeat and exile played a vital role in shaping and expressing a distinct Palestinian identity. A common narrative of suffering helped replace old local identities and instil a sense of national consciousness. The feeling of 'otherness' was exacerbated by the alienation and institutional discrimination felt within their Arab refugee host countries. The collapse of the Egyptian–Syrian union in September 1961 and the Arab defeat in the Six Day War of 1967 focused attention on Palestinian self-reliance, since pan-Arabism proved an illusion and their Arab brethren could not be counted on to deliver them.[128]

In the absence of state mechanisms normally utilised to inculcate memory and given the scattered nature of the Palestinian community, independent initiatives have been at the forefront of instilling *Nakba* memory. Refugee camps and centres in the diaspora have developed as 'communities of memory', while Palestinians have expressed their memories in a variety of ways, including oral histories, art, film, theatre, literature, and poetry, particularly the work of the late Mahmoud Darwish, who earned the title 'Palestinian national poet.' Memorialisation projects have sought to document destroyed localities, their histories, land registers, populations and principal families, agriculture, conquest by the Israelis and their current use of the land.[129]

The Palestine Liberation Organisation (PLO), though it supported some such projects like that of historian Walid Khalidi, has had an ambiguous relationship with the *Nakba* and the ethos of victimhood. Fatah, the leading faction within the PLO since 1969, was in 1959 founded as an organisation that championed revolution (*thawra*) and the liberation of their homeland through armed struggle. Sayigh argues that this armed struggle provided the central theme and practice around which Palestinian nation building took place.

> The heroic imagery and language of armed struggle gave new substance to the imagined community of the Palestinians. They now portrayed themselves as a revolutionary people waging an active struggle to determine their fate, rather than as a mass of helpless refugees passively awaiting charity handouts.[130]

Founded by members of the Palestinian diaspora, return to their stolen land became a supreme national goal, and the *Nakba* memory was a constant reminder of shame and a stimulus to action against their Israeli usurpers. An event referred to as 'the black day of disgrace and shame' did not fit neatly into this new revolutionary ethos, and the humiliating memory was in a sense officially repressed. The *Nakba* was not mentioned in either the 1964 or 1968 versions of the PLO Covenant, and was not officially commemorated by the PLO until its fiftieth anniversary in 1998.[131]

A second Israeli victory in the war of 1967 led to the further displacement of hundreds of thousands of Palestinians from the occupied West Bank and Gaza Strip, many becoming refugees for the second time. Since then, over 40 years of Israeli occupation has accentuated feelings of victimhood and perpetuated hatred of Israel. Continued combat with the occupying power, particularly during the second *intifada*, has intensified the *Nakba* memory for a new generation through identification with such earlier phases of the conflict; Israeli house demolitions have been described as a 'second *Nakba*'.[132] The construction and expansion of Israeli settlements in the West Bank has had the same effect, as new generations of Palestinians continue to see Israel as a colonial power that expropriates their land.

The difficult transition to co-existence

Though critical to the construction and maintenance of identity throughout decades of conflict, these narratives have constituted impediments to the development of discourses that emphasise a peaceful resolution to the conflict in the form of a two-state solution. With the onset of the Israeli–Palestinian peace process in 1993, there have been significant efforts to look beyond these narratives to a future based on mutual recognition and co-existence, but the challenges remain enormous.

Acknowledging the victimhood of the other has largely been absent on both sides. For Israelis, recognition of the Palestinians as victims of Israeli actions is tantamount to legitimising Palestinian claims and thereby negating or diminishing their own. Such acknowledgement would put into question the foundational myths of the state of Israel, alter the deeply rooted Israeli perception of what happened in 1948 and prior, and mean losing their monopoly on victimhood so central to the national narrative.[133] Segev observes a deep-seated, 'almost existential need to believe that Zionism had caused no injustice' to the Palestinians.[134] This is fuelled by the psychological threat that the more one comes to understand an 'evil' antagonist, the more one is likely to criticise and see 'evil' in one's own actions.[135]

Beginning in the late 1980s, a group of revisionist Israeli 'new historians' including Morris, Pappé, Segev and Shlaim have spearheaded efforts to critically examine their own national narrative. Though not all 'new historians' accept the term, the wider critical examination of Zionism, Israeli history and Israeli society has also been labelled 'post-Zionism'. Their corroboration of important parts of the Palestinian narrative, particularly concerning 1948, caused immense anger and controversy in Israel due to 'a perception that they endanger the boundaries of the current [Israeli] identity and are seen as a threat to Israelis' self-image'.[136] Pappé notes that in public debate, the enterprise 'has been denounced as a typical intellectual exercise on the part of self-hating Jews in the service of the enemy'.[137]

Just like the Israelis, Palestinians reflect and embody Arthur's phrase 'the egoism of victimhood'.[138] Palestinians generally fear that the acknowledgement of Israeli suffering, the Holocaust, or its impact on the Jewish community mindset constitutes sympathy for the enemy after a history of demonisation and self-portrayal as the victim of the other.[139]

Palestinians like Antonius and Said display understanding and sympathy for the plight of European Jewry, and consider their horrific history a disgrace to modern civilisation. Still, they cannot accept that this justifies the dispossession of the Palestinians, a result Antonius considers 'morally outrageous': 'the relief of Jewish distress may not be accomplished at the cost of inflicting a corresponding distress upon an innocent and peaceful population'.[140] Said emphasises the connection between the two national traumas, arguing that it is no less appropriate for Europeans and Americans today, who support Israel because of the wrongs committed against the Jews, to realize that support for Israel has included, and still includes, support for the exile and dispossession of the Palestinian people.[141]

That historical self-criticism is more prevalent on the Israeli side is not particularly surprising given the wide asymmetry between the two sides. Israel is a sovereign state that enjoys a high level of economic development, a higher standard of living, and whose citizens have been more exposed to Western critical thought and intellectual discourse, including ideas such as post-structuralism. Rynhold has identified a cultural shift from materialism to post-materialism in Israeli society, and convincingly argues that this fomented the development of a more liberal left-wing within the Israeli Labour Party and society as a whole.[142]

By comparison, the Palestinians are still an occupied and dispersed people yet to realise their national goals. Bar-On recognises that the 'deep and in many ways justified sense of injustice and suffering that Palestinians must confront every day and everywhere in their land makes it very difficult for Palestinian historians to be more impassioned when they investigate the roots of their humiliations.'[143]

Indeed, occupation has adversely affected the creation of uniform Palestinian national identity. Control of systems of education is particularly important in this regard. Throughout the twentieth century, Palestinian education has always been controlled by either the Ottoman Empire, or the British, Egyptian, Jordanian, and Israeli occupiers that followed, and only recently by the Palestinians themselves. Since education is and has always been a 'potent entry-point for nationalist ideas' – particularly when teaching the subject of history – this is a significant handicap for the development of national identity.[144]

The development of a national curriculum was one of the first important projects undertaken by the PA following its creation in 1994, and, according to Brown, the only one that ran on schedule. In his study of the curriculum, Brown finds that it is highly nationalistic, but positively so without being prone to incitement against Israel. Regarding their treatment of Israel and Jews, the textbooks are 'more remarkable for their omissions than for their content. Palestinian schools do not teach hate through their books.'[145] However, as Bar-On and Adwan suggest, the complete omission of Israel, Israeli suffering, and the existence of an alternative narrative can nonetheless be taken to reflect a culture of enmity.[146] Steinberg goes even further and argues that 'the language of hatred and rejection is dominant'.[147] As this brief cross-section of views illustrates, the issue is a contentious one since, significantly, the textbooks do not teach children how to think about resolving the issue of statelessness.

This ambiguity has reverberated through all sections of Palestinian society. For Yasser Arafat and the PLO, the transition from revolutionary freedom fighters to state-builders was not an easy one, and the tension between the ethos of armed struggle and the ethos of compromise peace has been palpable. The onset of pragmatism and the peace process ushered in a post-revolutionary era but, as Webman argues, this has not uniformly been the case, and the immaturity of the Palestinian national movement has been apparent.[148] It lacked a clear strategy to achieve independence and statehood, and the PLO struggled to reconcile their traditional position with a new vision. Consequently, without engaging the people in an open discussion on the substance of an acceptable peace, the Palestinian public has been left unprepared for the necessary compromises and trade-offs such an agreement will entail.[149]

The right of Palestinian refugees to return to their original homes within Israel proper, commonly known as 'the right of return', was one of the cornerstones of Arafat's political platform, appealing especially to the Palestinian diaspora. Former Member of Knesset and IDF Chief of Staff Amnon Lipkin-Shahak has acknowledged the difficulty this posed for Arafat:

> The idea of keeping refugee camps was a political idea, and I can understand it from the Palestinian point of view, to justify the conflict and to justify the resistance and to make it easy to recruit people for the resistance. Suddenly you tell them that you gave up their right? With all the education that you've built through the years on a number of generations that this is the main issue that you are fighting for? And believe me, Arafat never really believed – and I spoke with him more than once – that the Palestinian refugees would go back to Jaffa and Haifa. But for him it was a very important issue.'[150]

A substantial challenge to the power of Fatah and the PLO has been posed by Islamist groups like Hamas who reject any compromise with the state of Israel, an entity they do not recognise.[151] In the absence of established channels of Palestinian mass participation in national politics, alternative political forces had room to flourish.[152] An offshoot of the Egyptian Muslim Brotherhood, Hamas seeks to eliminate Israel through *jihad* and establish an Islamic state in Palestine. Islamist militants have employed armed resistance against Israel, most significantly in the form of devastating suicide bombings but also rocket attacks, which has effectively derailed the peace process at a number of important junctures.

Disillusionment with the peace process and the widespread corruption within the autonomous Fatah-led PA produced a resounding victory for Hamas in the Palestinian legislative elections in January 2006. Differences between the two over participation in the security forces and civil service turned violent, and in June 2007 Hamas militarily took control of the Gaza Strip. Initial hopes that political participation might moderate their ideological standpoint were overly optimistic,[153] though more radical groups such as Palestinian Islamic Jihad have nonetheless challenged their supremacy and provided a more aggressive alternative. While there have been episodes of pragmatism and negotiation with Israel, such as the prisoner exchange involving Gilad Shalit and ceasefires following flares in cross-border violence, Hamas has not abandoned armed struggle or recognised Israel. The ongoing divisions among Palestinians, both ideological and geographical, makes one question which group accurately represents and speaks for the majority of the Palestinian people.

In his analysis of the ending of civil wars, Stedman has identified the phenomenon of 'spoilers' and the crucial task of 'spoiler management'.[154] Spoilers are groups who believe that their power, influence, worldview, and interests stand to be harmed by the peaceful settlement of a dispute. Violence – whether in the sense of physical aggression or Galtung's concept of 'structural violence', the 'obstruction of human potential by economic and political structures and institutions'[155] – is employed by spoilers to sabotage the peace process and perpetuate the conflict. In terms of an identity-based conflict, these are segments of society that still reject territorial compromise on religious or ideological grounds, and link identity to possession of the land in its entirety.[156] In the Israeli–Palestinian context, these spoilers reject a two-state solution.

Like its Palestinian counterpart, Israeli society also contains a number of significant spoilers in the form of nationalist territorial maximalists, both religious and secular, who gained substantial political currency following the territorial conquests of 1967 and together formed the ideological Land of Israel Movement.[157] To distinguish this group from traditional Labour Zionism – which adopted a more pragmatic policy towards the Palestinians, realising the impossibility of fully implementing Zionist ideology[158] – Ram coined the term 'neo-Zionism'.[159]

The religious Zionist Gush Emunim movement began establishing settlements in the newly acquired territories, viewing victory in the Six Day War as a miracle indicating the coming of the Messiah. Settling the land was a religious duty, the next phase of redemption, and any withdrawal from it was against God's will.[160] Lacking a comprehensive strategy for the future of the territories, the attitude of the ruling Labour government towards them was ambiguous, ranging from opposition and confrontation to complicity, sympathy with their Zionist idealism, and active support.[161] Still, they ultimately helped build the system and the result was an increase in the number of settlers and settlements.[162]

Though a signatory to the Fourth Geneva Convention of 1949, which states that an 'occupying power shall not deport or transfer parts of its own civilian population into the territory it occupies', Israel argued that the West Bank was not occupied territory and that the Convention thus did not apply. By so doing, Israel defied the opinion of the international community and established facts on the ground in a way that would become familiar: according to Gorenberg, by the summer of 1977, there were nearly 80 settlements and around 11,000 settlers in occupied territory, not counting the new neighbourhoods in annexed East Jerusalem which housed 40,000 Israelis.[163]

Following the Likud[164] victory in the 1977 elections, which created a ruling government coalition of the religious and secular right, government support for settlement expansion was unabashed. Two days after his election victory, Prime Minister Begin told the settlers of Qadum in the West Bank, 'These are liberated territories, which belong to the Jewish people. The new government will call upon young people to come and settle the land.'[165] The Likud election manifesto was clear:

> The right of the Jewish People to the Land of Israel is eternal, and is an integral part of its right to security and peace. Judea and Samaria shall therefore not be relinquished to foreign rule; between the sea and the Jordan, there will be Jewish sovereignty alone.[166]

Territorial concessions in the Sinai – part of the Camp David Accords with Egypt in 1978 – became the impetus for the further political mobilisation of the settlers, who considered withdrawal a crime against the land and feared that Camp David would set a precedent whereby the West Bank would be relinquished in return for peace with the Palestinians.[167] Gush Emunim established an official settlement movement, Amana, and later the Yesha Council, a wider settler umbrella organisation, which includes more militant factions. Both were recognised by the Begin government, entitling them to state and World Zionist Organisation budgets.[168] Sprinzak argues that with the Yesha Council and political parties like the National Religious Party, Mafdal, and Tehiya, the settler movement and the 'radical right' was not a marginal political phenomenon, but a cabinet partner and a political organisation with a credible record of action.[169]

Furthermore, as Efron observes, the religious ultra-Orthodox have held the deciding votes in every election since 1977, when their main party Agudat Yisrael was persuaded to join Begin's government. Though a minority in Israel, ultra-Orthodox Jews wield a political influence vastly disproportionate to their electoral strength.[170] The Sephardi ultra-Orthodox party Shas has seen a steady rise in its political fortunes since its creation in 1984, and is one of the main political parties in Israel.[171] Significantly, the ultra-Orthodox oppose the division of Jerusalem, when Palestinians want East Jerusalem as the capital of their state.

According to the Foundation for Middle East Peace, by the end of 1993, the settler population in the West Bank, Gaza Strip, and East Jerusalem numbered 269,200. By 2008, after the evacuation of the Gaza Strip, the West Bank and East Jerusalem was home to 488,471 settlers.[172] The Palestinians and the international community have repeatedly described the settlements as obstacles to peace. In addition to the settlement enterprise, violence perpetrated by Israeli spoilers has had extremely negative consequences for the peace process. The assassination of Prime Minister Yitzhak Rabin on 4 November 1995 by religious zealot Yigal Amir was particularly devastating, and took place in an atmosphere of severe delegitimisation of Rabin's government by the radical right following the Oslo Agreement.[173]

Thus, although the asymmetry between the two sides is very pronounced and the occupation undoubtedly complicates the quest for peace, these difficulties are compounded by the fact that both parties suffer from serious cleavages within their societies. Intense competition exists not only between identity groups, but also within each identity group in a different way from most inter-state peace processes.[174] The notion of peaceful co-existence with a former enemy exposes internal differentiations and accentuates these cleavages, bringing spoilers to the fore.[175] An enemy and an active threat create unity and provide purpose, things that are difficult to supplant. It creates an extremely challenging situation for any leader attempting to sue for peace, as they are likely to face violent opposition from multiple directions.[176]

Bob Lang, a native of Manuet, New York, immigrated to Israel and Efrat, an Israeli settlement in the West Bank. He believes that the land is Jewish:

> If there is a Jewish people, Judea and Samaria are their home. To tell a Jew he cannot live in Hebron is to deny the existence of the Jewish people and the history of the Jewish people. Ninety per cent of the places mentioned in the Bible are in Judea and Samaria . . . It is Jewish land and I feel the history in my bones. I need no other guidebook here but the Bible. When the bulldozers are working to make new homes, they always hit ancient sites – and always those ancient sites are Jewish.[177]

Fakhri Kamel, a pharmacist in Jaffa, runs a shop that has been in his family for two generations and speaks bitterly about the past:

> Now the only thing that remains of Jaffa is the name. There is nothing left of the old Jaffa. The glorious days, the peace of mind, the people, they are all lost. Christian or Muslim, we were all Palestinians before 1948, and we were proud of it. When we travelled abroad, we said we were Palestinians . . . People lived in every corner. This is our country and I don't believe that God promised it to anyone else.[178]

These competing national narratives have taken many decades to develop and crystallise. They lie at the heart of the intractable conflict, and it is these identity politics that make it so hard to solve. Kriesberg emphasises four dimensions of reconciliation, key to a wider acceptance of the other: shared truths, justice, mutual regard, and mutual security. Realising these sometimes contradictory aspects is a gradual and extremely difficult process which takes time – decades or even generations – and is subject to the strains and tribulations of the continued conflict.[179]

While Pappé espouses the development of shared truths – a common bridging narrative shared by each community – and sees the emergence of post-Zionism and the 'new historians' as an important step toward this, Bar-On and Adwan do not believe that this is possible, apart from within a few exclusive and elite groups. The narratives are intertwined but are nonetheless distinctly separate and should be acknowledged as such.[180] Thus, each side does not necessarily have to accept the narrative of the other, but must at the very least acknowledge that a different narrative exists. 'If by "bridge" we mean develop greater mutual understanding and compassion, the answer is clearly "yes"; if the concept reflects a hope for a uniform narrative, the answer is clearly "no".'[181]

Erekat has identified this salient issue:

> I have predicted from very early on in this peace process, it's going to be painful, it's going to be long, because it's not about the ability of leaders reaching common ground. Common ground on what? Jews don't believe that Muhammad ascended to heaven from Jerusalem. Neither do Christians. Muslims will not change this. But both religions must accept that as a Muslim belief, and respect that ... People must change the way they have been thinking for many, many, many, many years. And without realising the bigger picture we cannot have peace ... I know that Christian and Muslim Palestinians will not convert to Judaism and become Israelis. Jews will not convert to Christianity and Islam and become Palestinians. So we know that. Now how do you prepare the atmosphere around us to accept this new reality? That's what peacemaking is all about.[182]

CHAPTER 2

THE EVOLUTION OF SWEDISH RELATIONS WITH ISRAEL AND THE PALESTINIANS: FROM A LABOUR LOVE AFFAIR TO THE TWO-STATE SOLUTION

If dialogue falls silent, only violence, doom, and madness remain.

– Olof Palme[1]

The ruling Swedish Social Democratic party has intervened in the Arab–Israeli conflict, particularly its Palestinian component, with a missionary zeal unequalled by any other European government.

– *The Jerusalem Post* – 11 February 1996[2]

Sweden's active foreign policy is the reason this small but outspoken Scandinavian nation is sometimes called the world's leading exporter of unsolicited advice.

– *The New York Times* – 16 December 1988[3]

Despite the geographical distance between Scandinavia and the land of Palestine, not to mention the manifold cultural and social differences, Sweden has developed strong bonds with both Israelis and Palestinians over the course of the twentieth century. The ongoing Israeli–Palestinian conflict has periodically made diplomatic relations akin to walking a tightrope between the two parties. This triangular relationship has fluctuated with the ebb and flow of Swedish, regional Middle Eastern, and wider international politics, and Swedish foreign policy has vacillated between being perceived as pro-Israeli and pro-Palestinian. A steady constant, however, has always been the promotion of dialogue between the parties and a negotiated solution to the conflict. This chapter will examine the development of Swedish politics towards the region, and outline how the attainment of a mediating role in the conflict has been made possible.

Swedish interest in the Holy Land has historically been predominantly theological, with a small number of religious emissaries and pilgrims making the long journey to Jerusalem from around the eighteenth century onwards. Unlike certain other Christian movements in Europe and the United States that focused more intently on Palestine, the Swedish Protestant State Church did not support the idea of a return to Zion. Sweden was prone to the religious and folkloric anti-Semitism which characterised Europe, and it was not until the late eighteenth century that borders were opened to small numbers of Jewish immigrants. Restrictions against Jews were gradually abolished through the mid-nineteenth century, and while both Yegar and Abadi both point out that the last discriminatory law preventing Jews from becoming government ministers was only abolished in 1951, they neglect to consider its wider content and thereby misrepresent it. The law stated that government ministers and certain other state employees (teachers, for example), had to be members of the Protestant State Church. It was not specifically aimed at Jews, as Yegar implies, but applied equally to all other faiths, Catholics, Muslims, anyone outside the Church. He further asserts that anti-Semitic thought remained prevalent in political and social circles, which is highly debatable.[4]

Although a policy of neutrality was in place during World War II, it is quite a chequered past in many respects. Some Swedes were sympathetic to the Nazis, the sale of iron ore to Germany continued during the war, and the German Army was allowed to use Swedish railways[5] to move troops and supplies, which facilitated Hitler's domination of the rest of Scandinavia. Like many other countries, Sweden watched in relative silence as the Holocaust unfolded in Germany and eastern Europe. Still, beginning in 1942, Sweden provided a safe haven for thousands of Jews from Norway, Denmark and Finland, and Count Folke Bernadotte played a part in the release and transfer of further thousands of prisoners from the Thereisenstadt and Ravensbruck camps in 1945, many of them Jews. King Gustav V sent a personal plea to the Hungarian Regent Horthy de Nagybanya 'to beg in the name of humanity that you take measures to save those who still remain to be saved of this unfortunate people'.[6] Most significant during this period were the actions of Raoul Wallenberg, a Swedish diplomat in Nazi-occupied Hungary, who protected thousands of Hungarian Jews under the Swedish flag. 1948 saw the introduction of laws prohibiting incitement against a people, and specifically imposed a prison sentence for the public display of anti-Semitism.

In 1947, Emil Sandström was chair of the first UN Special Committee on Palestine (UNSCOP) whose report on the state of affairs there constituted the basis for the UN partition plan of 29 November. The following year, the Norwegian Secretary General of the United Nations, Trygve Lie, asked Count Bernadotte if he would be willing to serve as UN mediator for Palestine. His reasoning for accepting the post, as explained by himself, went as follows:

> My first reaction was a feeling of immense gratitude to be considered for an assignment of such responsibility and complexity. At the same time, I naturally had feelings of doubt as to whether or not I should accept it. I knew, after all, that the chances of success were minimal. On the other hand, I believe that one cannot just undertake tasks on such a basis, and that one cannot be guided merely by considerations of personal prestige when it comes to such difficult endeavours.
>
> My knowledge of the situation in Palestine was undoubtedly superficial . . . Perhaps the fact that I had not previously dealt with the Palestine question was an advantage. There was, after all, a chance that an outsider like myself would be able to provide some new perspectives on the predicament, but I freely admit that the thoughtful work of countless previous commissions of inquiry weighed against such a possibility. My eventual acceptance of the post was primarily down to the critical nature of the issue and I could not therefore justify sparing any personal effort in working towards a solution.[7]

Clearly aware of his own shortcomings, Bernadotte nevertheless pursued his goals as stated in UN General Assembly Resolution 186, to 'assure the protection of the Holy Places' and 'arrange for the operation of services necessary to the safety and well-being of the population of Palestine', while promoting 'a peaceful adjustment of the future situation'.[8] His success was very limited. Although he managed to establish two periods of truce between Israel and the Arab states in June and July 1948, both of his proposals for a comprehensive settlement were rejected by the parties.[9]

Prime Minister David Ben-Gurion, Foreign Minister Moshe Sharett, and most Israelis in general were unimpressed with Bernadotte and considered his suggestions biased towards the Arabs. As Ben-Gurion confided to his diary, 'those who suspect that he is a Bevin agent are not too far off the mark'.[10] Without being a British 'agent', Bernadotte shared Bevin's view and 'believed that the [1947] partition plan had been a mistake, that the creation of a separate Jewish state was bound to lead to war, and that the creation of a unitary state "with far-reaching rights for the Jews" would have been preferable'.[11] On 17 September 1948, the day after he completed his second plan, members of 'The Fatherland Front', a group within the militant Jewish nationalist organisation Lehi, also known as the 'Stern Gang', gunned down Bernadotte at a roadblock in West Jerusalem. Among the Lehi leaders who tacitly authorised the assassination was Yitzhak Shamir, who in 1983 became Prime Minister of Israel.[12]

Unsurprisingly, Swedish Foreign Minister Östen Undén issued what Yegar has described as a 'very strong and unpleasant denunciation' of the assassination, implying that the Israeli government was in part culpable for its tolerant attitude towards the terrorists. The official Israeli report on the murder was received on 24 April 1949, but was deemed inadequate by the Swedish government, which also rejected Israeli explanations of difficulties surrounding the investigation. The Swedish attorney general said that the deficiencies of the report were 'in fact of so grave a character that doubts may well be held as to whether the Israeli authorities really intended to bring the enquiry to a positive result'.[13] The episode also had ramifications at the UN. Sweden abstained on a 1949 General Assembly vote on the admission of Israel, when another vote in favour would have meant *de jure* recognition of the new state. During the discussion, the Swedish ambassador condemned Israel for the measures taken in response to the assassination, while also making clear that it did not look favourably on the use of the episode by other states as arguments against Israeli membership, reflecting the duality of the Swedish position in this instance.[14]

In response, an Israeli investigative commission found Swedish accusations of negligence largely unjustified, although it agreed with some criticisms, including police negligence.[15] Following another report from Walter Eytan, the Director General of the Israeli Ministry of Foreign Affairs, Undén issued the following statement to the press: 'In accepting the expressions of regret and the apology conveyed by Dr Eytan on behalf of his government, the Swedish government considers the exchange of views on this matter as having reached its conclusion.'[16] Swedish *de facto* recognition of Israel came on 16 February 1949, while *de jure* recognition waited until 12 July 1950. Although officially shelved, the assassination would continue to cast a shadow over Swedish–Israeli relations, particularly during Shamir's premiership. At a commemoration ceremony dedicated to Bernadotte in Tel Aviv on 14 May 1995, Israeli Foreign Minister Shimon Peres reiterated Israel's 'vigorous condemnation' of, and 'profound regret' for, the murder, in the hope that the proceedings would 'heal the wound and bring this tragic incident to a final and definite close'.[17]

Otherwise, relations between the two countries were exemplary, primarily due to the centrality of the Labour movements in both governments. In Israel, the Mapai Party led by Ben-Gurion, the predecessor of the modern Labour party, had been the primary political party throughout the Mandatory period and continued its rule uninterrupted until 1977. Its Swedish Labour counterpart, Socialdemokraterna, the Social Democratic Party, shared its socialist foundational principles and enjoyed a similar longevity in government. Both movements were thus firmly anchored in their respective societies, and were closely identified with the state. The Israeli experiment in socialist state-building was widely admired in Sweden, particularly aspects such as the pioneering spirit of the *kibbutz* movement, which appeared to many to be a realised socialist utopia.[18]

The Social Democrats had positively acknowledged Jewish immigration to Palestine in a number of ways in the early twentieth century. Secretary General of the party, Gustav Möller, organised a conference in Stockholm in late September 1919 entitled, 'The position of the Jewish people in Palestine and other countries', for which he received strong support from party leader Hjalmar Branting to convince the Foreign Ministry to grant visas to the Zionist participants and delegates. In a letter to Möller and the party dated 9 October 1919, signed by the Jewish socialists of Poale Zion across western and eastern Europe, the United States and Palestine, they thanked unreservedly in gushing, flowery language for the party's assistance. Despite persistent organisational difficulties the conference had gone ahead, they said, thanks to the tireless efforts of the party on their behalf, itself a demonstration of their unbending moral support for their cause, for which they were eternally grateful. In the 1930s, a positive in-depth analysis of Labour Zionism in Palestine written by Joachim Israel also appeared in a party journal.[19]

On 12 June 1948, the Social Democrats sent a telegram to the Mapai party, expressing 'its good wishes and its feeling of solidarity with the working class in the State of Israel'.[20] During this period, the Swedish public as a whole rallied around Israel, which was perceived as the refuge of the persecuted Jewish people. The horrors of the Holocaust, still fresh in people's minds, and feelings of collective guilt associated with it were no doubt important factors contributing to this attitude. Svenska Israelhjälpen ('Swedish Israel Aid') was a large organisation with a powerful mobilising force comprising a number of Sweden's higher political hierarchy. Axel Strand, president of Landsorganisationen (LO), the main blue collar trade union, and Waldemar Svensson, the deputy chairman of Folkpartiet ('the Liberal Party'), were among its main proponents, together with Carl Albert Andersson, head of the Stockholm municipal assembly, various academics and the Archbishop of the state Church.[21] The roughly 1 million SEK (200,000 USD) it accrued between 1951 and 1952 was given to the *moshav* of Kfar Achim, just south-east of Tel Aviv and Jaffa, in addition to 75 Swedish wooden houses, most of which are still in use today. Kfar Achim was built in the spring of 1949 on the site of Qastina, a Palestinian village whose approximately 900 inhabitants were expelled by the Givati Brigade of the IDF on 9 July 1948.[22]

In a public appeal for Svenska Israelhjälpen published in a liberal magazine that Svensson edited, reference is made to 'Israel's present state of emergency' and the dire need of supplies for Jewish immigrants, emphasising that 'Israel, through its immigration politics, relieves the present dire refugee situation in the world.' No mention is made of the Palestinian refugees, nor is there any connection made between their refugee status and the establishment of the State of Israel. The Israeli perspective on the conflict appears to have been pervasive, with little consideration for the catastrophe that had befallen the Palestinians despite the official position of the UN. Zionist arguments, for example that Palestine was not particularly densely populated, that Palestinians had been ordered to leave by Arab leaders, and that the Arab world was certainly large enough to accommodate any refugees who had fled, appear to have been generally accepted by large segments of the Swedish public who were supportive of Israel.[23]

Unlike most of his fellow countrymen, Bernadotte came to appreciate the scale and importance of the refugee issue through first-hand experience, and emphasised the right of Palestinian refugees to return to their homes. He described the condition of the refugees in the West Bank as 'appalling', and wrote, 'I have made the acquaintance of a great many refugee camps; but never have I seen a more ghastly sight than that which met my eyes here at Ramallah.'[24] Bernadotte was known for his humanitarian work during World War II as president of the Swedish Red Cross, and believed wholeheartedly in the importance of humanitarian enterprises.

> Although it sounds strange, it has been a privilege to see for myself the conditions which afflict war torn countries. I consider it a privilege since it has made me appreciate how grateful one should be that one's own country and family have been spared the devastation of war.[25]

The return of Palestinian refugees was one of many objectives that Bernadotte could not accomplish.

Support for Israel continued to be the trend; Swedish–Israeli bilateral relations between 1950 and 1967 were generally excellent. Ties between the Labour parties were strong: government ministers from each visited the other; the trade unions, LO and Histadrut, maintained very close links; trade relations were solid; mutual tourism was increasing, cultural events were held and reciprocated, and a Swedish–Israeli friendship league was created in 1954. At speeches in Uppsala and Stockholm, Ben-Gurion stressed Israel's friendship with Sweden, expressed gratitude for Swedish aid to Jewish refugees during the war, praised international figures like Dag Hammarskjöld, Secretary General of the UN, and Emil

Sandström, and emphasised the shared social values and socialist visions of the two states.[26]

Swedish Prime Minister Tage Erlander returned the favour in 1961, when he went on the first official state visit to Israel. However, on the basis of observations by the British Ambassador to Stockholm at the time and others, Abadi suggests that 'there was little tangible in the bilateral relations', and that they were only promoting goodwill. But there was plenty of it; the British Ambassador reported that 'there is in Sweden a considerable fund of interest in and sympathy for Israel'. This was not directly translated into unconditional political support, however, and diplomacy toward the Middle East was generally quite cautious. Erlander had apparently made it clear prior to his trip to Israel 'that there would be no political talks whatsoever'.[27]

In a speech on 13 November 1955, Foreign Minister Undén argued that the main reason for the continued dispute in the Middle East was the refusal of the Arab states to recognise the reality of Israel's existence as an independent state. 'In Sweden, we have watched with respect and admiration while the Jews have created a modern socialist and democratic state, which has been able to give work and new courage to millions of Jewish refugees. It is obvious to us that Israel has justified its existence.'[28] The 1956 Suez crisis did, however, evoke a critical reaction from Sweden at the UN and dented the goodwill that had been accumulated up until then. Significantly, it reflected the anti-colonialism that would become the flagship of Swedish foreign policy. Personally, Undén considered it 'a fateful act of madness by the Israeli government'. His official statement was more diplomatic but clear nonetheless: 'Israel's preventive war against Egypt cannot be justified. That Israel has been subjected to numerous provocations from its Arab neighbours for many years is indisputable. But that did not entitle Israel to resort to war on Egypt.'[29] Sweden thus sought to reinforce the principles enshrined in the UN charter regarding the non-use of force, and continued to advocate a negotiated solution to the Arab–Israeli conflict.

Still, sympathy for the difficult Israeli situation continued to be evinced. In the late 1950s, while he was an up-and-coming young Social Democrat and secretary-cum-speechwriter to Erlander, Olof Palme spoke of a Jewish state plagued by 'hateful attacks from neighbouring states' and 'repeated acts of violence by Arab terrorists'.[30] In a debate on nuclear disarmament at the Swedish Social Democratic Youth League

(SSU) congress in August 1958, Palme argued in favour of global disarmament and referred to war and arms races as generally immoral, but specifically acknowledged the Israeli dilemma in the Middle East as a potential exception: 'For Israel, pushed against the sea, fighting for her existence, the highest moral norm is survival.'[31]

On the eve of the Six Day War, Erlander expressed great concern for Israel's security.[32] As in 1956, adherence to UN principles guided the official response. The Swedish government adopted a position that they felt would not in any way jeopardise the chances of a peaceful resolution to the conflict, and so avoided overt criticism of either party and apportioning blame for the start of the war. In a speech to the General Assembly on 23 June 1967, UN ambassador Sverker Åström said, 'we do not feel that the General Assembly has to act judge and to weigh the guilt and responsibility of those who are involved in the conflict'. Rather, he emphasised the Swedish government's belief in the tenets of the UN charter:

> we wish to affirm emphatically our adherence to the principle that no right to occupy and no right to annex territory can be based on military conquest. Troops that are stationed on foreign territory as a result of military action must be withdrawn. This principle, which is based on moral, legal, and political imperatives, must be unequivocally confirmed by the UN.

Åström went on to call for free and unimpeded access for all faiths to the holy sites in Jerusalem, and acknowledged the 'politically pregnant and immensely tragic human problem of the refugees', in addition to the right of all countries in the Middle East to exist in peace and security.[33]

Officially, this stance was due to the appointment in November 1967 of senior Swedish diplomat Gunnar Jarring as special representative of the UN Secretary General in accordance with Security Council Resolution 242, which was considered a position of great importance. Since the Foreign Ministry did not in any way want to affect or prejudice Jarring's mission, a position of official neutrality on the Arab–Israeli issue was adopted.[34] This is how Palme explained the Swedish position in a letter to a fellow Social Democrat on 13 November 1969. He said that the situation was extremely complicated, and would only go so far as to state that Sweden supported the Jarring mission and Security Council Resolution 242, the source of his mandate.[35] Jarring was thus at least in part used as an excuse to avoid adopting an outspoken position on a very sensitive and divisive subject.[36] As the results of the Six Day War became entrenched, the atmosphere did, however, gradually begin to shift away from its traditional pro-Israeli leaning to an increasing focus on the plight of the Palestinians. This was due not only to the onset of the Israeli occupation of the West Bank and Gaza, but also to developments within Swedish politics, particularly the rise to power of Olof Palme and the reconfiguration of Swedish foreign policy.

Olof Palme and 'active neutrality'

Neutrality has long been the cornerstone of Swedish foreign policy. However, it is important to clarify what this policy actually entailed, as the term 'neutrality' is slightly misleading in this context, and has indeed often been misinterpreted and misrepresented. Throughout the Cold War, the Swedish government adhered to a policy of non-alignment in order to be able to remain neutral in war. While wholeheartedly sharing the cultural values and fundamental democratic tenets of the West, Sweden was governed by the Social Democratic Party and geographically close to the Soviet Union. Between the democratic West and the communist East, there was little doubt where Swedish sympathies lay, but she was not formally aligned with either bloc to avoid being dragged into a superpower war. In that event, Sweden would maintain its neutrality. Should this neutrality policy fail and the country be attacked militarily, Sweden would defend itself. Although this applied to all states, strategic thinking always designated the Soviet Union as the primary threat, in which case they would also put faith in their good relations with the West to see them through.

Up until the late 1960s, Swedish–US relations were indeed exemplary, and it is not an exaggeration to purport that an alliance existed in all but name. The Social Democrats played a central role in the pro-Western International Confederation of Free Trade Unions (ICFTU), which essentially sought to stem the spread of communism worldwide. Significantly, there was close cooperation in the realm of intelligence. Försvarets radioanstalt (FRA), the Swedish National Defence Radio Establishment, was monitoring the Soviets – mostly with American equipment – and happily shared their intelligence with the Americans, who in turn sold them radar and other military hardware.[37] Today, we know that very secret and very extensive discussions took place between Sweden and NATO on cooperation in the event of war, including NATO use of Swedish air strips.[38]

This close cooperation notwithstanding, Tage Erlander, Prime Minister from 1946 to 1969 and a household name in Swedish politics, wanted the world to 'have faith in our assurances that our non-alignment [in peacetime] means that in the event of war we shall maintain our neutrality'.[39] Nothing was to be done to make the superpowers mistrust Swedish neutrality, nor create expectations that Sweden may deviate from its outlined policy. In his first major speech on security issues as Prime Minister in 1970, Olof Palme explained Swedish neutrality as follows:

> As the foundation of our foreign policy, we have chosen freedom from alliances in peacetime with the object of neutrality in war. This expresses our line of action in two different situations: when peace prevails and when war has broken out in our area. We do not join any military alliances. We stand outside any alliances in order to make our neutrality in the event of war credible already in peacetime. Neutrality policy ... has enabled us to preserve our peace ... [and] has contributed to calm and stability in our part of the world.[40]

The centre-right coalition government established in 1976 continued this neutrality policy, as did the later Social Democratic government under Palme upon its election in 1982.

In its capacity as a non-aligned state, Sweden exercised a completely independent foreign policy, which towards the end of Erlander's term may be best described as an 'active neutrality' policy. At a special party congress on 23 October 1967, Foreign Minister Torsten Nilsson explained the nature of 'active neutrality' more widely:

> We are in the process of developing an active opinion on foreign affairs ... Sweden's policy of neutrality has never meant passivity, and will do so even less in the future. On the contrary, we try – both within and outside the UN – to voice as actively as we can the values inherent in Swedish democracy that in our opinion are compatible with our responsibility for the vital interests of our people.[41]

At the party congress in June the following year, Undén reiterated that neutrality did not mean indifference or reflect a lack of opinion. Sweden was a small nation, but that did not relieve it of the obligation to make a stand. Rather, by making itself heard, Sweden could help to strengthen international opinion in favour of peace, democracy, and social equality. Such articulations of opinion would in no way contravene Swedish neutrality policy.[42]

As a small nation, Sweden called for adherence to international law, the UN charter, and UN resolutions in order to strengthen the public status of international law as a regulator of international political behaviour. This stance sought to strengthen not only Swedish security, but also international peace and security.[43] An important part of foreign policy was thus to encourage the universal observance of UN principles such as the non-use of force and the peaceful resolution of disputes, and to assist in upholding them in any way possible.

Palme, successor to Erlander as the head of the Social Democratic Party and as Prime Minister, was the main figurehead and proponent of 'active neutrality', instrumental to its articulation and development. Without a doubt, Palme was the most prolific Swedish politician of the twentieth century, not only domestically but, more significantly, internationally. Loved by his followers and hated by his detractors, it was difficult to be indifferent to the man; whether good or ill, he certainly inspired a great deal of emotion. A brilliant public speaker, this was his political trademark. Rather than only employing sheer logical argument to prove the superiority of one position over another, Palme's personal oratory style centred on evoking human emotions, and often made references to his own personal character, conviction, and feelings.[44]

In the opening line of one of his most famous speeches, delivered in front of an SSU congress in Stockholm on 12 May 1964, he proclaimed, 'Politics is to aspire to something.' In a reference to Goethe's *Faust*, he then articulated his own personal belief that 'if one were to remove emotional conviction as a source of inspiration, the politics of democracy would become dull and grey'.[45] As Jan Eliasson, UN Deputy Secretary General, former Swedish Foreign Minister, and close colleague of Palme's has explained, 'it was important for Palme not to give way on an issue where his political fervour was so strong and a lot was at stake'.[46]

His was a brand of politics guided by a sense of morality based on what he believed were basic social democratic principles, rather than subscribing to a particular Cold War power bloc. As he stated unequivocally on 19 April 1975, 'for the Social Democrats, neither capitalism nor communism offer acceptable solutions for our social problems'.[47] Quoting Leszek Kolakowski, Palme maintained that it was naïve to believe we can be free of ideology. 'We can never free ourselves from our values. Our values and emotional conviction can, however, be a guiding source of our long-term political goals and ambitions.'[48]

As a representative of the International Student Conference, Palme spent the summer of 1953 travelling across south- and south-east Asia, stopping in India, Sri Lanka, Burma, Thailand, Malaysia, Singapore, and Indonesia. He spoke with student representatives to gain a deeper understanding of the political and social problems that plagued the developing world:

> Above all, we spoke about poverty and nationalism in Asia, and how the new societies should be structured . . . Socialism's demand for social fairness was an obvious starting point. There was no aggression in our relations, rather a feeling of commonality in our values and practical demands. Madness would be overcome; the poor people would chart their own course. My friends spoke tirelessly about contemporary reality and developed their dreams for the future.[49]

These experiences had a profound impact on him, and crystallised his perspective on international politics. Colleagues and friends of his have all said that Palme reacted very forcefully to oppression and violence against the poor and vulnerable, no matter where in the world it was happening. There was in him a strong personal feeling of sympathy for the subjugated, and he felt compelled to fight their corner.[50] As much as he helped shape Swedish politics, he also reflected a wider social mood. He represented a new generation of Social Democrats who advocated a more international brand of social equality and solidarity, and he gave them a bold voice with which to speak. For Palme, foreign and domestic policy both had to operate on the same basic principles of justice, democracy, and freedom, as these were universal values that had the same currency at home and abroad.[51] This was the theme of his May Day speech of 1968, with specific reference to the developing world.

> It would ring false if we worked for social equality domestically without a thought for the millions of starving people throughout the world. Similarly, it would ring false if we were to advocate help for the world's poor if we simultaneously let class cleavages and differences in income grow at home. There must be a clear and indisputable connection between what we strive for at home and what we stand for internationally. That is what gives stability to a political programme.[52]

Foreign policy was thus a crucial arena for Palme. Eliasson has argued that Palme fundamentally wanted to 'internationalise' Sweden. He was eager to show the world that Sweden had not only an identity, but also a role and a responsibility, all of which underpinned his demand for international solidarity.[53] Consequently, a number of key issues came to characterise Swedish foreign policy. Foremost among these were decolonisation and the need for national liberation. Often used as battlegrounds in the Cold War proxy conflict, Palme argued that Sweden had a moral responsibility to help developing states achieve real independence and self-rule. The developing world had to be afforded the democratic right to determine their own future, and Sweden offered political and economic solidarity towards this end. Rather than going capitalist or communist, Palme believed that developing countries would see the merits of the Swedish model for establishing egalitarian socialist societies and emulate it. Alongside democracy, the integrity and rights of small states as enshrined in international law was paramount, together with human rights and wider social equality. Furthermore, he was an ardent advocate of the peaceful resolution of conflicts and sought to enlist Swedish assistance in such endeavours wherever possible.

In the early 1960s, foreign aid became an important aspect of Swedish foreign policy. Written in 1962, government proposition 100 held that foreign assistance was primarily a matter of ethical behaviour and solidarity. The ambitious target it stipulated was to donate the equivalent of 1 per cent of Sweden's GDP in foreign aid every year, and thereby seek to improve the standard of living among the poor of the world. It was acknowledged that monetary aid alone would not cure all ills in and of itself, but should stimulate independent development initiatives with a view to improving self-sufficiency; in other words, the aid was to enable them to help themselves. Self-ownership of this process was considered paramount, and there were initially few restrictions on the use of funds or stipulations on purchasing from Swedish companies. At a time when foreign aid was a method whereby the superpowers brought developing nations in Africa and elsewhere into their fold as proxies, Sweden advocated independence and financial freedom for them to choose their own path. Palme said that 'the African peoples' struggle for freedom shall be supported on their own terms, on Africa's terms. Attempts to use African countries as pawns in a battle for power must be resisted to avoid a new scramble for Africa between the rival superpowers.'[54]

The Swedish International Development Agency (SIDA) was founded in 1965 as part of a reshuffle of the former government aid agency, and in 1968, Riksdagen, the Swedish parliament, decided that the 1 per cent goal should be enacted by 1974–5 years' budget. It was eventually reached only one year late, in 1975–6.[55] While concerns regarding the Swedish economic capacity to accommodate such a policy did cause a great deal of domestic debate and controversy,[56] internationally it was the choice of recipients that raised a number of eyebrows. Although Tanzania was unanimously accepted as the first recipient, aid to countries like Cuba and North Vietnam, and national liberation movements like the ANC in South Africa, FRELIMO in Mozambique, MPLA in Angola, PAIGC in Guinea Bissau, and ZANU and ZAPU in Rhodesia was all the more controversial.

Palme considered colonialism the scourge of the world, a system of injustice and warfare which had to be overcome. Moreover, it only served to bolster the communist cause, an anti-democratic system that Palme detested. In Malaysia, Palme observed, 'It is a strange paradox that the British government spends millions of pounds on killing a few communists in the jungle, which simultaneously produces an increasing number of them at the universities of Malaya.'[57] This reasoning also applied to Vietnam, an issue which put Palme and Sweden in the international limelight.

On 30 July 1965, Palme gave an incendiary speech at a congress of the Union of Christian Social Democrats in Gävle. It was a bold declaration, signalling the onset of 'active neutrality', a new era of outspoken Swedish foreign policy. The overriding theme was one of national self-determination and de-colonisation in Asia and Africa, with strong linkage to issues of poverty and equality. Palme stated his conviction that 'the struggle for national freedom is inextricably linked with the pursuit of social and economic emancipation. This pursuit of emancipation is the hallmark of the world today.' He was adamant that national liberation movements across the world deserved Sweden's support, for they were going through the same process Europe had gone through many years earlier:

> We should recognise a lot of this. What we see in the world today are more or less the old banners of the French revolution, calling for freedom, equality, and fraternity. What we are seeing is the rise of people against the upper classes. What we hear are the same demands for freedom and equality for the masses that once ignited hope and stimulated faith in the future among the growing Labour movements across Europe. The difference is that today's demands are at least in part directed towards us. The basic moral values of social democracy outline our duty to stand on the side of the oppressed against the oppressors, with the poor and downtrodden against their masters and usurpers.

Continuing in the same vein, he eventually specified the focus of his speech:

> I don't know if the farmers in Vietnamese villages – for it is after all mostly Vietnam that I have spoken about – have any utopias or dreams for the future. The impressions one gets convey a sense of hopelessness and resignation, of confusion and despair over a political power struggle which spills over into their lives. If they do dream of a future, it is probably a simple one: a peaceful environment, without starvation, where their human worth is respected. To them, no doubt that utopia seems distant and improbable.[58]

He went on to emphasise what he saw as the parallels between the Vietnamese struggle for a distant utopia and that of the pioneers of the Labour movement a century earlier. As with most of Palme's speeches, there was a heavy emphasis on morality, and the use of a moral compass to guide policy. He issued a damning indictment of colonialism, both old and new:

> The old colonial powers and industrial nations of the West have a sinful record in Asia and Africa that stretches far into the past. With the onset of the industrial revolution, liberal ideals of

> freedom began to gain currency in Europe. But the same industrial revolution also drove an overseas colonialist expansion to access raw materials, bringing oppression in its wake. It resulted in a cutting hypocrisy. While preaching ideals of freedom for its own citizens, these states simultaneously intensified their repression of the colonial subjects under their control. An English Queen could superciliously claim that 'all political power exercised over people should be to their benefit' while her governors and regiments in India brutally put down an attempt by Indians to exercise their legitimate rights. This contrast between word and social and political reality has been a constant burden for the old colonial powers. We can still find it in the world today.[59]

Palme created an intense controversy on 21 February 1968 during a massive protest against the Vietnam War in the centre of Stockholm. In solidarity with the Vietnamese, Palme walked side by side with the North Vietnamese ambassador to Moscow at the head of the demonstration. Although he himself always claimed to have been unaware that the ambassador would be attending, most commentators agree that this is highly doubtful. He explained the reason for his attendance to his close colleague, Thage G. Peterson: 'It was so natural for me, given my disposition towards freedom and justice, but what I felt deep inside was that I wanted to participate in the Vietnam protest. Nothing could have stopped me.'[60] His speech to the masses in attendance was a brutal indictment of the war in Vietnam:

> Democracy is an exacting system of government. It demands respect for others. One cannot force a system of government upon a nation from outside. The people must have a right to decide over their own destiny. It therefore presupposes the national right of self-determination. Democracy demands justice. One cannot gain a people by filling the pockets of those who are already rich while the poor are driven into ever deeper distress. One cannot meet the demand for social justice with violence and military power. Democracy presupposes social liberation. The goal of democracy can never be reached by means of oppression. One cannot save a village by wiping it out, setting the fields on fire, destroying the houses, capturing the people, or killing them.

He went on to condemn French and American colonialism in Vietnam, describing them as 'foreign intruders' who had consistently stood in the way of free elections and a united Vietnam. The regime in South Vietnam, characterised by 'corruption, inefficiency' and 'indifference to social demands', was the antithesis of democracy:

> The United States maintain that they want to defend the democratic rights of the people of Vietnam against foreign intruders. But if one is to speak of democracy in Vietnam, it is obvious that this is represented in a considerably higher degree by the FNL than by the United States and its allied juntas ... A regime which requires the aid of more than 500,000 American soldiers to be able to survive one single day has not got the support of the people ... On what grounds can we deny the right of the Vietnamese people to choose their own regime? It cannot be the object of democracy to make itself a guardian for other peoples. On the contrary, it is an abuse of the fundamental ideas of democracy ... This democratic opinion does not consider the American war in Vietnam support for democracy, but a threat against democratic ideas, not only in Vietnam but also throughout the world.[61]

To Palme and a substantial segment of the Swedish public, the war was 'a revolt against those who oppress fundamental social and human rights' with 'deep roots among the people'.[62] His image was that of a resistance leader, a supporter of national liberation, and a tireless anti-apartheid campaigner. According to Palme, socialism 'obliges us to make common cause with the oppressed and fight on their side against the powers which exploit them'.[63]

The intense American bombing of North Vietnam over Christmas 1972 was too much for Palme to bear. In a statement, he said:

> One should call things by their rightful name. That which is now going on in Vietnam is a form of torture. Military motives for the bombings cannot exist ... It cannot reasonably be based on Vietnamese intransigence at the negotiating table ... These actions are intended to torture people, torture a nation in order to humiliate it, force it to submit to power. That is why these bombings are an outrage. Modern history is full of such deeds.

> There are often names connected to them. Guernica, Oradour, Babij Jar, Katyn, Lidice, Sharpeville and Treblinka. Violence has triumphed. But judgement has been levelled against those responsible. Now there is another name to add to the list. Hanoi – Christmas, 1972.[64]

In an interview with *Time* magazine in 1973, he explained the language he had employed. 'I didn't make a direct analogy ... You can't compare military commanders or political systems. What I wanted to illustrate is the effects on human beings of mass violence and the enormity of what was happening during the bombings of Hanoi ... To make people listen and understand you have to use fairly strong language.' Palme thought these actions were particularly difficult to digest given his personal affection for the United States.

> We have been used to looking to the United States for moral leadership and authority when it comes to questions of peace and the preservation of basic human values ... And just because of this we feel our sorrow and our disappointment to be so great when something like the bombings of Hanoi and Haiphong happens.[65]

Pierre Schori, a close associate of Palme's, a government minister, and later UN ambassador, saw first-hand the 'passion and anger' which the war ignited in Palme, as he struggled to reconcile it with his love for the United States.[66] Palme was genuinely hurt by accusations of being anti-American, which was not at all the case. Eliasson explains that it was rather

> a matter of necessary reaction to blameworthy superpower behaviour, not about the USA or Americans generally ... He believed that it was a question of international law and human rights, of the integrity of small states, and the importance of standing firm even against a superpower. Next time, it could be the Soviet Union involved in a crisis in our immediate vicinity.[67]

Contrary to the claims of some conservative Swedish politicians at the time, particularly Sven Wedén of the Liberal party, the Swedish stance on Vietnam did not raise fundamental doubts about Swedish neutrality. True, it prompted several diplomatic crises with the United States, which saw them recall their ambassador multiple times and freeze high level relations for as long as 15 months after Palme's 1972 statement, but Swedish neutrality itself was never in question.[68] Kissinger confirmed this fact in the late 1970s, and maintained that a difference of opinion between friendly nations was not out of the ordinary. Any 'punishments' above and beyond diplomatic posturing would have been unwise, he said, as Swedish security policy contributed to stability in northern Europe, a point the Swedes had made repeatedly.[69] Trade relations and defence cooperation were not affected and remained strong.

Another common conservative claim that the United States and the West were singled out for condemnation above and beyond all others does not stand up to scrutiny. In his empirical study on the frequency of Swedish international criticism between 1947 and 1990,[70] Bjereld has found that, second only to South Africa with a staggering 138, Sweden criticised the Soviet Union the most, with 51 instances of criticism, compared to 38 for the United States and 22 for both superpowers jointly.[71] Just as Western transgressions of human decency were harshly criticised, so were actions by the communist Eastern bloc and the undemocratic nature of those regimes. Controversial issues that were perceived to be morally indefensible were heavily and harshly criticised, regardless of who was on the receiving end of this criticism and liable to get upset.

Ehnmark explains that

> what made Palme so controversial in the realm of foreign affairs was that he was simultaneously anti-communist and anti-imperialist. It was unusual then. You were either one or the other. Consequently, everyone was furious. The anti-communists could not forgive his criticism of the West for their colonial wars and articulating the needs of the developing world during the Cold War. Many of the anti-imperialists could not forgive his criticism of the Eastern dictatorships. But his dual criticism was consistent throughout.[72]

On 19 April 1975, in a speech to the Stockholm Social Democratic Association, Palme described the communist leadership in Czechoslovakia as 'beasts of dictatorship', representatives of a system that did not instil any hope for a future based on democracy and social justice, but whose security apparatus violently repressed 'reactionaries' who sought to express their distaste towards the regime.[73] At the 1979 Riksdag debate on foreign policy, Palme spoke of the dangers of the communist system:

> The communist states lack the necessary level of social and political support to develop a social polity. The absolute power of the police state cannot guarantee serenity and stability, much less economic growth. Instead, it can constitute a security threat, both domestically and internationally.[74]

Sweden strongly condemned the Soviet invasion of Afghanistan, for reasons nearly identical to those that underpinned criticism of the Americans in Vietnam. In a speech to the Stockholm Social Democratic Association's representative assembly on 12 January 1980, Palme explained these reasons to his audience. Primarily, the rights of small states were again being 'threatened and trampled [upon]' by this 'brutal aggression, a flagrant violation of every nation's right to self-determination, a violation of international law. A military intervention in another nation's domestic affairs can never be justified. A people's liberation must be its own work.' Such behaviour was entirely consistent with previous superpower actions:

> we have now been offered another example of how little the rights of small states mean, when their strivings are in conflict with the guarding of spheres of influence by the superpowers and what they judge to be their vital interests ... In Hungary in 1956 and in Czechoslovakia in 1968, too, we saw Russian tanks rolling in. And in the Dominican Republic and in Indochina we saw American marines intervening as intruders. It is indeed terrifying how little tolerance the superpowers show the people within their own power sphere. The Soviet Union could not tolerate the liberalisation in Hungary by Imre Nagy, could not tolerate the attempts to create socialism with a more human face in Czechoslovakia. Now it obviously could not tolerate Muslim nationalism in its southern neighbouring country.[75]

Furthermore, it stoked tensions between East and West, threatening détente and thereby heightening the likelihood of a continued arms race rather than a move towards mutual disarmament. Palme argued that not only was it a blow in the fight against colonialism, international poverty and human rights violations, but an assault on a non-aligned state and a threat to the wider non-aligned movement.[76] Just over two years later, this position was reiterated and reaffirmed at a party hearing on human rights jointly organised with LO, where Palme proclaimed that the continued Soviet presence in Afghanistan would continue to be a threat to international peace and détente.[77]

With the benefit of hindsight, it is easy to criticise the romanticist socialist logic employed by Palme and the Social Democrats towards the developing world and consider it naïve. It was based on an honest belief that the Labour structures Sweden had employed to develop into the modern welfare state envied by so many could be effectively exported elsewhere.[78] More or less all of the African recipients of Swedish foreign aid failed to live up to expectations: Julius Nyerere's brand of African socialism (*Ujamaa*) had devastating economic and agricultural effects in Tanzania; Angola, Guinea-Bissau, Mozambique and Zimbabwe have been continuously ravaged by brutal civil wars; governmental practices are far from democratic and their human rights records are poor.

Palme himself was very aware of these dangers. Towards the end of the 1970s and in the early 1980s, he became increasingly pessimistic and saddened by the violence that unfolded.[79] Still, Palme and the Social Democrats believed passionately that the right to determine one's own future was paramount, that self-determination was a just cause, and that independence was the basis for social and economic development. Independence had to come first, and peace would hopefully be the end result.

Other principled stands, however, were vindicated. The outspoken Swedish position on Vietnam was ultimately proved correct. As Walter Mondale admitted on a visit to Stockholm in 1979, and Robert McNamara subsequently expressed in his reappraisal of the thinking behind the war, *In Retrospect*, 'you were right – and we were wrong'.[80] Similarly, the fierce criticism of totalitarian fascism in Europe and the fundamentally self-destructive nature of communist systems further east has been substantiated. The world united to put an end to South African apartheid, while nuclear disarmament continues to be strongly advocated by many. But of paramount importance, for the purposes of this book at least, is the eventual international and Israeli acceptance of the Swedish stance toward Yasser Arafat and the Palestinians.

Palestinians as a people with legitimate national rights

In line with 'active neutrality' and the values that Swedish foreign policy sought to represent, policy towards the Israeli–Palestinian conflict was gradually altered to reflect the new reality following the Six Day War. This was the essence of the message conveyed to Israeli Foreign Minister Abba Eban when he visited Stockholm in early May, 1968. Although Foreign Minister Torsten Nilsson stressed the friendly nature of Swedish–Israeli relations, he also added that new factors were present.[81] Indeed, as the Israeli occupation of the West Bank and Gaza Strip became increasingly entrenched and showed no signs of being renounced, prior perceptions of the parties were re-evaluated. Although most of the older generation of social democrats still strongly supported Israel and close contacts between the two Labour parties were maintained, the newer generation represented by Palme increasingly objected to Israeli policy towards the Palestinians and eventually began to specifically acknowledge their national rights. But while criticism of Israel became more pronounced, its right to exist was never in doubt.

While the Jarring mission kept official pronouncements devoid of any real criticism of either Israel or its neighbours, opinions were expressed domestically and privately. In an article published 17 September 1967, Palme noted that 'in the Middle East, Israel has triumphed militarily in a war. Negotiations and peace, however, are absent, and there is no doubt that talks are hindered by, among other things, the hate and devastation bred by humiliation and poverty.'[82] Although he did not go on to clarify this statement further, this was in all likelihood a reference to the conquered Arab territories.

Just over a month later, at the special Social Democratic Party congress where Nilsson announced an increasingly 'active opinion on foreign affairs' in line with 'the values inherent in Swedish democracy', he offered his view on the Arab–Israeli conflict:

> The Arab states saw before their eyes how a modern welfare state was built up in the centre of a poor and backward area. An irreconcilable atmosphere of revenge was stirred up. Hundreds of thousands of Arab refugees were condemned to a comfortless refugee existence while awaiting to be able to return to their former home. Fundamentally it is a social problem that has to be solved.

He noted that Sweden had at that stage contributed 12 million SEK toward the problem, which had to be dealt with immediately in the interests of 'this unfortunate group of people'.

Nilsson went on to express admiration for Israeli democracy and socialism, but was concerned for their future. He feared that Israeli leaders would view their new borders as offering strategic advantages, rather than acknowledge the longer term danger inherent in strengthening the Arab lust for retribution.[83] Several years later, Palme echoed this view in a confidential report to his Party executive:

> my view, since 1967, is that Israeli policy has been flawed. Rather than maintain their irreconcilable stance to avoid budging a millimetre in the way of concessions or offers, they should use the position of strength they gained from the Six Day War in order to settle things and relinquish occupied territories, and try to create international guarantees ... It is no secret that Jarring was not given a millimetre by the Israelis to negotiate with ... He had started the Arabs down that path, but he never received anything from the Israelis. I have no intention of stating that publicly, but I want to say it here.[84]

A significant landmark was reached in the early 1970s when the notion of a Palestinian state began to be publicly voiced. At the end of January 1970, a small delegation from the Social Democratic Party visited Israel for talks with their Labour colleagues like Prime Minister Golda Meir, the new Party Secretary Lyova Eliav, and the commander-in-chief of the occupied territories Shlomo Gazit, among others. According to Schori, a member of the Swedish delegation, the trip was an important catalyst for a much more nuanced line of thought on the Palestinian issue.[85] The confidential summary of their discussions submitted to the Party executive outlines a difference of opinion within Israel about the future of the Palestinians and the occupied territories: 'A growing opposition to the government line is demanding that the national identity of the Palestinian Arabs is acknowledged.'

This was certainly the line taken by Eliav, who in the spring of 1969 had published a series of articles collectively titled, 'New targets for Israel.' He summarised his position thus: 'The first thing we have to do is to admit that the Palestinian Arabs exist as a new nation. The sooner we admit this fact and their existence, the better it will be for us, for them, and for the state. Secondly, Israel must make it clear to the world that we have no intention of annexing the territories.'[86] The report refers to this as 'a new positive line in the political debate in Israel', indicating a clear preference for such an outcome.

This was in stark contrast to Meir's stance on the issue. She was asked if a national Palestinian identity existed, and 'after much hesitation' replied that 'if the Arabs in the West Bank and Jordan make an arrangement with Hussein and then re-name themselves Palestinians then fair enough. If we achieve peace that way, I'll be the first to congratulate the King of Palestine.' This Labour policy, known as the 'Jordanian option', served as a compromise to smooth over internal rifts within the Labour party vis-à-vis the Palestinians. According to the Israeli representatives who were party to the conversation above, it was the first time Meir had ever accepted the use of the term 'Palestinian' in conversation.[87] She was otherwise adamant, privately and publicly, that no 'Palestinians' existed, that it was not a legitimate term, and that the Arabs of Palestine were merely Southern Syrians or Jordanians without a separate national identity.

After attending the Socialist International party leaders conference on the Middle East in London in November 1973, Palme reported back to the Riksdag:

> If we want the [Socialist] International to play a constructive role, we must naturally take as a starting off point our solidarity with our Israeli Labour friends. But we must also have contacts with the Arabs. They must also be included in any constructive peaceful solution. You cannot simply view the Palestinians as refugees. In the public debate, they have now acquired a national identity, become a people.[88]

The occupation was increasingly viewed as a sword of Damocles hanging over Israel's neck. At the same conference, Palme articulated this position to Meir. The future, he said, was working against Israel. It was in Israel's long-term interest to make peace with the Arab states generally and the Palestinians more specifically, even though it would require painful concessions. In demographic terms, Israel was surrounded by millions of Arabs, a number that stood to increase over time together with their military capacity. A time would eventually come when their potential would be extremely dangerous to the Jewish state unless peace agreements existed between them. Meir disagreed vehemently, arguing instead that Israel's future based on deterrence was bright.[89]

Not only was the occupation perceived to be endangering Israel's long-term security, but it was also seen to reflect very poorly on Israeli democracy. Just as Palme had been 'saddened and disappointed by the contrast between America's ideals of freedom and the reality persisting in Vietnamese villages',[90] there was a parallel sense that Israel was depriving the Palestinians of the legitimate freedoms that they themselves enjoyed and claimed to value in principle. This perspective does not appear to be clearly understood by neo-conservative historians such as Wistrich, who has branded Palme 'anti-American' and 'an Israel-hater of purest Social Democratic vintage'.[91] Both of these accusations are wildly off the mark, particularly considering the previous decades of pro-Israeli Social Democratic policy which Palme had subscribed to. If anything, Palme was a great admirer of Israel, another small socialist state.

Just weeks prior to the Six Day War, Palme spoke at a gathering in Stockholm to celebrate Israel's nineteenth anniversary. He praised Israeli success in their state-building enterprise: the development of communal agricultural systems like the *kibbutz*; industrialisation; the rapid transition from a developing to a developed country; and not least the integration of Jewish refugees from all over the world, which Palme viewed with deep 'admiration'. Israel was an example which the developing world could learn from, an illustration of 'the sympathy that one always feels for the small nation that seeks to exercise their right to shape their own destiny.'[92] The Israeli ambassador thanked him unreservedly for his 'magnificent' speech.[93] Notably, there was no mention whatsoever of the Palestinians.

Still, Palme spoke presciently of the dangers of aggressive, intolerant, expansionist nationalism, and called instead for 'internationalism':

> What the future requires of us now is above all to spread the idea of solidarity and co-operation, which has taken root in individual nations, beyond borders. Our main national pursuit should be to try to enact in real terms the idea of peace and security between

peoples ... To gain strength, [internationalism] requires a respect for the identities of peoples and their differences.[94]

In exactly the same way that his stance on the Vietnam War had not been based on any anti-Americanism whatsoever, nor was his view on the Israeli–Palestinian conflict based on anti-Israeli bias or anti-Semitism. In each case, it was not about being for one side against the other, but a matter of speaking out for an oppressed people who were being denied their rights.[95]

In several speeches throughout 1973, but particularly in his address to the UN General Assembly on 11 October, Foreign Minister Krister Wickman was very critical of Israel and IDF actions against the Palestinians. To the Riksdag on 21 March, he described Israeli reprisals against terrorism as 'severe countermeasures ... that are more likely to aggravate existing disputes than to provide real security against violence'. In front of the UN, 'reprisals' or 'severe countermeasures' were referred to more strongly as 'counter-terror', and the Palestinians were officially mentioned for the first time: 'ever since the foundation of Israel, the future of the Palestinian Arabs has been uncertain'. The matter of the occupation appears to have been prioritised and separated from the overall Arab–Israeli conflict context. There was no clear acknowledgement of Egyptian and Syrian aggression in the 1973 Arab–Israeli War, and Wickman held the line that condemnation of one side would not contribute to a peaceful resolution. Following this logic and the continuing policy of deferring to the Jarring UN mission, Sweden abstained on most bills introduced by the Arab states condemning Israel.[96]

While on an official diplomatic visit to Algeria in November 1974 at the invitation of President Houari Boumedienne, Palme was introduced to Arafat at an official dinner. Although he himself claimed that Arafat's presence took him by surprise – as with the North Vietnamese ambassador to Moscow in Stockholm in 1968 – this has been disputed by Carl Lidbom and Schori who were both present that evening. According to them, Boumedienne asked Palme if he had any objections to the attendance of the 'special guest', to which he replied that it was not for him to say, but Boumedienne's prerogative as host to invite whomever he wished. The matter was largely out of his hands, as he could not reasonably refuse to attend. Palme did, however, find it very interesting to meet one of the main protagonists in the Arab–Israeli conflict.[97]

In a report following his encounter with Arafat in Algiers, Palme articulated his views on the changing status of the Palestinians: 'More and more, we have come to realise ... that there is also a Palestinian people, a separate people who therefore have legitimate national interests that need to be guaranteed somehow.' A one-state solution was 'not realistic', and so Palme saw no reason not to support the establishment of an independent Palestinian state in the West Bank and the Gaza Strip. A two-state solution was the most 'logical' solution: 'Israel must be a separate state', but for them to colonise or annex the West Bank would 'only encourage continued warfare, as it is not and never has been Israeli territory'.[98]

In a speech to the UN on 21 November 1974, UN Ambassador Olof Rydbeck expressed the first official Swedish support for a Palestinian state, a policy that was confirmed in the Riksdag by Palme the following day. He stated that the Swedish view, 'based on demands not only for justice, but also realism', required that all parties recognise the political identity and national rights of the others. While Resolution 242 and the non-acquisition of territory by force was central to any solution, Palme said that Resolution 194 regarding the Palestinian refugees from the 1948 war could not be implemented to the letter, given how circumstances had changed since it was passed. A compromise solution had to be reached, involving a combination of repatriation to Israel, resettlement elsewhere, and compensation.[99]

One year later, on 11 November 1975, Palme reaffirmed the Swedish position when he addressed the UN. Israel, like all other states in the region, had the right to live within secure and recognised borders. Still, the occupied territories had to be returned in compliance with UN resolutions. 'The Palestinian people have a political identity and a just demand for national self-determination. As long as they are denied this right, the conflict will not be resolved.'[100] The first condemnation of Israeli settlement policy in the occupied territories was issued in the UN the following year.

To fully understand the relationship between Sweden and the PLO, and Palme and Arafat, it is necessary to return to Palme's Riksdag statement from 22 November 1974. There, he highlighted the continuity of Swedish activity in the Middle East, from Sandström and Bernadotte to Jarring:

> These efforts by Swedes under UN auspices are closely related to the politics of the Swedish government. From our point of view, it has been important to work for peace and reconciliation, which requires respect for the interests of all parties involved. For this reason, we have endeavoured to maintain contacts with all parties on the basis of trust and good faith.

After condemning terrorism, a tactic deemed unjustified under any circumstances, he explained in detail the reasons for inviting the PLO to the UN General Assembly debate on Palestine:

> This decision is based on our firm conviction that all parties to the conflict must be involved in its resolution. The Palestinian Arabs are clearly a part of this. Today, the PLO appears to be the most authoritative representative of the Palestinian Arabs. This understanding has been confirmed by all the Arab states.
>
> We also supported the participation of the PLO because we believe this organisation should appear before the UN and specify which solution it finds reasonable and realistic. Important aspects of the PLO programme stand in stark contradiction to our own view of the problem. It is clear that this organisation has adopted violent methods which we must reject, just as we have objected to widespread Israeli military reprisals. However, it is imperative to take advantage of PLO statements expressing a desire to reach a peaceful resolution of the conflict. Without creating unrealistic expectations, we believe that only by taking advantage of every sign indicating a willingness to compromise from both parties can one work toward a political solution.[101]

Palme further expressed this to the party executive: 'One must in some way communicate with the representatives of a people ... We have never said that the PLO is the sole representative', only that 'Arafat is apparently one representative of the Palestinian people who enjoys strong support throughout the Arab world ... Dialogue is a prerequisite for peace.'[102] So on 4 December 1975, Sweden cast the decisive vote in the UN Security Council in favour of inviting the PLO to address the Council and discuss the situation in Middle East. This constituted a qualitative step in the modification of Swedish policy, particularly when seen in conjunction with Palme's meeting of Arafat.[103]

As leader of the opposition, Palme strongly criticised the 1982 Israeli invasion of Lebanon in speeches given on 1 July[104] and 7 August.[105] In gross violation of the UN and international law, he said, Israel had launched an 'indefensible' war against the PLO and the Lebanese that would stain its reputation for a long time. He did not excuse or condone violent attacks against Israelis, but did not consider the invasion a proportionate response: 'The PLO has made many serious mistakes; many disgusting acts have been perpetrated in their name. But there has been a development within the PLO toward an increasing desire to negotiate and respect Israeli rights which are to us self-evident.' Acts such as the attack on the Israeli ambassador to London, the immediate trigger of the invasion, were committed by a minority, and such a disproportionate military reaction would harm Arafat and the moderates who were calling for a peaceful resolution to the conflict. 'Israel should have learnt from her own people's history that an entire people cannot be exterminated. One cannot solve the Palestinian question by destroying the PLO'; 'It is impossible to exterminate a belief, to crush a dream – the belief in national identity, and the dream of a state of ones own.'

It was a sincere and genuine belief in the need for dialogue that led the Union of Christian Social Democrats to invite Arafat to Stockholm in January 1983, a decision that sparked fierce domestic debate. The Jewish community, in association with the Sweden–Israel Society and a number of churches, organised a protest meeting in one of Stockholm's main churches, Storkyrkan, held on 13 April. Their motto read: 'Against violence and terror. For Israel's right to security. For the Palestinians' right to self-rule – in peace with Israel.'[106]

Although not invited, Palme arranged to speak on behalf of the Social Democrats and defend their decision to invite Arafat. Certain members of the pro-Israeli audience vocalised their discontent; his speech was regularly interrupted by shouts and jeers. It honoured and praised the legacy of senior PLO member Issam Sartawi and former president of the World Jewish Congress and World Zionist Organisation Nahum Goldmann, two men on opposing sides who had both advocated a negotiated two-state solution.

Sartawi paid dearly for his conviction: just a few days earlier, on 10 April, he was gunned down in Albufeira, Portugal, by men from

Abu Nidal's rejectionist faction, so staunchly opposed to peace or any accommodation with Israel that they had left the PLO. For roughly a decade Sartawi had represented the moderate wing that Palme sought to bolster. Prior to his death in 1982, Goldmann had called for the mutual recognition of Israel and the PLO. Since the days of the British Mandate, he believed that an Israeli state, existing in peace within secure and recognised borders, could only be achieved if the Palestinians too enjoyed the same right of national self-determination.

Palme wanted to keep their legacy alive:

> It is in this tradition and vein that we Nordic Social Democrats are modestly trying to make a positive contribution towards peace ... Today, we told Arafat and representatives of the PLO, as we have always said, that Israel has the right to a state within secure and recognised boundaries ... The PLO must recognise the state of Israel ... The legitimate Palestinian demand for recognition of their national rights can only be realised through dialogue aimed at reaching a political solution ... Israel must recognise the right of the Palestinians to determine their own future. The Palestinians have the right to a homeland, to their own state that exists in peace, side by side with Israel in the spirit of the original partition plan, on the lands that Israel has occupied since 1967. It is fruitless to refuse to speak with the representatives of the Palestinians ... We are convinced that dialogue and talks are necessary and that a political solution is an ethical duty. It is on the basis of this belief that we have invited Yasser Arafat to Sweden. In the same way, we will continue our discourse with our friends in Israel.[107]

Aside from Eliav and a likeminded minority on the Zionist fringe, most Israelis saw this as a betrayal. Their traditional social democratic allies were now perceived to be working against them in favour of their existential enemy, Arafat and the PLO. While Meir considered Erlander a faithful, devoted, ideological friend of Israel, she could not say the same of Palme, with whom she at best had a 'love–hate' relationship.[108] In the mid-1970s, Meir and Foreign Minister Yigal Allon sternly expressed their disappointment over Swedish support for the PLO to address the UN, calling it a 'cowardly' and 'opportunistic' act of submission to the

Arab oil weapon. Furthermore, they believed it encouraged Palestinian terrorism intent on destroying Israel. Meir thought Israel's old 'friends in Europe' had deserted them, and now voted for Arafat, whose hands were 'full of blood'.[109]

Following Arafat's invitation to Stockholm in 1983, the Director General of the Israeli Foreign Ministry, David Kimche, told the Swedish ambassador to Israel, Thorsten Örn, that they considered it an act of 'political immorality' that dealt Swedish–Israeli relations 'a very severe blow'. Arafat's visit, he said, would only harm peace efforts, and that without changes in the Palestinian Charter, the PLO could not be deemed to have fundamentally changed their approach.[110] These opinions were shared by prominent pro-Israeli voices in Sweden, such as Per Ahlmark, leader of the Liberal Party. He was, as a matter of fact, one of the first Swedish advocates of a Palestinian state existing side by side in peace with Israel. But, as he explained to *Svenska Dagbladet* ahead of Arafat's visit in 1983, 'If one wants this [two states], then every encouragement of the PLO is a step in the wrong direction. The PLO Charter calls for Israel's destruction.'[111]

The conservative coalition governments that were in office between 1976 and 1982 – of which Ahlmark was a prominent member – had followed the established Social Democratic policy toward the Arab–Israeli conflict. The same principles still applied, but criticism of Israel was slightly less frequent, the emotional tone of Palme's government was adjusted somewhat, and there was limited interest in the PLO. Both Israelis and Palestinians had the right to live in peace and security within secure, recognised, and negotiated boundaries of two mutually recognised separate states. Foreign Minister Ola Ullsten continuously expressed concerns that Israeli actions in the occupied territories – continued settlement expansion, for example, and the Knesset law of 1980 that altered the status of Jerusalem – were contradictory to the aim of granting the Palestinians autonomy as expressed in the Israeli–Egyptian Camp David accord, while he simultaneously condemned certain Palestinian factions for resorting to violence. 'A political settlement cannot be achieved by force', he said, 'but through concessions and compromise by Israelis and Palestinians alike.'[112]

In his analysis of Swedish Middle East policy, Bjereld concluded that the change in policy was not due to public opinion, but a result of decisions at a governmental level. Public support for Israel remained quite strong, but generally failed to influence foreign policy.[113] Although the OPEC oil embargo undoubtedly affected the foreign policy thinking of all Western industrial states – and it would be naïve to think otherwise – it is nonetheless equally erroneous to suggest that it was the main reason for interest in the Palestinian cause. Not only did the realisation of the Palestinian situation significantly pre-date the oil embargo, but it was also entirely consistent with the wider principles of Swedish foreign policy.

The Israeli Labour Party declared that Swedish support for the PLO meant she could not claim neutrality in the conflict.[114] In the foreword to Yegar's *Neutral Policy*, Dror reiterates this point, observing that Sweden 'adopted a very forward policy, such as in relations with the PLO, while *claiming to maintain neutrality* [emphasis added]'.[115] This is truly a misguided analysis.

Firstly, Swedish neutrality policy, as explained above, did not mean shying away from the world of foreign affairs or declining to express opinions about international politics. Neutrality policy meant that Sweden was a non-aligned nation, striving to be neutral in the event of a war between the two superpowers. Acknowledging the existence of the Palestinians as a people and initiating relations with the PLO in no way contravened Swedish neutrality policy. Rather, it demonstrated a key function of the policy, which was that it enabled Sweden to have relations with anyone she wanted.

Secondly, even if one were to use the traditional meaning of the word, relations with the PLO would not be a violation of neutrality. True neutrality warrants relations with both parties to a conflict in order not to automatically appear allied with one side. Furthermore, this is a particularly curious claim given the exemplary nature of Swedish-Israeli relations up until the mid 1970's, a period which saw few Israeli complaints about Swedish neutrality.

Given its nature as a relatively wealthy non-aligned small state, Sweden sought to maximise its potential to affect world politics by maintaining good relations with other small states, and building a non-aligned counterweight to the Cold War superpowers. Moreover, as a country without a record of colonialism and without power ambitions or vested strategic interests, Palme thought that Sweden was particularly well suited to defend the interests of small states across the world, so much so that circumstances created a responsibility to do so.[116]

By engaging with the developing world in a way few other Western countries did, Sweden created excellent contacts and became a bridge between the wealthy and the poorer non-aligned states, acting as an intermediary for their leaders to interact with the rest of the world. This was particularly helpful in the case of countries that a superpower like the United States could not publicly be seen to interact with. Indeed, this reasoning formed the basis of the first of a number of Swedish intermediary roles in the Israeli–Palestinian conflict.

CHAPTER 3

'QUIET DIPLOMACY'

The Swedish Foreign Minister, Sten Andersson, was praised yesterday by George Shultz, the US Secretary of State, for his 'constructive, professional, careful and admirable' help in the delicate diplomacy which led to the change in the public stand of the Palestine Liberation Organisation.

– *The Independent* – 17 December 1988[1]

I believe we've arrived at the root of the problem. We have learned that our rejection of you will not bring us freedom. You can see that your control of us will not bring you security. We must live side by side in peace, equality, and cooperation.

– Ahmed Qurie (Abu Ala)[2]

Oslo is no one's idea of a good peace, except for the alternatives.

– Robert Rothstein[3]

On the night of 28 February 1986, Olof Palme was shot dead by an unidentified assassin as he left a cinema in central Stockholm with his wife. At his funeral, soon-to-be Conservative party leader Carl Bildt said,

> There is no doubt that Palme was a great man in the realm of Swedish foreign policy. He left a distinctive mark on Sweden's international engagement, and put Sweden on the map in many countries where Sweden otherwise stood for nothing but trucks, tennis and Vikings. He made Sweden bigger.[4]

Ingvar Carlsson inherited both of his offices as Prime Minister and leader of the Social Democratic Party. The two men were highly different in their personal style and political focus. Unlike Palme, Carlsson was not overly interested in foreign affairs, and left that domain squarely at the doorstep of Foreign Minister Sten Andersson. A disciple of Palme's, Andersson was passionate about the Middle East, specifically the Israeli–Palestinian conflict, and was keen to be the bearer of his dead friend and mentor's legacy.

Prior to his appointment as Foreign Minister in 1985, Andersson had long been involved in the Social Democratic Party. He had been its Secretary General from 1962 to 1982, and a member of the Riksdag since 1966; he was a charming, battle-scarred political veteran, always amicable and making jokes. Within the Israeli Labour Party, he was known as a true and faithful friend of Israel. Like so many others of his generation, he was strongly affected by the horrors the Jewish people had suffered during the Holocaust. He identified with the Israeli pioneering spirit, and was a keen admirer of their socialist state-building experiment. He even sent his teenage son to work on a *kibbutz* for a summer as a learning experience.

As with Palme and many other Social Democrats, the occupation and the 'brutalisation' of Israeli politics towards the Palestinians altered the equation. Andersson considered it a very real threat to Israeli democracy and the exercise of democratic values. At a meeting with Vice Premier and Foreign Minister Shimon Peres during a visit to Israel in March 1988, he told him, 'You have set a very high democratic standard for your own people. Now, the world is waiting for you to recognise the rights of the Palestinians, in accordance with the principles Israel herself represents.'[5] Still, unlike Palme and Schori, Andersson's personal reputation had not been besmirched by close contacts with Yasser Arafat and the PLO. That situation, however, would soon change drastically.

Following Palme's death, Dr Eugene Makhlouf, the PLO representative in Sweden, wrote to Carlsson and the Social Democratic Party to express his condolences and his hope 'that the party will not bury with Mr Palme the aims and goals to which Mr Palme dedicated his life'. Bo Toresson, Secretary General of the party, wrote a reassuring reply the following day. 'I can assure you that the Swedish government's position regarding the Palestinian question has not changed. The future Swedish policy on the question will not be different from the policy under the leadership of Olof

Palme. You may rest assured that this shall be evident in due course.'[6] Toresson cannot have known quite how right he was.

Foreign Minister Andersson and a number of diplomats, including among others Anders Bjurner and Mathias Mossberg in Stockholm, and Stig Elvemar at the Swedish UN mission in New York, were keen to re-focus attention on the Israeli–Palestinian conflict after a period of relative Swedish inactivity in the area. Mossberg had recently served at the Swedish Embassy in London, where a number of conversations with the British Foreign Office had revolved around the idea of gaining a firmer understanding of what was actually going on in the occupied West Bank and Gaza Strip. The idea was adopted enthusiastically in Stockholm, and a decision was made to devote the yearly Swedish statement in the UN General Assembly debate on the Middle East to the matter.[7] Elvemar, an Arabic speaker who had spent many years stationed in the Middle East, had since the early 1980s advocated a sharper focus on the Middle East, particularly Lebanon and the occupied territories. In New York, he set to work on a speech which to this day largely continues to define Swedish policy toward the occupation.[8]

On 1 December 1987, Swedish UN Ambassador Anders Ferm took to the podium at the UN and delivered this incendiary speech.[9] Far from a collection of diplomatic platitudes and political niceties, it was intended to expose the misconduct of the Israeli occupation. Ferm made it very clear that Sweden considered the ongoing occupation an unacceptable transgression of international law, in terms of the Israeli refusal to acknowledge the applicability of the fourth Geneva Convention to the territories, and the acquisition of territory by force. 'There cannot be two sets of international law in the world, one for Israel and one for the rest of us.' He criticised 'a general lack of respect for human rights in the occupied territories', pointing to 'deportations, detention without trial, demolition of houses, house arrests', and the 'harsh methods used ... in attempts to subdue demonstrations and other forms of legitimate protests'.

Israeli settlement construction was 'a crime directed against the Palestinian people, their property and their land' which aggravated tensions, and for which there could be 'no justification'. In addition to the annexation of East Jerusalem and the Golan Heights,

> these and other unlawful Israeli policies and practices affecting the physical character and demographic composition of the occupied

> territories inevitably give rise to serious concerns as to Israel's ultimate intentions. These practices and the long duration of the occupation suggest a deliberate policy of creating faits accomplis.

In other words, as Mossberg explains, 'what we more or less told the Israelis was, "We know what you're up to. This is no temporary occupation. Rather, the evidence points to the fact that you intend to keep these territories."'[10] Just as Palme had suggested to Israeli Prime Minister Golda Meir nearly two decades earlier, Ferm argued that the Israelis had become 'the oppressors of another people, thereby, in the long run, creating a situation which might constitute a threat to Israel itself.'

Once again, Sweden recognised 'the right to self-determination and to statehood of both the Israelis and the Palestinians', that 'there is room for two peoples, two nations, and two states', living in peace within secure and recognised borders. Ferm reiterated the longstanding Swedish position that 'a just and lasting solution . . . cannot be based on violence or military superiority', but must be a negotiated solution involving the PLO and the Palestinians. 'Israel refuses to negotiate with representatives of the PLO. If there is a genuine will to achieve a peaceful solution to the conflict, parties to that conflict should not simply refuse to sit down and negotiate with one another. If it had been the policy of parties to conflicts to exclude their enemies from peace negotiations, no peace treaties would ever have been signed.' While a mechanism for potential negotiations had not been agreed upon, Ferm conveyed Swedish support for the idea of an international conference under UN auspices.

The Palestinian observer stood up and shook Ferm's hand as he walked to his seat; the Israeli UN Ambassador, Benjamin Netanyahu, was incensed. The speech led to an intense two- to three-hour long debate on the Middle East in the Riksdag, held on 9 February 1988, where fundamental questions were raised about Swedish policy. Did Ferm's speech truly reflect the views of the government? Did it constitute an official policy change? What was Sweden prepared to do to aid the peace process and support an international UN peace conference, and how would the government support moderate forces in the region? Andersson dealt with these issues in his address:

> The stands made on various issues in the UN, whether through speeches or votes, are always the government's. It is not a question

> of an individual delegate's personal opinion, whether it's our UN Ambassador, other diplomats, or members of the Riksdag who comprise our UN mission. The formulation of Sweden's speeches and decisions on votes are made in close cooperation between the UN mission and the Department of Foreign Affairs. It is the government who instructs the UN to act in a certain way. I thereby hope that it is clear that that which is sometimes referred to in the press and elsewhere as 'Ferm's speech' is the Swedish government's speech.[11]

Andersson went on to say that it was nothing but a continuation and restatement of years of Swedish policy toward the conflict. He repeated Ferm's criticisms of Israeli actions, particularly the expansion of settlements and the violent reaction to the Palestinian *intifada*.

> It is because of Israel's refusal to respect what are to us basic and extremely important principles of international law – and Israel's refusal to acknowledge the applicability of international law to the occupied territories – that Sweden criticises Israel. Our tone is now sharper than before for the simple reason that our statements and pleas, and those of other countries, have fallen on deaf ears.

The sanctity of international law as an instrument to protect the rights of small state was raised, a principle that was in Sweden's interest to defend. Another such principle was the peaceful resolution of conflict and advocacy of dialogue between enemies. These had also been themes in Palme's speeches throughout his leadership.[12] It was a thorough, unequivocal statement of policy reminiscent of his spirit.

Kerstin Ekman of the Liberal Party agreed that Israel's friends had to be allowed to criticise Israel, but said this needed to be done in a fair way, with respect to the historical conflict context. She considered the government's position an extremely one-sided betrayal of Israel, and warned that anti-Semitism was once again rearing its ugly head. While she later denied that the accusation of anti-Semitism was directed against Andersson personally, that was not how he saw it, and it bothered him greatly. Defending himself, he described his personal affinity for Israel and his many trips to the country, in both a private and political capacity, and noted how the position of many Israelis toward the Palestinians had changed. What was needed, he insisted, was dialogue. 'I am travelling to Israel on 7 March to meet Shimon Peres and the Palestinian leaders. I am modest enough to realise that Sweden cannot play a decisive role, but our duty is to support the forces seeking a positive development for both nations.'[13]

An old friend of Andersson's since 1963, Peres represented the more progressive, peace-attuned Labour wing of Israeli politics that Sweden wanted to support. Prior to Andersson's trip, Peres and his Labour colleague, Minister of Defence Yitzhak Rabin, had accepted the 'Shultz proposal', a re-hashed version of the autonomy plan included in the 1978 Camp David accord between Israel and Egypt. However, Yitzhak Shamir, Prime Minister and leader of the ruling Likud party, rejected it. Yossi Beilin, Peres' protégé, admitted to Andersson that a growing faction within the Labour party was calling for negotiations with the PLO, but that they were not quite ready yet. As the opposition, Peres and Labour were not in a particularly strong political position.

At the Swedish general consulate in East Jerusalem, Andersson spoke sternly with local Palestinian leaders about the need to take responsibility and fight terrorism, to the point where consul Arnold Hjertström became slightly nervous and apologetic. Mossberg recalls that 'Sten tried to maintain an evenly balanced line' toward both parties.[14] The mood of self-pity and helplessness in the face of the occupation normally expressed by the Palestinians had been replaced by a wave of optimism, unleashed by the *intifada*. Finally, a popular movement had emerged aimed at ending the occupation and establishing a Palestinian state. An increasing readiness existed both within and outside the PLO to recognise Israel, and the Palestinians requested that Sweden take a more active role in the search for peace.[15] As he stood on the front steps of the Makassed hospital in Jerusalem, having witnessed first-hand the human cost of the Israeli repression of the *intifada*, Andersson swore in Swedish and was visibly upset. 'I will never forget the look in the eyes of the injured boys and the children in the refugee camps', he later said in an interview.[16]

Upon returning to Stockholm, Andersson decided to establish what became known as 'studiegruppen', 'the study group', a secret task force operating above the traditional bureaucratic structures and lines of communication, which included, among others, Bjurner and Mossberg. Given the weak position of the Labour party and the need to encourage the idea of Israeli acceptance of the PLO – Israeli law made it illegal for citizens to have any contact with the PLO whatsoever – the study group drew the conclusion that the best way forward was to approach the Americans, try to initiate a dialogue between them and the PLO, and thereby affect a change in American policy.[17] The road to Jerusalem, they believed, went through Washington, the only source of real leverage against Israel.

In addition to the facilitation of an official contact channel between Arafat and US Secretary of State George Shultz, it was suggested that a meeting should be arranged between Arafat and a number of prominent American Jews with close ties to Israel. As Andersson explained,

> We became more and more convinced that US public opinion – and more particularly the American Jewish opinion – had a crucial role to play. If a dialogue could be established between prominent American Jews and prominent PLO leaders, we believed this could contribute to increase prospects for a change in the US attitude towards the PLO. The need for confidence building meetings between the PLO and American Jews was immense.[18]

This idea was not an entirely new one. It had been voiced in late 1982, and been developed between the Swedish Foreign Ministry and senior PLO member Issam Sartawi in preparation for Arafat's visit to Stockholm in 1983. That initiative died with Sartawi when members of Abu Nidal's faction gunned him down in Portugal.[19] Unlike Sartawi, it was now revived.

Others also entertained the same idea. Muhammad Rabie, a Palestinian academic based in the United States who enjoyed close personal contacts with PLO leaders, was working with Shai Feldman, an Israeli academic, representatives from the National Security Council (NSC), and William Quandt, a former official for Middle East affairs at the NSC, on precisely this issue. Working more or less at the same time as the Swedes, their work was promising and generated useful input into the process, but was ultimately unsuccessful on its own.[20]

In April 1988, Andersson went to Washington DC and met with Secretary of State George Shultz on the balcony of the State Department reception room. Although he did not properly respond to the idea of a meeting between American Jews and Arafat, Andersson 'could read in his eyes what he thought': interest weighed down by scepticism, but not disapproval.[21] So during the latter half of 1988, Swedish diplomats engaged in periodically intense shuttle diplomacy between the United States, Sweden, and the PLO to get everyone on board and reach agreement on the substance of the discussions.

Ulf Hjertonsson, Deputy Chief of Mission at the Swedish Embassy in Washington DC, was asked to compile a list of possible American participants for a meeting with Arafat. Three agreed to participate in a personal capacity, all affiliated with the International Centre for Peace in the Middle East (ICPME): Drora Kass, the ICPME executive director in the United States; Stanley Sheinbaum, a Democratic publisher, economist, and philanthropist based in Los Angeles; and Rita Hauser, a prominent Republican attorney from New York who had formerly served as the US representative to the UN Commission on Human Rights.[22]

Meanwhile, Andersson was communicating with Arafat through letters, urging him to take advantage of the political opportunities created by the *intifada*. On 22 June, the *New York Times* published a statement by one of Arafat's spokesmen, Bassam Abu Sharif, which called for a two-state solution and implied that the PLO might be ready to recognise Israel. Andersson urged Arafat to endorse the statement, and said he understood that he may need 'an appropriate international framework' to do so. To this end, he proposed the idea of a meeting with American Jews in Stockholm. Initially unconvinced, Arafat agreed to the idea in October after a month of contacts between the Swedish Foreign Ministry, Makhlouf, and the PLO leadership in Tunis.[23]

In Algiers, the Palestinian National Council (PNC) met on 15 November 1988, and voted in favour of a statement accepting UN Resolutions 242 and 338, the principle of a two-state solution, and a condemnation of terrorism. Although Hauser had tried to elicit a more positive reaction to the Algiers decision from Richard Murphy, head of the Middle East desk at the State Department, he made it clear that the United States could not in any way lessen their conditions for establishing relations with the PLO: an acceptance of Israel's right to exist, Resolutions 242 and 338, and the renunciation of terrorism. Via the Israeli Ambassador to Stockholm, Moshe Erell, Peres sent a letter to Andersson explaining the Israeli view on the PNC declaration. He protested that 'the critical and careful balance represented by

Resolution 242 was violated and distorted to the point of threatening to undermine the only commonly accepted basis for a solution', and that 'terrorism inside Israel and the territories was specifically legitimised'.[24] Israel and the United States clearly shared the opinion that the PLO needed to be more precise in its formulation.

On 21–23 November, secret preparatory meetings were held at the Grand Hotel in Stockholm between the three Americans, Khaled al-Hassan, head of the PNC Foreign Relations Committee, Makhlouf, Hisham Mustapha, and Afif Safieh. After a short welcoming address, Andersson left the proceedings, while Bjurner and Mossberg were invited to stay. What followed was a difficult morning session marked by Palestinian irritation and 'mutual mistrust'. The Palestinians described the difficulty involved in negotiating the PNC declaration, voiced their opinion that the PNC decision in Algiers contained all the relevant points, only expressed in their own language, and bemoaned what they considered American arrogance. Over lunch, Andersson tried to ease the mood by suggesting that he personally represent the understandings they reached, in the form of a short summation ostensibly authored by Andersson and signed by the parties. This preliminary document containing some clarifications on the Algiers text was produced over the course of two days, and became known as the 'Stockholm document'.[25] The Palestinians returned to Tunis to have it approved.

When Bjurner went to Washington to present it to the Americans, Murphy and Shultz were impressed with the text. It was a vast improvement on the Algiers declaration, easily the best they had seen from the Palestinians so far. They asked the Swedes to continue their work, and gave their blessing for a meeting between the Jewish-American group and Arafat. They urgently wanted to know whether Arafat would back it.

Meanwhile, in talks with al-Hassan and later Makhlouf in Stockholm, Andersson, Bjurner, and Mossberg were trying to ascertain precisely this. It became clear that for a future meeting where Arafat might endorse the document, he wanted an official invitation from Andersson and the Swedish government. While he was interested in an official trip to Sweden, he was less keen on meeting Americans who were not government officials. Andersson, who politely reminded Arafat that a meeting was a prerequisite for an official trip, rapidly issued an official invitation. A few days later, Arafat replied positively via Makhlouf and, after some discussion regarding possible dates, a meeting was scheduled for 6 December 1988, in Stockholm between the Jewish-American group, expanded to include Menachem Rosensaft and Abraham Udovitch, and an official PLO delegation led by Arafat himself.[26]

When Swedish Ambassador Wilhelm Wachtmeister informed Shultz about the upcoming meeting and inquired as to the American reaction should Arafat accept the text, Shultz invited him to come to his home. Wachtmeister found that Shultz had prepared a letter to Andersson containing a draft formulation of what he wanted from Arafat, together with an American commitment to initiate dialogue should his conditions be met. Hjertonsson was dispatched immediately to Stockholm to personally deliver the letter, per Shultz's request. This clearly constituted official American backing, should Arafat raise concerns regarding the nature of the American 'delegation' in Stockholm.

The negotiations on 6 December produced further refinements to the 'magic words' Shultz had proposed, with Bjurner acting as intermediary between the PLO and Washington. Arafat was reluctant, however, to make the official announcement without running it past the PLO Executive Committee, and requested 48 hours to do so. Bjurner and Hjertonsson exerted pressure on Yasser Abed Rabbo and Mahmoud Darwish to convince Arafat to make the announcement that same day, but had to settle for a letter to Andersson signed by Arafat containing the necessary statement and a commitment to 'work to have it issued officially after being presented to the Executive Committee later on'.[27] Hjertonsson reasoned that 'Arafat could be so slippery ... so we at least had a written promise from him to do this. It would be bad for him if this came out, so to speak, if he then backed out and did not deliver.'[28]

Arafat was then expected to make the necessary statement in front of the UN General Assembly in Geneva on the evening of 13 December,[29] but his speech in Arabic did not use the precise agreed upon language. 'When we analysed the text, we found everything the American administration wanted was in the text, but he had split it up and he had not used the same words.'[30] As a result, the State Department rejected the speech as insufficient, which launched an extremely intense and difficult 24 hours of negotiations. Andersson, Bjurner and Mossberg conferred with Arafat and various PLO spokesmen, while Hjertonsson functioned as the link between Bjurner and Murphy at the State Department, and the exact language was eventually ironed out after many exchanges. A press conference originally scheduled for the morning of 14 December was continuously put back until 20:30 in the evening. Frantic last-minute adjustments saw Bjurner running with handwritten notes to Arafat's aides, who passed them on to their boss up at the podium.[31] Arafat then uttered the necessary words, although when totally rejecting all forms of terrorism, it sounded like he said 'tourism'. As this unfolded, Hjertonsson had Murphy on the phone, who asked Shultz, 'Shall we take that?' 'Yeah, yeah!' said Shultz, 'Now we are on, we'll take it.'[32]

Rational yet almost mythical trust

The fundamental basis upon which Swedish mediation rested throughout this process can be summed up in one word: trust. Andersson himself understood the situation thus:

> The problem which existed, which we could help to solve, was that the USA and the PLO wanted to initiate a dialogue, but serious mutual mistrust existed between them. In such a situation, a third party is required whom both parties trust implicitly. Both Shultz and Arafat took great personal risks during this process. They would not have dared to do so had they not trusted us completely.[33]

As a small state without specific national interests in the Middle East, merely an interest in upholding the principles of international law and the peaceful resolution of disputes, Sweden was well poised to mediate.

Primarily, this was a facilitative role consisting of relaying messages between the parties, creating the procedural framework for their interaction, and providing a secret venue. During this period, the Swedes were commonly referred to as the 'postman'. They did, however, move beyond a pure facilitative role and engaged in a more active formulation strategy. In negotiations in Stockholm and Geneva, the Swedes suggested modifications to the language of statements in order to find a mutually acceptable formulation.[34]

Additionally, Swedish diplomats on occasion had to convince the parties to go ahead with the process when they were having cold feet. The day before she was set to go to Stockholm for the first meeting in November, Hauser suffered from serious doubts and told the Swedes that she would not be attending. As the more right-wing of the group and an influential heavyweight in the New York Jewish community, she was concerned about the negative backlash she stood likely to incur from her participation. The Swedes reasoned that it was precisely these associations that made her a crucial member of the team, in order to provide a more bipartisan Jewish perspective and influence public opinion more widely. So Hjertonsson hurried from Washington to New York on the first morning shuttle to speak very seriously with Hauser. Yes, she was undoubtedly taking a personal risk, but he assured her of the necessity and longer-term significance of the meeting. Ultimately, she came over to Hjertonsson's reasoning and flew to Stockholm that same afternoon, but took some convincing.[35]

The Swedes had to lean on the Palestinians to get them to meet the necessary requirements throughout various stages of the process and refine their language when necessary. Over breakfast with Arafat on 14 December, Bjurner applied pressure of a personal and emotional nature, making it clear to him that he was letting down his friend Andersson who had worked extremely hard on his behalf and had much vested in this endeavour.[36]

Moreover, Sweden provided an insight into the American political mindset that may not always have been self-evident to the Palestinians. Andersson certified that US representatives stood in the shadows of the initiative when Arafat questioned the unofficial American delegation. However, the Americans did not abide by the reciprocity of the arrangement and read their public statement, which Shultz had sent with Hjertonsson to Stockholm, like they said they would. Rather than build confidence, this 'only reinforced PLO suspicion and deepened its mistrust of US intentions',[37] and also reflected badly on the Swedes. Thankfully, the historical strength of Swedish–Palestinian relations was enough to overcome this hiccup.

For Arafat and the PLO, trust in Sweden and the Social Democratic Party in particular went back many years to the days of Palme, as we have seen. Although rational in terms of Swedish policy, Arafat also seemed to have an exaggerated, almost mythical, trust in what Sweden could achieve.[38] In addition to the broader national level, Andersson knew that in order to play an intermediary role, confidence in him as an individual was crucial. Through policy statements and multiple trips to Tunis and the occupied territories, he demonstrated continuity with Palme's policy and developed an excellent standing among the Palestinians, particularly Arafat, with whom he had a close friendship. Andersson showed a genuine personal and emotional concern for Palestinian problems, just as Palme had.

After the initiation of dialogue with the United States, Arafat continued to seek Andersson's counsel on a number of issues. In his memoirs, Andersson describes a moment in late 1989 when the Egyptians were trying to finalise the details of a peace plan Sweden had been working on. He happened to be in Cairo, at a meeting organised for all Swedish ambassadors to the Middle East, and received a call from the Egyptian Foreign Minister, Esmat Abdel Meguid, urgently requesting his help.

> You have to come to my office today and meet Arafat and I. After repeated attempts I have almost managed to reach an agreement with the PLO. You are the only one Arafat trusts. Please come so I can read the agreement to the both of you, and you can say it's OK! Then Arafat will accept it!

Andersson obliged. During the meeting, he sat next to Arafat, who held his hand 'as a sign of trust and friendship', as Meguid went through the agreement.[39]

The initiation of relations with the United States was a truly important breakthrough for the Palestinians and the PLO. As they sometimes expressed it, this was their 'passport to the world'.[40] Significantly, it was essential for any kind of dialogue with Israel aimed at progressing toward a negotiated resolution of the conflict. Sweden had played a pivotal role in the establishment of these ties, something that the Palestinians would never forget. A close relationship with Sweden was maintained and, like the friendship between Andersson and Arafat, would continue to be of value in the peace process, as we shall see.

As for the Americans, this close cooperation with Sweden vastly improved relations between the two countries. Although the rift during the Palme years was substantial, it was largely a diplomatic marker that did not affect essential defence or trade relations. Nonetheless, it was a strained past. Middle Eastern diplomacy practically became a driving factor in bilateral relations. This was facilitated by the excellent personal relationship between Andersson and Shultz, who seemed to have a strong mutual admiration for each other. In the aftermath of Arafat's declaration in Geneva, Shultz hailed the 'constructive, professional, careful, and admirable' role Andersson played in the delicate diplomacy, while the latter believed that the relationship he had with Shultz was unprecedented between Swedish and American foreign ministers.[41]

While personal relationships existed between Swedish and American diplomats and relations were improved, these too should not necessarily be exaggerated as crucial factors. Ultimately, the Americans realised that Sweden could serve their interests. It is possible that other secret, more direct channels of information existed between the State Department and the PLO beyond the Rabie–Quandt connection, but any public visibility, during or immediately after, would have been damaging for the United States.[42] The Swedish historic relationship with the PLO was well known, and the Americans were aware of the trust that existed between them. Sweden thus became an interesting piece of the puzzle, and could help the Americans in a manner that was of relatively low risk to the latter.[43] Success would not only be a welcome accomplishment, but would also provide cover for the other secret contacts; should it fail, the United States would not be publicly implicated in any way and could deny any official involvement in the Swedish efforts to improve communication between Palestinians and American Jews. For both Americans and Palestinians, Sweden was thus undoubtedly a friendly nation, which eased the process immeasurably, but above all she was a useful partner in foreign relations.

For many Israelis, the initiation of US–PLO relations was a very bitter pill to swallow. Peres described it as 'a black day in the history of Israel'.[44] Apart from certain segments of the left, the Israeli political establishment was furious with Sweden. Not only had they been among the first to acknowledge the PLO, but now they had aided and abetted their existential foe in initiating relations with their most important ally.[45] This further dented Swedish–Israeli relations, which had been rocky for almost two decades. Both Peres and Foreign Minister Moshe Arens declined official invitations from Andersson to visit Sweden, and it was not until May 1990 that President Chaim Herzog made the trip. Once again, there was the feeling that a former friend was now working against them.

Prior to his appointment as Foreign Minister, Andersson had made himself fairly unpopular in Israeli Labour circles by retracting an invitation to attend the May Day celebrations in Stockholm in 1982. He feared that an Israeli presence would be gravely unpopular given their invasion of Lebanon. While one can perhaps understand his reasoning, the Labour party quite rightly took offence at being tarnished with the Likud brush. They largely shared the Swedish assessment of the war, and were speaking out against Operation Peace in Galilee. Andersson's continued advocacy of Palestinian self-determination and Palestinian rights, in addition to criticism of Israeli conduct in the occupied territories, were interpreted as indisputable signs of a strong pro-Palestinian bias, which added to his unpopular image.[46]

Shultz appears to have shared this assessment towards the end of the process. On 14 December in Geneva, the day after Arafat had made his unsatisfactory speech and a few hours before he said the 'magic words', Andersson had used his speech to the General Assembly to speak for Arafat. He made it clear that, as he understood it, the PLO leader had met American requirements for dialogue, if in his own way: 'This [Arafat's speech] can, in our view, not be misunderstood, not even by the most suspicious', he said, in a clear reference to the Americans and the Israelis.[47] Although he never seems to have publicly shared his view, Shultz confided in his State Department colleagues that he believed Andersson had become partial, and that Sweden could no longer be trusted as a mediator.[48]

Although many Israelis and Americans sincerely believed this, some of the criticism appears to have been public posturing, depending on which side of the political spectrum it was coming from. Despite the fact that direct communication was possible after the crucial first breaching of the barriers separating the United States and the PLO, the Swedes were needed from time to time to ease interaction, and act as a sort of 'midwife' through the initial stages of relations. They were also highly involved in trying to iron out conditions for a Middle Eastern peace conference, and the mechanics of democratic elections in the West Bank and Gaza. After the PLO rejected what has become known as the 'Shamir plan' in the summer of 1989, Peres, peacenik Nimrod Novik and other Israelis of a similar ilk were in Stockholm for a meeting of the Socialist International Middle East committee.

Publicly, Peres spoke sternly: 'The Swedish Social Democrats and the government do not have a friendly attitude toward Israel. Sweden must understand the Israeli perspective, not merely the PLO's, otherwise

Sweden cannot play a role as a mediator in the Middle East.' Privately, however, he was much more accommodating. Over dinner, Peres and Novik secretly enumerated ten points where they could make some concessions and narrow the gaps between Israeli and Palestinian positions, and asked the Swedes to present them to the PLO. Novik explained that as far as he was concerned, 'we knew that Sweden was on an excellent footing with the PLO, and trusted that they would accurately communicate our position to the PLO leadership'.[49]

Simultaneously, Andersson and the Swedes also tried to help establish direct contacts between the Israeli Labour party and the PLO, but this was dangerous for both parties and thus very difficult to manage. Contacts were maintained with Arafat and the PLO, Peres and the Israeli Labour party, and Meguid and the Egyptians, without producing much in the way of concrete results.[50] Andersson met with Peter Wallensteen, professor of peace and conflict research at Uppsala University, to discuss the prospects of using an academic setting to further advance the 'quiet diplomacy'. Wallensteen agreed to hold a secret academic seminar in late June 1990 for this purpose.

Israel was represented by, among others, Knesset member Dedi Zucker and Ari Rath, the former editor of *The Jerusalem Post*, while the Palestinian team included PLO members Safieh and Nabil Shaath in addition to academics like Hanan Ashrawi and Sari Nusseibeh. Kass and Sheinbaum also participated as 'neutrals'. Discussion focused on mutual recognition and the economic benefits of cooperation, and positive relationships, both personal and societal, were generally the theme of the seminar. However, the initially promising prospect of further contacts was soured by the PLO's support for Saddam Hussein following his invasion of Kuwait in August. The themes of this 'academic diplomacy' would be revisited and developed further, but not in Sweden.[51]

Astute and thoroughly active diplomacy by the new US Secretary of State James Baker – complicated by a 'stonewalling' Shamir, supported by a right-wing government, which left Baker feeling 'battered, beaten, and betrayed'[52] – would eventually lead to the Madrid Conference at the end of October 1991. This conference constituted a 'rare and interesting example of a mutually enticing opportunity, in which it is the prospect of a better situation for the parties at the end of the negotiations which pulls the parties to the table' rather than the immediate threat of a worse situation.[53] The Gulf War had highlighted the difficulty of the

American strategic relationship with Israel in regional Middle Eastern politics. Israel had acceded to American requests that they refrain from retaliation after being hit by Iraqi missiles, and were dependent on the United States for its defence, an uncomfortable departure from their traditional emphasis on military self-sufficiency. Shamir was thus susceptible to American pressure.

The Palestinians, by contrast, were hurting a lot after the PLO's catastrophic decision to support Saddam Hussein and Iraq in the Gulf War. They had fallen out of American favour and lost the bulk of their financial support from the Gulf States. As a measure of their desperation to reverse their fortunes, the PLO consented to Palestinian participation in a process from which they themselves were excluded. When they later participated in the Oslo negotiations, these concerns also helped bring about flexibility and substantial concessions to Israel.[54] Both parties were at a low ebb, and in no position to work directly against American mediators.

The proceedings in Madrid were tense and strained, a testament to the extremely sensitive, emotional, and complex nature of the undertaking. Fisk has described the first session in Madrid as 'little more than a disgrace':

> Had I not been there, I would never have understood the nature of the venom that the Arabs and Israelis displayed towards each other. It was not so much the mutual accusations of 'terrorism' that created so shameful a spectacle. It was not the extraordinary decision of the Israeli PM to stomp out after making the first speech because, he claimed, he wanted to return to Israel by the Sabbath. Nor was it even the Syrian foreign minister's decision to brandish an old British mandate poster of a young Jewish 'terrorist' called Yitzhak Shamir. It was because the Israelis and Arabs used the peace conference to talk about war.[55]

Still, as a first real official interaction, Madrid broke quite a few taboos, and served to legitimise the very notion of Israeli–Palestinian negotiations. Given the extreme animosity and hostile atmosphere that existed, and that Shamir had no appetite for it whatsoever, that Madrid was convened at all was in itself significant. But while American pressure had formally brought selected representatives to the table, it was not applied to force any concessions in the negotiations.[56]

The preparatory period, during which the form of Palestinian representation and members of the delegation were being agreed upon, was a learning phase which revealed much about what was needed to break the impasse between the parties. As American negotiator Aaron Miller observes in his analysis, though US–PLO relations had been formally opened, they had been suspended in June 1990 after Arafat refused to expel a group of Palestinians from his Executive Committee after a failed terrorist attack. Thus, despite the original recognition, the team was still plagued by a poor American understanding of the Palestinian position and a lack of 'credible or serious' channels of communication.[57]

Similarly, the subsequent negotiations in Washington and the multilateral working groups also shed light on the limits of that framework and the procedural requirements for advancing the peace process. These public channels mainly served as forums for political posturing to sceptical domestic constituencies extremely sensitive to any concessions or renunciation of principles. This prevented any real discussion of the issues, since negotiators were weary of giving away too much and being personally associated with controversial positions. To borrow a formulation from Corbin, 'a war of microphones was being waged' which, over months of talks, 'degenerated into sour name-calling by both sides'.[58] Also, since Israel refused to accept any PLO participation in Madrid or Washington, Palestinian negotiators always had to consult representatives in Tunis, who were reluctant to move at all in a process from which they had been excluded. Clearly, facilitative mediation and 'quiet diplomacy' were vital.

Sweden, however, was no longer in a position to play that role. The Social Democrats lost the 1991 election to the Conservative party and the new coalition government, led by Prime Minister Carl Bildt, changed Swedish foreign policy orientation in two significant respects. Firstly, the geographic focus. Sweden was looking to join the European Union. Given the political earthquake that was the collapse of the Soviet Union and the tremendous changes taking place in Europe, this was the number one priority. Nascent democratic governments across central and eastern Europe had to be stabilised and required political and financial support. The Baltic States were of particular interest.[59] This was deemed a far more pressing concern than the far-flung Israeli–Palestinian conflict.

Secondly, the Swedish stance towards the PLO was re-evaluated. Foreign Minister Margareta af Ugglas made it clear that the new government would conduct 'a more balanced policy', and that there would be no more 'kissing of Arafat'. While the basic principles of Swedish policy did not change, it was certainly an adjustment of rhetorical tone and public appearance. af Ugglas told the Riksdag that she would 'not associate with representatives of the PLO the way Sten Andersson did . . . It is important that the government avoid measures which damage relations with Israel. We do not wish to reinforce the image of Sweden as closely tied to Yasser Arafat and the PLO.' Riksdag member Hadar Cars of the Liberal party thanked af Ugglas for her statement, which he said constituted 'a radical change compared to the Palme-Andersson-Schori era'.[60]

Andersson, keenly aware of what to expect from the Conservative and Liberal parties, tried to make alternative arrangements to fill the void created by his departure. After the election results were confirmed, Andersson and Prime Minister Carlsson called their Norwegian Social Democratic friends Jan Egeland and Thorvald Stoltenberg to 'pass on the torch', urging them to take on the role that Sweden had been playing. This move was based not only on their natural party commonality and friendship, but a history of contacts regarding the Middle East.

For many years, Sweden had advocated a more unified Scandinavian foreign policy, in the belief that increased co-operation and co-ordination between small states could help maximise the collective political pressure they could bring to bear. In terms of relations with the Palestinians, Sweden was the most outspoken advocate and tried to bring the others into the fold. Norwegian and Danish Social Democratic party leaders were present for Arafat's first visit to Stockholm in 1983, and were also involved in the earlier planning stages. On New Year's Eve 1982, former foreign ministers Knut Frydenlund of Norway and Kjeld Olesen of Denmark met secretly with Arafat in Tunis. As the Swedish Social Democrats had returned to power while the Norwegian and Danish parties were in opposition, Stockholm was deemed the appropriate venue. Not only was a party in power the most attractive host for Arafat in terms of status, but they would thereby also avoid protests from governments in Oslo or Copenhagen who did not wish to welcome the PLO leader.[61]

Stockholm was also a more natural location since Swedish policy towards the conflict was more strongly rooted in international law and human rights than its neighbours'. For the Norwegians in particular, Palestinian statehood was not a given. Norway had been one of the last European countries to establish official contacts with the PLO, and Waage has described Norwegian policy toward it as 'highly restrictive'.[62] Sweden was the driving force behind this policy throughout the 1980s and tried to move the Norwegians closer to their position. Although Stoltenberg and his countrymen eventually became more amenable to the idea, the Swedes originally had to drag the Norwegians 'kicking and screaming' into the field.[63] Relations between the Norwegian Social Democrats and Palestinians existed, primarily in the way of trade union initiatives and some foreign aid,[64] but were nowhere near as strong as the Swedes'. Close co-operation between Sweden and Norway in the Middle East arose towards the end of the decade, with many bilateral meetings and joint meetings with both Israelis and Palestinians.[65]

Historically, like the Swedes, the Norwegian Social Democrats had extremely close ties to the Israeli Labour party,[66] but they stayed the course and had not re-evaluated their position the way their Swedish colleagues had done during the 1970s. It was obvious to Andersson that Sweden had now exhausted the goodwill that remained among most Israeli politicians. Norway, on the other hand, had excellent political capital in Israel and was a trusted friend. When Andersson contacted Egeland and Stoltenberg, he simultaneously advised the PLO to approach Oslo for the kind of assistance Sweden had previously been rendering.

This was not an alien idea to them. Arafat first approached the Norwegian government in 1979 and then multiple times throughout the 1980s with requests to act as a channel for negotiations with Israel, but to no avail. Strong relations with Israel and the United States, and a general international reputation for 'decency', made the Norwegian option appealing to the Palestinians.[67] The additional endorsement from a friend like Andersson can only have helped their stance. An institutional trust in Norway thus existed among both parties. More important, however, was the mutual faith in one Norwegian individual in particular, the key to the Oslo channel: Terje Rød-Larsen.

Larsen and the Oslo channel

Unwittingly, the Norwegian Ministry of Foreign Affairs took one of the first steps towards creating the Oslo channel when it posted diplomat Mona Juul to their embassy in Cairo in 1988; Larsen was Juul's husband, and he accompanied her to Egypt. As the founder and director of Norwegian social science think-tank FAFO, Larsen took the opportunity to initiate a study of welfare and living conditions in the neighbouring Gaza Strip. In this capacity, he travelled widely across Israel and the occupied Palestinian territories, creating some important personal relationships with senior Israeli and Palestinian officials and deepening his understanding of the conflict.

In addition to these personal relationships, Larsen's wife Juul would be the linchpin to engender contacts at the highest level. When Sweden deferred their role to Norway at the end of 1991, PLO delegations started travelling to Oslo rather than Stockholm to discuss direct contact with Israel and seek financial help to see them through their post-Gulf War crisis.[68] Among the Palestinians was Ahmed Qurie (Abu Ala), a prominent banker who, as the head of the financial institution of Fatah, SAMED, was effectively the PLO Finance Minister. In late February 1992 he met with Deputy Foreign Minister Egeland and Juul, who now worked in the Foreign Minister's secretariat, to solicit financial support. Juul in turn introduced Abu Ala to her husband, and the two found in each other a kindred spirit. They kept in contact over the phone, and Abu Ala invited Larsen to Tunis, an invitation he did not feel he could act on until the data from his study on living conditions was safely in Oslo.[69]

On 29 April 1992, Larsen met with former Finance Minister and Knesset member Yossi Beilin at an Indian restaurant in Tel Aviv: 'I met him for the first time and we started discussing the Washington talks which were going on ... We completely agreed that this was being mishandled, and that it couldn't lead anywhere. We particularly discussed that there had to be secret talks, that there had to be pre-negotiations in order to build confidence, and it would have to be a kind of gradual approach to it.'[70] Off the back of this meeting, Larsen arranged for Beilin to meet Faisal Husseini later that month at the American Colony Hotel in Jerusalem. For the following six months, Yair Hirschfeld, a close academic associate of Beilin's with whom he had been working since the early 1980s, and his colleague Ron Pundak, served as his non-official long arm into the Palestinian community. They engaged in an intensive dialogue with the local Palestinian leadership, including Hanan Ashrawi, Husseini, and Sari Nusseibeh.

Rabin and the Labour party won the Israeli elections in June, which greatly increased the chances of establishing direct contacts with the PLO. Although an excellent opportunity, the Norwegians were slightly apprehensive of a potentially negative American reaction to their involvement, so Egeland and Juul travelled to Washington to make inquiries. After lunch at the Norwegian Ambassador's residence, Deputy Assistant Secretary of State for Near Eastern Affairs Dan Kurtzer was pulled aside and asked what the American attitude would be to a possible Norwegian back channel between Israel and the PLO. Kurtzer replied that he could not immediately speak on behalf of his government, but offered Egeland his personal view:

> Don't ask. Go for it. Just do it. We're not going to do it. And the way Washington works, it's unlikely that anybody's going to stop you. It's not that they're going to wake up one morning and say, "Don't let Norway do this." They probably won't pay much attention to it, or they'll dismiss it, or they'll watch it with bemusement, but nobody's going to stop you.[71]

On 12 September, while on an official visit to Israel, Egeland and Juul attended a secret meeting with Larsen, newly appointed Deputy Foreign Minister Beilin, and Hirschfeld in an effort to try to establish a secret channel of negotiations parallel to the Washington talks.[72] It was a meeting of likeminded individuals who agreed on what was needed, although doubts existed as to specific Israeli and Palestinian representation. Beilin agreed to meet Husseini, but the latter repeatedly declined to meet in Jerusalem or travel to Oslo, so the meeting never took place, for reasons that would soon become clear.

At the multilateral working groups in Ottawa held parallel to the Washington talks, Larsen and Juul were participating in the working group on refugees. From their experiences there, the couple realised that the PLO had complete control over the entire negotiating process in Ottawa. 'Abu Ala ... was actually sitting in his hotel room directing the negotiations via mobile telephone; there wasn't a word which was said which was not approved by him. But he then in turn reported to Abu Mazen [senior PLO official Mahmoud Abbas] who was sitting in Tunis – it was complete Tunis control.' They also deduced that the same reasonably applied to the bilateral talks in Washington. 'Mona and I, we drew the conclusion that Tunis would never allow an agreement to take place unless the PLO were an official part of it, because that would basically be political suicide for Arafat and the PLO.' Thus, the same powers had also forbidden Husseini from establishing a secret channel with Beilin in Oslo, fearing that his participation would undermine the PLO.[73]

Hirschfeld and Pundak had also reached this conclusion. 'The message from the local Palestinians was that on all issues, if we would like to see progress, we must speak with the PLO.'[74] At the end of November, they were discussing ways to break the gridlock with the Palestinians, and Ashrawi suggested establishing an official back channel. Different configurations were discussed, and the Israelis raised the idea of meeting Abu Ala, to which the Palestinians responded positively. Abu Ala had namely attracted a lot of interest in the Israeli peace camp due to a paper he wrote on economic interdependence and co-operation between Israelis and Palestinians, which fit quite nicely with Peres' vision of a 'new Middle East' economic zone. Among all these parallel lines of thought which had thus far been developing almost separately, there was a convergence of thinking among Israelis, Palestinians, and the Norwegians.[75]

A meeting of the multilateral working groups took place in London on 3–4 December, which provided an opportunity for a secret meeting. Hirschfeld had been in Switzerland for a meeting on water issues and continued on to London, ostensibly to discuss the financing of various academic projects with Larsen, but really to meet Abu Ala. As a facilitator, Larsen supervised their initial encounter at a hotel in London, which was made to look like a chance run-in, but then let them speak privately later that evening, where they agreed to try to pursue their contacts further in Oslo.[76] At the end of December, Larsen finally took Abu Ala up on his offer and travelled to Tunis, where his host took him to see Arafat. Together, they decided to establish a secret channel of negotiations under Norwegian auspices. The PLO leader spoke of his disappointment that their traditional facilitator, the Swedish Social Democrats, had been ousted from power, and said, 'Mr. Larsen, Norway must now take over Sweden's role. I hope you will convey this message to your government when you return.'[77]

Regardless of what Arafat may then have thought, the Oslo channel was not a government initiative. This is not to say that the Norwegian government was uninterested in an intermediary role in the Middle East. Stoltenberg was a close friend of Sten Andersson's and had been involved in the discussions leading up to Arafat's visit to Stockholm in 1983. When the Madrid conference convened, Stoltenberg had instructed Egeland to offer Norwegian services in the form of modest confidence-building measures between the parties.[78] These attempts had not produced any concrete results, but quite clearly brought the option to Arafat's attention once again. The Norwegian Ministry of Foreign Affairs supported Larsen's initiative and were kept abreast of it, but were not an integral part of it at this early stage. The Ministry has officially stated that they 'had a very limited involvement in the secret negotiations'.[79] FAFO, with Larsen at its helm, was the organiser on the Norwegian side, and was responsible for liaising with the Israeli and Palestinian parties and co-ordinating with the Ministry of Foreign Affairs. Egeland's presence during the preparatory stage and a few of the initial meetings in Norway demonstrated official support and inspired faith in the effort.

The fact that it was a FAFO initiative also ensured full deniability, an integral component that the parties insisted on and the Norwegian government could not provide as readily. Rather than appearing to be anything official, meetings hosted and funded by a non-governmental organisation would merely be deemed academic exercises or discussions. Working through a think-tank like FAFO would help them 'avoid the reporting and filing routines which civil servants are bound by' and maintain complete secrecy.[80] All expenses (flights, transport, hotels, and food) were paid by FAFO, and the first drafts of the Declaration of Principles (DoP) were written on FAFO stationary so that they would look academic should they somehow circulate beyond the intended inner entourage.[81] No paper trail was to point anywhere except FAFO. The Israelis were taking great risks by talking to the PLO, and should the talks leak and become public, Beilin insisted that he had to be able to deny any knowledge of them.[82] Similarly, while the PLO obviously wanted to be negotiating directly with Israel, they did not want to be seen doing so behind the backs of the Americans, the Jordanians, the

Syrians, and others. Arafat in fact suggested they have the US Consul General to Jerusalem participate as an American representative, but as Kurtzer had told Egeland, there was no American enthusiasm for this track, nor was there to be any involvement.[83]

Aware of the intense nature of the enmity that existed between the conflicting parties and having observed the dysfunctional charade unfolding in Washington, secrecy was of the utmost importance. In private discussions, groups of Israelis and Palestinians would attempt to overcome these hurdles through clear, frank, honest communication and the creation of mutual trust and respect, isolated from the external pressures of their societies and the asymmetry of the conflict. From the outset, Larsen had a very particular conception of his role in the Oslo channel, together with Juul and Egeland.

> [We] developed this philosophy that we should not participate in the talks. They could brief us afterwards, we could be go-betweens if they wanted to get some new information ... and to clear up misunderstandings ... We defined ourselves as go-betweens and facilitators, but not as negotiators. We basically said, 'You own the problem, you develop your notion of how this should be done.'[84]

The Norwegians were there to smooth things out, interpret or clarify positions, and explain the difficulties of one side to the other, but not get involved in the real substance of their negotiations.

The first session was held on 21–22 January, 1993, at Borregaard and they continued sporadically until 1 May. Hirschfeld and Pundak represented the Israeli side, with Abu Ala representing the Palestinians together with Hassan Asfour and Maher al-Kurd. Larsen was always present at the chosen location, Borregaard, Sarpsborg, or elsewhere, and Juul or Egeland stopped in from time to time, but care was taken not to have anyone from the Foreign Ministry there regularly lest they be spotted. Larsen would share meals with the parties, encourage them, and generally strove to create a relaxed, friendly atmosphere.[85] This became known as the 'Oslo spirit', and the Norwegian played his role exceptionally well.

The Norwegian mediators benefited from an immensely fortuitous set of personal connections. Although he himself was not directly connected to the Ministry of Foreign Affairs, Larsen's wife Mona Juul was (she was also a close friend of Stoltenberg's), so essential information pertaining to the back channel could be shared informally without having to go through official channels and without raising undue suspicion.

This familiarity was maximised upon Johan Jørgen Holst's accession as Minister of Foreign Affairs in April 1993. Holst was a very close personal friend of both Larsen and Juul, and they spoke practically every day.[86] In early April, Larsen and Juul invited Holst and his wife Marianne for a traditional Easter dinner at their flat in Oslo. During the meal, Larsen informed Holst about the secret talks that he was orchestrating, and wanted to introduce him to Abu Ala. Holst, however, thought that it seemed 'too fantastic' and declined to be intimately involved at that point. He said, 'No, I will not proceed on a failure', but signalled that should the process begin to yield serious results, then he would join the proceedings and his Ministry could shepherd the group through the final stages.[87]

Larsen suspected that this guarded pessimism was also shared by Stoltenberg, who 'didn't believe at all that this would succeed'. He 'actually never met Stoltenberg thoughout this process. Not ever.'[88] Stoltenberg clearly felt that using Egeland as his envoy was sufficient. By contrast, Holst became personally involved in the Oslo channel and played an increasingly active role. Eventually convinced that this was more serious than he had first thought, he altered his original stance demonstrably by attending the fifth round of talks held on the weekend of 8–9 May. Here, Abu Ala took Larsen aside and explained that, as productive as their talks with Hirschfeld and Pundak had been, they needed official Israeli representation in order to advance the dialogue. Larsen assured him that they would address his concern, and that Holst 'had agreed to take whatever initiative he could to avert the collapse of the negotiations'.[89]

Larsen flew to Israel and met with Beilin, who in consultation with Rabin and Peres appointed the Director General of the Foreign Ministry, Uri Savir, to be the Israeli chief negotiator. Here, Larsen was instrumental to convincing both parties that the other was acting in good faith, and that these were serious discussions with real representation on each side. Waage surmises that Holst's presence was a further incentive for the Israelis to make their participation official.[90]

Holst, the official conduit

From then on, Holst was a central figure in the dialogue, together with Larsen and Juul. In mid-June, Holst travelled to Israel and Tunis to definitively confirm the high level of commitment to the channel from Peres, Rabin, and Arafat. When the Palestinians then issued an extensive set of demands for modification of the DoP draft on 10 July 1993, at Halvorsbøle, the Norwegians began a period of intensive contacts between Tunis and Tel Aviv and Jerusalem, meeting each side, passing messages between them, conveying positions and personal impressions. While Holst stayed in Tunis, Larsen and Juul joined him for meetings with Arafat where they discussed the channel in detail, including points of disagreement between the parties in the DoP. The couple personally delivered letters from Holst to Peres and vice versa after each of their discussions, and repeated this pattern. They presented an encouraging image of their meetings, conveyed thoughts of the leaderships and negotiators, emphasised the positives that had been put on the negotiating table, and reassured each side that the desire to reach an agreement was genuine.[91] Although both parties still paid lip service to the Washington talks, it became clear that rather than transfer the results from Oslo over the Atlantic, it would be the main forum for striking a deal.

Beilin noted that Holst was prepared 'to do everything in his power to prevent collapse of the talks', offering to deepen his role as mediator, but was not invited to formulate compromises or adjust positions.[92] Indeed, Larsen corroborates this. As rounds of talks were held over the summer of 1993, he sometimes took the parties to Holst's villa en route to Fornebu airport, where they gave him 'an oral briefing ... and sometimes copies of the documents which were negotiated ... but there were no negotiations'. Larsen emphasised that the Foreign Minister was not substantially involved in any negotiation or formulation, 'not at all, neither in reality nor formally, not in any shape or form'.[93]

In mid-August, Peres was on an official tour of the Scandinavian countries and telephoned Holst, asking to meet him secretly in Stockholm that night in order to finish finalising the DoP. Holst was in Iceland, but dispatched Larsen to Stockholm to make the arrangements. Larsen concocted a cover story to tell the Swedes, embellishing a bilateral complication between Israel and Norway over heavy water which Holst needed to iron out secretly with Peres in Stockholm before the Israeli Foreign Minister continued to Norway. This way, the Norwegians and Israelis were given complete secrecy at Haga Slott, an old royal manor turned government guesthouse for foreign dignitaries in Stockholm, guarded by the Swedish secret service. Unbeknownst to their Swedish hosts, the DoP was largely ironed out over the phone between Stockholm and Tunis in the early hours of 18 August. The Swedish contribution did not extend beyond picking up the phone bill.

In Stockholm, Peres did not want to speak to Arafat himself, so insisted that Holst be his mouthpiece. Israelis Joel Singer and Avi Gil, in addition to Larsen and Juul, were present and offered advice, while Rabin was in Israel, ready to be consulted when necessary. On the other end in Tunis, Abu Ala was on the phone:

> I listened to the proposals put to us by Holst, consulted with Arafat and our group of advisors [including Abu Mazen, Hassan Asfour, and Yasser Abed Rabbo] and then conveyed the Palestinian position back to Holst. Meanwhile, Holst was passing our proposals to Joel Singer, who, in turn, would consult Peres, after which Holst would give me their reply.

This dynamic persisted throughout the morning. Abu Ala goes on to describe the role played by the Norwegian Foreign Minister, which he considered 'of the highest importance':

> Using all his charisma and his impressive diplomatic skills, Holst played a crucial and decisive role. He was an honest broker who transmitted and reported all the various proposals impartially from one side to the other, refraining from any interference. He kept a careful balance between the role of neutral mediator and that of an active player. He put forward all the alternative formulations that were offered, without showing any preference or personal choice.[94]

This was a further development of Holst's role, and there is no doubt that it was a crucial one and that he played it well. But like Abu Ala, Larsen maintains that 'it was not a negotiation on the Norwegian side', they were simply conveying positions.[95] Waage, on the other hand, suggests that Holst upgraded his role to that of formulator ('formulation being one of Holst's strongest suits').[96] In his account of the negotiations, Abbas notes how

> we saw them go beyond the role of host providing conditions of comfort and total secrecy for the negotiators, right up to direct intervention between the negotiators: to reconcile viewpoints and provide suggestions, alternatives and sometimes different scenarios. They adopted the role of a full partner in the negotiations.[97]

Holst himself said that 'in some phases, you could quietly suggest compromise formulas and mediate between positions which diverged more than compromise could sustain'.[98]

Although Larsen admits that they did occasionally discuss the wording of positions with the Israelis and volunteered some suggestions, he describes their impact as 'marginal'.[99] A few days later in Oslo, when the DoP was on the verge of being signed, disagreements surfaced between Abu Ala and Savir, and the two began negotiating once more. At this juncture, Holst 'came in with some suggestions', which made Larsen 'furious, frankly', because he 'thought it was counter productive to come in and intervene'.[100] More substantial involvement above and beyond facilitating communication or passing positions went against the ethos that had originally guided Larsen's initiative.

Following the conclusion of the DoP, Holst was then heavily involved in the negotiations over mutual recognition between Israel and the PLO. Aggestam argues that this role was possible thanks to the increase in Norwegian credibility from the previous phase.[101] As Waage suggests, Holst's 'personal prestige was now even more on the line' since the Oslo channel was no longer a secret, so his main concern was to 'protect the Norwegian peace project and Norway's role ... determined not to let the Oslo DoP go unsigned simply because the mutual recognition text was not agreed upon'.[102] Israeli officials like Beilin attest to the devoted activity of Holst during this phase, observing that Holst 'threw the full weight of his energy and expertise into the issue of mutual recognition, and the phone lines to Tunis and Jerusalem were hot'.[103]

In addition to the two letters of mutual recognition between Arafat and Rabin, which were the fruit of negotiations on 9–10 September in

Paris, a letter was drafted from Arafat to Holst containing commitments to call on Palestinians to take steps towards normalising life and to reject violence and terrorism. Another letter was to be written from Peres to Holst committing Israel to allow Palestinian institutions in Jerusalem to remain open.[104] Beilin recalls that during this phase, 'in the point of exchange of letters between the PLO and Rabin, Holst played the role of mediator rather than a facilitator for sure'. Whereas his influence had otherwise been 'mild', here Holst was acting as a formulator, suggesting alternative wording, which 'was very important'.[105]

Abbas acknowledges that there was a genuine human emotional involvement in the process from the Norwegians, an 'inner motivation' which went beyond pure political cynicism.[106] Although undoubtedly true, personal egos did come into play and soured the otherwise excellent relationship in the Norwegian camp. Primarily, this was due to Holst, who tried to make the process more his own than it had been. As he had made clear to Larsen earlier in the year, he was keen to take on a more substantial role only if the talks were succeeding, naturally eager to capitalise politically on the success of Larsen's initiative and maximise his own political prestige. Had he judged that the talks were not serious, or if they petered out naturally, Holst would have wanted nothing to do with them.

Crucially, when the DoP was being finalised and Holst sought to intervene more substantially, an additional rift was caused by a press conference where he attempted to alter the image of the Norwegians and the negotiations. At the expense of Mona Juul, he assigned an imagined role to his wife Marianne, who, although involved in FAFO, had not been a crucial part of the team. Holst led the press to believe that negotiations had been conducted in their home, when, as Larsen explained, only briefings and social meetings had taken place there, and further that Holst's young son had been a 'diplomatic ice-breaker' of some importance. The story had been altered to appear a 'homely Norwegian saga of two families who had brought the warring sides together', with photo spreads of the whole Holst family, prompting 'disbelief, anger, and embarrassment amongst everyone who really knew what had been going on'.[107]

Additionally, Holst ran into trouble when he tried to put an exclusively Norwegian stamp on the process. When everything was presented publicly at the aforementioned press conference, former Foreign Minister

Stoltenberg was furious that Holst had not mentioned anything of the historical background, the co-operation with the Swedes that had substantially brought the Norwegians into the fold. Stoltenberg called upon the Prime Minister Gro Harlem Bruntland to make sure that Holst publicly recognise the historic Swedish involvement, which he then reluctantly did.[108]

The similarities between the intermediary roles played by Andersson and Holst are many. Both acted as messengers between their respective parties, passing positions between them; both were the recipients of written commitments from each side that they would not make directly to each other; both applied what personal pressure they could on Arafat to be flexible and make the necessary concessions and decisions; both became very actively involved in their respective endeavours. Andersson and his colleagues acted as formulators in Stockholm and Geneva by modifying the language of statements, as did Holst when he worked on the letters of mutual recognition.

If proof were needed of his hard work, one need only look at his deteriorating health. The stress of the process took its toll on Holst, who suffered multiple heart attacks due to serious exhaustion and eventually passed away on 13 January 1994. Despite this loss, Norway remained involved in the peace process, which was deemed a foreign policy priority of the highest order. It initiated the group of international donor countries known as the Ad Hoc Liaison Committee (AHLC) in October 1993, which is the main financial mechanism of the peace process responsible for aid guidelines and policies to build economic, technical, and administrative infrastructure in the West Bank and Gaza. The Local Aid Co-ordination Committee (LACC), a substructure of the AHLC, is co-chaired by Norway, the UN, and the World Bank and co-ordinates the activities of aid agencies with the PA.

Additionally, Norway has led the working group responsible for the development of a Palestinian police force, and the Norwegian Agency for Development and Co-operation (NORAD), a part of the Foreign Ministry, has been heavily involved in plans for development aid, working with Norwegian NGOs, for example.[109] Initially the organiser of Norway's role in the AHLC, Larsen then became the UN co-ordinator in the occupied territories, overlooking AHLC projects, and has remained involved in the region ever since in a variety of capacities.

As a result of the Oslo Agreement, the Norwegian global diplomatic profile exploded overnight. Oslo became known as the 'Capital of Peace', and the Norwegians were invited to mediate or participate in peace processes all over the world, including Colombia, Cyprus, Guatemala, Sri Lanka, Sudan, the former Yugoslavia, and many others.[110]

Oslo's Achilles heel: the lack of a coercive arbitrator

Since the signing of the DoP on the White House lawn on 13 September 1993, 'Oslo' has become a bit of a dirty word in the Israeli–Palestinian conflict. The initial hope and positivism heralded by Oslo disappeared, submerged in rivers of blood and broken pledges. The mutual trust that the agreement had looked to instil was lost amid years of violence, mutual violations of agreements, and mutual recriminations. A vast number of studies have been written about the failures of Oslo,[111] and many point out weaknesses inherent in the structure and (lack of) substance of the agreement itself. Most of those involved in the negotiations have no illusions about this. Larsen freely admits that 'of course, according to ideal standards, it's lousy! I mean there's no state, there's no refugees, there's no Jerusalem, there's nothing.' Many critics have said '"you should have had settlement freeze, refugees, Jerusalem, borders, everything," yes of course. But it was impossible.' Under the circumstances, given the limited 'ripeness' that existed, 'Oslo was the best possible outcome you could get'.[112]

This is particularly true given the nature of the identity-based conflict in which the parties are embroiled. For years, each has done its utmost to deny the legitimacy of the other. Mutual recognition of the other as a people was a crucial and necessary first step in order to embark upon conflict resolution. This is what makes Oslo so significant.[113] While many Palestinians remained extremely critical of the agreement for its lack of substance and specifics,[114] Saeb Erekat, a Palestinian negotiator at the Washington talks, explained why it was so significant for him as a Palestinian:

> I asked to read the agreement. I read the first paragraph and I accepted it. It says the Government of Israel, GOI, and the Palestine Liberation Organisation, PLO, the representative of the Palestinian people, and I saw the term 'Palestinian people' and

> PLO and I said I accept. Because in my mind, this is Zionism: Zionist movement in 1897, people with no land, a land with no people; we did not exist, that's number one. Balfour declaration, we exist, but as subhuman, the white man's burden. Then we became refugees, then we became terrorists, and now, they're telling us we're people, that's it, I accept. I accepted Oslo fully because of this sentence. Because I know this was the major turning point in Zionist and Western thinking. We did not vanish as Palestinians. This was my triumph.[115]

Whatever weaknesses one points to in the Oslo Agreement, it is not fair to fault the Norwegian intermediaries for them, as it would be a misrepresentation of the Norwegian role. In her analysis, Waage criticises Larsen and his associates for running the errands of the Israelis, being biased towards their positions, and reproducing the political asymmetry that existed between the parties to the conflict. She berates the Norwegians, who 'acted on Israel's premises, bowed to Israel's "red lines"' and 'bent over backwards to accommodate Israel's security concerns'.[116]

Larsen dismisses her assertions of pro-Israeli bias, insisting that 'we would criticise one and we criticised the other. And later I've been in the privileged position that I've been made *persona non grata* by both Arafat and Sharon . . . So I mean we have always been extremely fair with all parties, brutally I would say. And it was the same in Oslo.'[117] Unable to influence the political asymmetry, he instead worked within his means to focus on achieving process symmetry by treating each negotiating team with minute equality, down to the very last details.

Though Waage obviously has a point, it is not entirely clear how the Norwegians could have influenced the positions of either party. No amount of gentle persuasion would have made either party accept terms which they thought fundamentally unacceptable. Waage herself admits that they had no 'muscle' to alter the situation: 'Norway could not alter the power asymmetry between Israel and the Palestinians', and 'it could not force solutions on unwilling parties. Israel was the stronger party, with a clear national security agenda, and it was not willing to concede much. The PLO was the weaker party, willing to accept little in order to avoid further marginalisation.'[118] She appears to exaggerate the extent of Norwegian involvement on substance, evaluating a facilitative mediator on the terms of a coercive one. Larsen insists that 'it was only marginally that we had anything to do with the substance, because we defined our role as facilitators and go-betweens, and not as negotiators'.[119]

In cases of asymmetric conflict, mediators with coercive powers have an increased ability to generate symmetry, but, in this instance, the prime candidate, the United States, was incapable of playing the role that was required to move the process forward. Their mediation strategy was not attuned to the needs of the process, and they could not be the discreet facilitator the situation called for, whereas Larsen's Norwegian initiative was contextually appropriate and perfectly within their means. The American State Department was dismissive of the Oslo channel, and generally neglectful of the Israeli–Palestinian track.

This was not due to ignorance of goings-on in Oslo. Up until May 1993 when the Oslo channel was upgraded, the Norwegians and Israelis regularly briefed Deputy Assistant Secretary of State Kurtzer on their progress. He in turn wrote up memos of these briefings and circulated them to a small circle, the 'peace team', including Secretary of State Warren Christopher, assistant Secretary of State for Near East Affairs Ed Djerejian, Martin Indyk at the National Security Council (NSC), and Dennis Ross and Aaron Miller, who in June 1993 became Head and Deputy Special Middle East Co-ordinator respectively under President Clinton. The only reaction from this group was that Oslo did not constitute anything particularly serious.[120] On the face of it, these were discussions between Israeli academics and PLO officials, without the backing of Rabin. Other nascent dialogues also existed between Israelis and PLO members like Nabil Sha'ath, so there was not necessarily a reason to think anything of Oslo specifically.

As soon as the talks were upgraded on the Israeli side, the Norwegians, on advice of the Israelis, did not let the Americans know this new development. Rabin reportedly wanted to keep them in the dark, afraid that they would leak information. Following Savir's first meeting with Abu Ala in Norway, Holst went on his first trip to Washington as Foreign Minister to meet with Christopher. After their meeting, Holst rang Beilin to brief him: 'I told him [that there was progress on the Oslo track]. He didn't press me, and my impression is he thinks Oslo is just a talking-shop. He doesn't know about Uri [Savir].'[121] In early August, however, Beilin himself briefed Kurtzer on the latest developments, who in turn informed Christopher and the peace team. The seriousness of Oslo should thus have been clear.

In their analysis of the period, Kurtzer *et al.* argue that a significant American error was a failure to fully understand Rabin's intentions and strategy.[122] Rabin had decided that he would negotiate with both the Syrians and the Palestinians simultaneously, and proceed with the track that showed the most promise. On the basis of a mistaken reading of Rabin's calculations, American attention was focused entirely on the negotiations between Israel and Syria.[123] As Indyk explains, 'the key to understanding what happened in the summer of 1993 is that Bill Clinton's highest priority was Syria and Yitzhak Rabin's was not'.[124]

This was a failure to correctly assess the impact of Rabin's immediate political priorities on wider strategic thinking about Arab–Israeli peace. Although Rabin shared the broader strategic American assessment that peace with Syria should come first, he had vowed prior to his election to lessen Israeli control over the lives of the Palestinians, whose plight had been showcased over seven years of *intifada*. 'Rabin was essentially choosing between a quick and advantageous deal with the Palestinians, albeit with Arafat, and a drawn-out negotiation with [Syrian President Hafez al-] Assad', and opted for the former. The Israelis knew Arafat was desperate to do a deal and took advantage of the fact.[125]

Rabin had in fact signaled a real interest in an alternative Palestinian track. In Washington in late February 1993, Rabin had a breakfast meeting with the American peace team, minus Christopher, where he bemoaned the negotiations with the unempowered local Palestinian delegation. The American team concluded that direct talks with the PLO were clearly on his mind.[126] Despite this, with knowledge of Oslo's existence, there was no reaction and no heightened interest in the endeavour.

Even after Oslo became public, the Americans continued to focus on the Syrians, much to the dismay of Kurtzer and Miller, the two members of the American peace team who had long advocated a focus on the Palestinian track. The aftermath of Oslo meant that Israel would have to give up territory to the Palestinians, rendering a withdrawal from the Golan – the necessary ingredient in any deal with Syria – practically unthinkable. They felt that an opportunity with the Palestinians was being squandered. 'Even if you're persuaded that Syria is the outcome that you're looking for, since Rabin has signed onto this and has told you he's not doing Syria, make this work. Take it over.' But 'it didn't happen.

The team was uninterested, by and large.'[127] Kurtzer further suggests that the 'double whammy' of not being able to broker a deal with Syria and having the Norwegians involve themselves in what was traditionally their domain put the Americans into 'a very reactive mode'.

There was little inclination to adopt a framework that they had not negotiated themselves, a particularly lamentable decision since it was precisely in the implementation phase that American coercive power would have been of real use.[128] When carrots and sticks were required, few others could wield the same power as the United States, but the Clinton administration decided against it, limiting their role to that of a facilitator.[129] Miller agrees that the real problem during this period was the change in the US perception of its role in the peace process.

> The combination of the 'do it themselves' Oslo process, Rabin's reflexive opposition to a strong American role, and Clinton's 'reverence' for the {Israeli} Prime Minister, as Dennis {Ross} put it, conditioned us in the early years to act as a very cautious and deferential facilitator. 'Rabin didn't want a mediator,' Dennis recalls. 'He wanted us to be the facilitator or the intermediary,' at least with the Palestinians. This seemed to make perfect sense then. Oslo was their breakthrough, not ours.[130]

The Americans briefly intervened to avert a crisis after Baruch Goldstein killed 29 Palestinian worshippers at the tomb of Abraham in Hebron,[131] and were a limited presence prior to the signing of the Gaza–Jericho agreement on 4 May 1994, but there was no substantial involvement on the Palestinian track. In some respects, this was not an issue. Israelis and Palestinians were negotiating themselves and both insisted that American envoys not get involved. As with the Norwegians, the Americans were not present in the negotiating room, a rule that remained in force up until August 1995, when the Interim Agreement known as 'Oslo II' was being ironed out.[132] Savir writes that, up until then:

> I had been updating Ross by phone. He made a point of encouraging the negotiators and expressed his appreciation that we were solving our problems without the United States' active

> intervention. Whenever Ross visited Israel with Warren Christopher ... the atmosphere of these trilateral meetings tended to be relatively stiff. Nevertheless, the Americans were delighted, they said, by the 'chemistry' between the two delegations and the degree of creativity they displayed.[133]

In early August, Ross had angered Savir and Abu Ala by speaking directly with Peres and Arafat, essentially going over the heads of their negotiating teams. When he defended himself, pointing out that he was only helping them resolve the gridlock, Savir told Ross

> something revealing about most successful negotiations: his relationship with his negotiating partner had to take precedence over everything else. If Abu Ala felt a third party was undercutting him, then, in Uri's words, "solidarity with Abu Ala" was more important.[134]

Still, in mid-August the Eilat and Taba talks reached a point where even Savir felt the Americans needed to be involved as a lever. To progress on the issue of water, Ross proposed a trilateral US, Israeli, and Palestinian committee to focus on allocation rather than ownership of the aquifers themselves.

> The committee had another purpose: to signal to Arafat that there would be a more intrusive US role from here on. I knew that he would see a committee with US participation as a new lever to get the Israelis to fulfil their promises on further redeployments (FRDs) and other issues, and that Peres and Uri would see it as an additional lever to ensure that Arafat lived up to his commitments. I considered it a way to facilitate agreement, not as a fundamental transformation of our role. We could not take the place of the two sides as they negotiated.[135]

Ross observes that Arafat and Rabin seemed to have had an 'implicit deal' that acknowledged the lack of more pervasive ripeness for conflict resolution: 'You don't push me beyond where I can go with my opponents and I won't push you beyond where you can go with your settler constituency.' With the benefit of hindsight, he laments that 'while tactically useful, this complicit bargain was strategically damaging. Israeli settlement activity convinced Palestinians over time that the process was a sham, and gave Arafat, at least in his mind, an excuse not to fulfil his responsibilities on security.'[136]

Oslo – and then later the Israeli–Jordanian peace treaty – provided proof that Middle Eastern states can reach landmark agreements without an American mediator. The strategy of 'quiet diplomacy' employed by Andersson continued to yield dividends when practised by Larsen, Holst, and the Norwegians, and demonstrated the importance of procedural aspects in difficult negotiations.

It became abundantly clear however that the implementation of Oslo and the later interim agreements could not merely be left to the parties themselves, but required more robust international involvement. Both sides violated Oslo in both letter and spirit. The Palestinians ignored the strengthening of armed militias, and failed to collect and control illegal arms. Violence and suicide attacks against Israelis contravened their vow to put an end to terror and, on the whole, the option of armed struggle was never truly abandoned. Furthermore, widespread corruption undermined Palestinian efforts to create effective government institutions.

The Israelis disrupted timetables of redeployment, refused to withdraw from territory as agreed, and reneged on prisoner releases; checkpoints and roadblocks designed to enhance security impeded Palestinian transportation and economic links; though not explicitly forbidden under the terms of the agreement, Israel did nothing to halt the expansion of illegal settlements in the West Bank but in fact accelerated their pace. Both parties turned a blind eye to incitement against the other, undermining the mutual recognition that was the hallmark of Oslo.[137]

A major failure of the Oslo Agreement was the absence of effective systems of monitoring to ensure compliance, resulting in a lack of accountability. While the Americans were not the official underwriters or guarantors, they could and should have played this role. The United States did not monitor performance and enforce commitments the parties had made to each other, allowing destructive developments to continue unchecked, thereby eroding confidence and trust among the parties.[138]

Indyk believes that America's greatest contribution to peacemaking lies in using its power and resources to shape a positive and supportive environment, rather than engaging in the details of the negotiations themselves. He points to Clinton's commitment to 'minimise the risks' of those making peace, and the American influence exercised on Arab leaders, but bizarrely, accountability does not appear to have been considered a key for a 'positive and supportive environment'.[139] Kurtzer explains that the need to 'keep the process alive' became more important than ensuring strict compliance:

> The view at the time was very much if we push these guys too hard, the process may collapse, and we'll figure out how to fix this stuff later on. Rabin for example had so captivated President Clinton that Clinton was not going to press Rabin to dismantle settlements or to stop settlement activity. When Rabin says to him, 'Don't worry about it, I'm going to have to deal with this later, why should I have a crisis now?', Clinton says, 'Alright, I accept that.' You know, he's a politician after all, why have a crisis before it's time. The attitude towards the violence on the Palestinian side was a little bit tougher, but even there, there was always an excuse – fragility, or weakness, or internal problems, so it became keeping the process alive for the sake of the process, without understanding that there was this build-up of bad behaviour that was actually weighing down the process.[140]

Fundamentally, Oslo was not the product of a shared vision, but a shared interest. Arafat and the PLO were primarily interested in political survival. Keen to neutralise Hamas, their Islamic fundamentalist rivals in the occupied territories, the pragmatism displayed in Norway was a move in a quest for political supremacy. Israeli Prime Minister Yitzhak Rabin was aware of the danger posed by groups like Hamas, and a sense of realism made him opt to deal with Arafat and the PLO. Peace with the Palestinians was seen as the best way to counter the rise of Islamic fundamentalism.[141] Aside from this mutual interest, Rabin also saw signs of erosion and fragmentation in Israeli society. He confided to Israeli diplomat Shlomo Ben-Ami that the mobilised and pioneering society of old had 'lost its fighting spirit', and that he was doubtful if they could continue to withstand the future threats facing them.[142]

This lack of a unified vision was ultimately harmful to the process. As Rynhold highlights in his analysis, a constructive ambiguity prevailed, which acted as 'destructive ambiguity' by masking the substantial gulf between each side's conceptualisation of what mutual recognition meant in practice.[143] Consequently, the interim mechanism posed serious difficulties. A number of Israeli and Palestinian academics and politicians, however, sought to move beyond the thorny interim stage and narrow the gaps that existed on final status issues. In their quest to loosen this Gordian knot, they once again needed the help of a discreet small-state mediator.

CHAPTER 4

THE 'BEILIN–ABU MAZEN UNDERSTANDINGS' OR THE 'STOCKHOLM DOCUMENT': A TRYING TIME FOR TRACK II

What was important for us was that it {the channel which produced the Beilin-Abu Mazen Understandings} was facilitated by Sweden. I mean, it is not big sums of money but it is money . . . It was an unofficial channel, they provided all the facilities for it, and the secrecy, and the security. So it worked.

– Yossi Beilin[1]

The project has helped clarify the issues, set the parameters, and define the realms of what is possible and desirable in seeking a peaceful resolution of the conflict. The concepts and outcomes contained in the document have set the agenda for public and official discussions on final status issues.

– Report from the 'Stockholm group'[2]

The Palestinian people feel victimised by this 'peace process'. . . reinvented all the time to suit Israel. And America thinks all the time that as long as there is a 'process', God is in his heaven.

– Hanan Ashrawi[3]

Oslo produced euphoria among many of those who had been striving for peace between Israel and the Palestinians. Mutual recognition suggested that a corner had been turned, heralding a new spirit of mutual co-existence between the two peoples and aimed to recalibrate the zero-sum attitude that had long been the norm. The Oslo process was based on gradualism, a theory that espoused a step-by-step process of interim agreements moving towards a complete conflict-ending final status agreement. Gradually intensifying cooperation and the implementation of interim agreements at each stage would build trust between the two parties and replace old antagonism. This air of partnership nurtured by tangible positive results for both sides would then make compromises on the hard final status issues such as borders, refugees, and Jerusalem more forthcoming.

Theoretically, the logic was sound enough. What emerged, however, was a situation that Israeli head negotiator Uri Savir has described as 'a kind of purgatory between conflict and cooperation'.[4] The open-endedness of Oslo exacerbated the sense of uncertainty on both sides, and meant that each looked to keep its options open and improve their negotiating position.[5] In the words of Robert Rothstein, 'it promised negotiations on all the critical issues but it couldn't and didn't guarantee any of the outcomes each side desired, and neither side was able or willing to take the risks implicit in betting on the success of the peace process'. The peace process thus 'became the continuation of conflict by other means'.[6]

While Savir believed in the interim process, many did not.[7] Two such individuals were Yair Hirschfeld and Ron Pundak, the two Israeli academics who had been the original participants in the Oslo channel. Hirschfeld believed that

> there was no need for an interim agreement. There was a need for a Declaration of Principles (DoP), and then go directly to permanent status, because we thought that major issues that were kept open – Jerusalem, refugees, security, settlements, territory – they were open wounds, and if you don't deal with them, they will come back at you, and unfortunately we were right.[8]

Pundak shared these fears, and additionally saw the need for a clarification of the basic principles that would inform a final status agreement. He believed that 'gradualism was the right thing to do', but 'only if you know where you're heading. You cannot move gradually to a non-existent target ... An interim agreement with no final principles is very, very difficult to be implemented in a positive and honest way.'[9]

Yossi Beilin, deputy Foreign Minister and the first official mentor of the Oslo channel, agreed with these assessments. Acutely aware that extremists on both sides would do their utmost to kill the process, he knew they could not afford to drag their heels for years before beginning work on final status.[10] Although it provided for an interim period, the terms of the Oslo Agreement also enabled immediate discussion of final status issues, stipulating that final status talks were to begin *no later* than 4 May 1996. In order to prepare for these negotiations, they sought to reach an agreement with the Palestinians on the principles of final status, to be used as a basis for future formal negotiations.

After the Oslo Agreement had been concluded, Beilin travelled to Tunis in October 1993 to speak with Arafat. Hirschfeld and Pundak did the same, though separately from Beilin. The message they brought, however, was the same. They wanted to start work on permanent status through a secret channel similar to the one that had been so effective in Norway, and were looking for Palestinian partners to engage with. Arafat agreed with the idea. At a conference in the United Kingdom in May 1994, Pundak met Ahmad Khalidi, a Palestinian academic. The two met again later that summer in London, joined by Hirschfeld and Hussein Agha, another Palestinian academic based in the United Kingdom. Together, they developed a joint proposal for a secret channel.

This channel was envisioned as an adaptation of the successful Oslo model. The four academics required a facilitator to host their secret discussions on permanent status, but were not looking for a formulator or a manipulative mediator. They intended to find an external academic sponsor for their project, something akin to the way FAFO had functioned in the Oslo channel, but circumstances presented a slightly different opportunity. As Agha and Khalidi have explained, 'the Swedish connection was essentially fortuitous'.[11] In June 1994, at a conference in Stockholm organised by the American think-tank Search for Common Ground, Agha met with Margareta af Ugglas, the Swedish Foreign Minister, and Ann Dismorr, her Private Secretary and later Deputy Director of the Middle East desk at the Ministry of Foreign Affairs with special responsibility for the peace process.

Agha had a heated argument with af Ugglas about the effects of EU membership on Swedish neutrality.[12]

The following day, Agha approached Dismorr with the proposal, who, together with State Secretary Lars-Åke Nilsson, in turn presented it to af Ugglas. She remembered Agha from the day before, and her reply was immediately positive. It was an offer she could not refuse; Dismorr has explained that the proposal was from the outset so well thought out and credibly presented that there were no doubts whatsoever about accepting it. Since it was a joint proposal, the two sides did not require any complicated diplomatic integration on Sweden's behalf to make it happen. A general election was looming, set for 18 September 1994, but the view was that this was something Sweden should be involved in, regardless of which political party was in power.[13]

According to Khalidi, 'if Hussein [Agha] hadn't been at that meeting, there was no reason for us to go for the Swedes in particular. It could have ended up anywhere else, or nowhere ... It wasn't as if we sought them, it just sort of fell into our lap, as it were.'[14] Agha thought simply, 'I was there, I had a proposal with me, I said I might as well give it a try, and it worked.' He was aware of the historical Swedish contribution to the peace process and the role played by Sten Andersson, and although this was at the back of his mind, it did not directly inform the decision to approach the Swedes.[15]

After having found their host, Khalidi went to Gaza later that summer to inform Arafat about the project, whereupon Arafat assigned Abu Mazen to act as the PLO liaison. On the Israeli side, Beilin was the official sponsor, and the teams agreed to keep their respective sponsors abreast of developments. Should any understandings be successfully produced, the sponsors would present these to their leaders and seek official endorsement of them for use in the formal final status negotiations. Although Arafat was clearly on board, Israeli Prime Minister Yitzhak Rabin and President Shimon Peres were unaware of the initiative.

In part, Swedish acceptance of the proposal constituted an admission of error on behalf of the same government that in 1991 neglected to follow the Social Democratic tradition of active involvement in the Israeli–Palestinian conflict. This step back had cut off a key avenue of Swedish foreign policy, one that generated a lot of high profile diplomatic interest and publicity for the country. They had served as a focal point for knowledge on the region, built up an excellent contact network, and were visited by many international Middle East policy chiefs for consultations, but much of this political capital was then squandered. Mathias Mossberg, a former Swedish ambassador, is very critical of this decision, describing it as a 'very bad business idea'.[16] When the Norwegians achieved the great breakthrough in Middle Eastern peacemaking and reaped tremendous international rewards, it stung the Swedish Foreign Ministry severely. A palpable level of neighbourly rivalry existed, and in some circles there was a sense that the breakthrough should have been Sweden's. The Israeli–Palestinian peace process became one of the 'sexiest' political topics on the international agenda, making the Swedes eager to get back in the game.

While af Ugglas had not been willing to maintain former Foreign Minister Sten Andersson's close relationship with Arafat, this opportunity presented a remarkably different scenario compared to earlier Swedish activity. This was an initiative jointly authored by Israeli and Palestinian academics to advance thinking on final status, presented directly to the Foreign Minister. It did not favour one side or the other, and so could not reasonably harm relations with either party, an issue that af Ugglas had previously raised in regard to the Israelis. Furthermore, there was no suggestion of hosting contacts at the highest political level and, anyway, Arafat had since achieved a much higher level of international legitimacy. More widely, af Ugglas' traditional Conservative attitude towards the Palestinians generally had been altered during her time in office, due in no small part to her relations with Hanan Ashrawi, a woman who had truly impressed her.[17]

The elections had a significant impact on the composition of the Swedish team of sponsors. The Social Democrats won, necessitating a handover of the initiative. Beilin had been concerned about this eventuality and contacted an old friend of his, Pierre Schori, who was a prominent figure in the foreign policy wings of the Social Democratic party and, Beilin reasoned, undoubtedly an influential member of any future Social Democratic government.[18] At a meeting 'between four eyes' in Stockholm on 23 August 1994, Beilin informed Schori about the secret channel and requested that he should do everything in his power to continue support for it should his party return to power. According to Schori's memo of the meeting, circulated only to party leader Ingvar Carlsson and Sten Andersson, Beilin stressed the secrecy surrounding the channel, noting that very few people on either side were aware of it. It also appears that the Conservative government had agreed to sponsor the channel to the tune of 600,000 SEK (80,000 USD).[19] Schori assured him, 'Of course, if there is something like this we shall cherish it and continue it, no problem, no question about it.'[20]

The exact sequence of events during this transitional phase is not entirely clear. What emerged, however, was an arrangement extremely well attuned to the needs of the initiative. Lena Hjelm-Wallén became the Foreign Minister in Carlsson's new government, and was very supportive of the channel. She did not, however, have a great deal of experience in the Israeli–Palestinian conflict, and was thus not a natural candidate to supervise the talks. Andersson, given his experience of mediation in the late 1980s and the strong relationships he had built up with the Palestinians, was in a far better position to do so. He had previously been made aware of the idea through Schori and was briefed again more thoroughly by Hjelm-Wallén, who supported his involvement in the matter. At the Casablanca conference on the economics of the Middle East and Northern Africa, held on 30 October and 1 November, Andersson represented the Swedish government as a special envoy and, while in the region, held meetings with Arafat and Beilin.[21] It was not until 1 December, however, that Andersson's position as official government envoy on matters pertaining to the Middle East peace process became permanent.[22]

Amid all the governmental changes in the wake of the elections, there was also a change in leadership at the Olof Palme International Centre (OPIC), an NGO founded in 1992 as an amalgamation of the International Centre of the Swedish Labour Movement and the Peace Forum of the Swedish Labour Movement. The new director, Sven-Eric Söder, was a Social Democrat who had been involved in Palestinian–Swedish NGO relations since the 1980s, and he sought to prioritise the region in OPIC's work. Aware of his experience and excellent connections, Söder suggested that Andersson become the new OPIC chairman. Andersson accepted, and assumed the position in early November.

OPIC then became the primary sponsor for the talks. In fact, though unaware of the initiative at the time, the idea of establishing a secret channel was very much on Söder's mind when considering candidates for the position of chairman. A dominant idea behind the appointment was that Andersson and OPIC could play a similar role to that of Larsen and FAFO in the Oslo channel.[23] As with Oslo, a non-governmental sponsor provided deniability should the channel become exposed. Despite being transferred overseas to the embassy in Geneva, Dismorr remained in her original role as coordinator, taking time off to attend each round of meetings in Stockholm. Her, Andersson and Söder formed the main troika of facilitators. Although all of these changes were taking place, the academics did not get any sense of discontinuity from their hosts. From their side of the fence, these transitions passed very smoothly.[24]

Though the Stockholm talks were modelled on the Oslo channel that preceded it, they nonetheless differed widely in a variety of ways. At the level of the mediator, they progressed in near polar opposite ways. As described in the preceding chapter, Oslo began as an informal, exploratory Track II discussion under the stewardship of Larsen and FAFO, with Foreign Minister Holst gradually intensifying his role towards the end of the process. In Stockholm, however, the talks were initially sponsored by the government but then transferred over to the OPIC. Had both parties officially adopted the results of the talks, the Foreign Ministry would have assumed a leading role in the implementation process as one of the heads of the proposed International Commission for Palestinian Refugees (ICPR), but this point was never reached.[25] Like the Norwegians, though to a seemingly smaller degree, the Swedes looked to ensure a continued role in the future.

Oslo also began with very different levels of representation from the parties themselves. The original presence of Abu Ala versus Hirschfeld and Pundak, an official versus academics, suggests that the Palestinians from the outset viewed this channel as more of a back channel than a Track II exercise. They continuously insisted the Israelis upgrade their delegation to officials and demonstrate that the channel was serious, thereby creating an official back channel. Abu Ala was furious when he learned that, despite the assurances of the Norwegians, the Israeli academics were not speaking for Peres and Rabin.[26] The Palestinians saw its potential differently to the Israelis and the Norwegians, who saw it as a Track II that could potentially produce results to benefit the main Track I negotiations in Washington, but not a back channel in its own right.

The Stockholm talks were more of a classic Track II situation. They began at a level of parity, two academics speaking with two academics. Pundak remembers that the atmosphere in Oslo was 'a bit more rigid because we had to report to the two officials', while 'Stockholm was much more relaxed because of the composition of people.'[27] At the level of sponsorship or political anchoring, however, there was more of an imbalance. 'On the Israeli side it was Track II because with all due respect to Yossi Beilin, he wasn't seen as a decision maker.'[28] Abu Mazen, on the other hand, was more of a political heavyweight, widely considered the second highest in the PLO hierarchy after Arafat. However loosely Arafat and Abu Mazen followed it, it was still anchored in the highest echelons.

Initially, there was no clear unified vision as to what they were in Norway to achieve. Stockholm was very different. As Pundak explained, 'When we entered Oslo we didn't know where we were going – with Stockholm, it was very clear what we were aiming at.'[29] The academics agreed to try and reach an understanding on the basic principles of the core final status issues which could serve as the basis for official Track I negotiations on permanent status. It was to be a preparatory document, a 'pre-framework agreement', a short cut to final status. Just as Hirschfeld's original text had been used as the basis for the Oslo agreement and modified by Savir and Singer, he envisioned a similar use of a future Stockholm document.[30] The team's targets later had to be adjusted somewhat to suit the circumstances. As it became increasingly clear in early 1995 that Rabin was facing domestic political problems, 'the concept became more one of giving Rabin some tool with which he could go to the elections and say to his electorate, "Listen, I have the means of coming to a final status agreement with the Palestinians."'[31]

Thus, whereas the origins of Oslo may be described as academic, the same cannot be said of Stockholm, despite the fact that it was being conducted by academics. Both channels benefited from the guise of academia but, although it was non-officials speaking to non-officials, Stockholm had an overt, strictly political purpose from the beginning. Hirschfeld suggests that 'it was something between Track I$\frac{1}{2}$ and Track II, but it was more Track II than Track I.'[32] Phrased slightly differently, Agha and Khalidi refer to this as a 'pure' Track II, but the essence remains the same.[33]

In total, the group met for about 21 secret sessions from September 1994 to October 1995, held at a variety of hotels, villas, and secluded conference centres in and around Stockholm, transported and guarded by agents from the Swedish secret service, SÄPO. Diplomat Mikael Dahl assisted Dismorr with the organisation and logistics for the first two or three meetings. Andersson then joined Dismorr, as did Söder, and their participation was welcomed by all parties. The Swedish liaisons were responsible for the logistics, accommodation, and all other arrangements the talks required. A permanent fixture at their meetings, they were on hand to assist in any way possible without imposing themselves. The Swedes ate meals with them between sessions, acting as friends, occasional buffers, and confidants, contributing to the relaxed atmosphere. In this capacity, they played a very similar role to Larsen and the Norwegians in the Oslo channel, although the Swedish task was significantly easier given that all the participants were already well acquainted and required no tense introductions.

According to the Palestinian participants, the Swedes played their role very well.

> It has to be said, the Swedes put an enormous effort into this. It wasn't just being nice, or hosting us for dinner. There was security, we had bodyguards ... we were very well fed and shod. They went out of their way to make it comfortable and to free us from any kind of concern besides our work, and it clearly involved a lot of effort.[34]

Agha particularly remembers Andersson's contribution to the proceedings:

> I must say his involvement all through was very, very light handed. He never tried to take sides at all. His only commitment was to the cause of peace. Privately, he was very reassuring, of course, but he did not interfere in any of the meetings. Whenever there were arguments, whenever the atmosphere was heated, he always tried to cool it down without taking sides, and by stepping back from the substance and trying just to save the moment. And he was very good at that.[35]

Discussing the dynamics of the Swedish role, Dismorr identified 'a very important balancing act' between being supportive and actively encouraging, but not pushy.[36] The Swedes were available for discussion or consultation on any issue, and the parties would sometimes request their opinion on certain aspects of proposals, but it was always the parties' prerogative to do so.[37]

> Maybe that's why it worked so well, because there was great mutual trust regarding this process, but the parties always set the limits. They decided. We gave this support, economically, administratively, and psychologically and so on, but in no way did we ever make any demands for formal briefings or guarantees that this was anchored in the highest political echelons.[38]

The parties periodically briefed the Ministry of Foreign Affairs, in addition to their informal exchanges with the hosts.

Had the parties requested a stronger Swedish role, there is no doubt whatsoever that the Swedes would have been happy to provide it, but that did not happen. Hirschfeld was representative of the prevailing attitude:

> In Oslo, I insisted that with all due respect to our Norwegian friends, the Norwegians would be not in the room, and in Sweden, in Stockholm, I insisted that with all due respect to Sten Andersson and Ann Dismorr, that if we were serious they should be not in the room. Because I said this is an Israeli–Palestinian affair, and we have to come to terms.[39]

Similarly, Beilin stated that 'the very important thing in these kinds of negotiations is secrecy, security, and a venue. That's what we got. We didn't search for somebody wise enough to help us, to solve our problems.'[40] In this case, the Swedish role did not exceed that of a facilitator. Nonetheless, on the basis of Bercovitch's definition of mediation, facilitation – though not as involved as other more classic strategies – still constitutes mediation.

Secrecy was paramount throughout, and was maintained thanks to the efforts of SÄPO and the small closed circle of people who were aware of the channel. There was, however, one scare on 21 February 1995, which was beyond their control. An article mentioning Israeli–Palestinian talks in Sweden appeared in *Svenska Dagbladet*, one of the main Swedish daily newspapers. 'It was a real fright over breakfast to see "Stockholm talks, Middle East",' Dismorr said, 'but when the trail went cold the journalist abandoned it.'[41] The story was in reference to a meeting between Beilin and Nabil Shaath in Stockholm in mid-February, which took place parallel to the talks between the four academics. Beilin had participated in a number of secret meetings with Shaath and General Abd al-Razzak Yihya, the PLO's chief military advisor, in the presence of Andersson and Schori, both in Stockholm and in Israel. Here, conversation centred on the final status issues.[42]

At an event in Gaza on 27 February, Shaath pulled aside the Swedish general consul to Jerusalem, Karin Roxman, and asked how the press had got wind of this meeting. She said she had no idea, and was just as surprised as he was. Beilin speculated that the leak came either from Eugene Makhlouf, the PLO representative in Stockholm, or the Israeli embassy there.[43] Either way, Shaath appeared very perturbed by the leak and the questions that arose from it. Roxman reported home that 'Shaath emphasised how important the discussions in Stockholm had been, and seemed very pleased with the arrangements, including the presence of Sten Andersson.'[44]

As Beilin explained to Schori at a meeting 'between four eyes' in Jerusalem on 11 April, these talks were not viewed as a priority. Shaath was an 'effective and knowledgeable' Palestinian spokesperson, an important figure to include in any deepening and political anchoring of the Stockholm document, but he would be sidelined for the time being if necessary. Furthermore, Beilin argued that these meetings provided useful cover for the secret track, the avenue which he deemed more important. If questions were asked about any activity in Stockholm, they could refer to those meetings.[45]

Agha, Khalidi, and Abu Mazen saw things very differently. The academics were upset by what they perceived as an attempt by Beilin to bypass them. Khalidi suspects that 'Beilin wanted to test other waters. He may have felt that he didn't want to put all his eggs into this particular basket ... I think he was trying to see whether he could get something better somewhere else.'[46] Agha had been informed of the meetings through Palestinian sources, and 'was told to put an end to them, because Abu Mazen did not like to have the channel disturbed by Nabil [Shaath]'.[47]

Similarly, when Faisal Husseini joined the group to discuss the issue of Jerusalem in June 1995, Abu Mazen told Agha and Khalidi not to have such meetings. Contrary to Beilin's argument, Abu Mazen was concerned that multiple channels with additional participants would jeopardise the secrecy of the Stockholm group. Additionally, having multiple channels dealing with the same issues was not seen as an ideal dynamic. Agha confronted his Israeli colleagues about the meetings with Shaath.

> They tried to belittle it and say that nothing happened. I had the minutes of the meeting, so I took them out and I started reading them, and I told them that we cannot have the two tracks simultaneously and that they had to choose. It didn't take much choice, they immediately chose to have our track.[48]

This episode illustrates the premium attached to absolute secrecy, but also provides an insight into the thinking of both Abu Mazen and Beilin. Of the two sponsors, the latter was much more involved than the former.[49] Beilin initially only followed the channel in a personal, not official, capacity, but nonetheless took a very active interest. His position as a government minister and a personal friend of Hirschfeld and Pundak made this helpful ambiguity as sponsor possible. As demonstrated, he was much more pro-active than his Palestinian counterpart, and in addition to exploring other avenues he also participated in a number of the Stockholm group's meetings.

Abu Mazen left Agha and Khalidi to work more or less independently. Since they were not formally operating on behalf of the PLO yet were still trusted by them, 'the Palestinian team thus had a wider mandate and was often able to develop its lead positions without constant consultation or supervision by the leadership'.[50] Agha has explained that 'our relation with Abu Mazen was not such that we used to ask his permission, or that we used to coordinate with him during this process. It was not like that at all'. They would inform him of developments 'from time to time' whereupon he would comment 'in very general terms' and express his opinion on matters like the involvement of Husseini and Shaath.[51]

This was decidedly not a reflection of the esteem in which Abu Mazen held the channel, but merely a procedural concern. If anything, Abu Mazen thought it far more significant than either Agha and Khalidi, who did not always feel that the talks were proceeding seriously. 'Every time we questioned it with the leadership, especially Abu Mazen, they reassured us that it's more serious than we think it is.'[52] Abu Mazen was namely convinced that Rabin must have been aware of their work through his own intelligence sources and was waiting to see what they would produce.[53]

As for the Swedish hosts, Andersson, Dismorr, and Söder joined the academics for a number of meetings with Arafat, Beilin, and, later on in the process, with Peres. The Swedish presence at such meetings was not in order to involve themselves in the actual substance, but to demonstrate clear support for the ongoing efforts of the Stockholm group. Though their presence was largely symbolic, they underscored the seriousness of the discussions being held by the academics, and emphasised the need for such enterprises to both parties. Furthermore, close relationships based on trust, such as that between Andersson and Arafat, were reinforced and further developed.

At the later stages of the talks, Hassan Asfour, a member of the Palestinian Legislative Council (PLC), joined the discussions in Stockholm and in Israel as a 'non-official official' to offer another opinion on the document.[54] On 31 October, a lengthy session was held at the ECF offices in Tel Aviv to finalise a draft document to present to both leaders, described by Beilin as a kind of unofficial ceremony.[55] In addition to the two sponsors and the four academics, Asfour and Beilin's long-time associate Nimrod Novik were also present. The last draft of the document bore the date 1 November 1995.[56] At a meeting in Gaza shortly afterward, the Palestinian team – Abu Mazen, Agha, Asfour, and Khalidi – and the Swedes presented the document to Arafat and Abu Ala. Andersson asked Arafat if he was willing to accept it as a basis for negotiations, and if they could proceed to the Israelis with it as planned. Arafat replied, pointing to his colleagues, 'If these spies want to continue, then it's fine with me, you can continue.'[57]

While the highest level of the Palestinian leadership had always been informed of the talks, the Israeli leadership had not been. The plan was to present the working paper to Peres on 8 November, since Beilin believed that Rabin would ask him to obtain a reaction to it from Peres first before reading it himself. Moreover, he thought going straight to Rabin would offend Peres, given their political rivalry at the head of the Labour party, and make him feel that he was being circumvented.

Still, given his position as Prime Minister, the Beilin–Abu Mazen Understandings were tailored towards Rabin and what the academics thought he was willing and able to accept. Publicly, he had expressed his position on a number of final status issues which reflected the contents of the document. The academics and their Swedish hosts believed this was a sign which in part vindicated Abu Mazen's belief that Rabin was secretly aware of their work through Mossad or other intelligence sources. In this way, Rabin was influenced by the discussions in Stockholm and simultaneously affected them.[58] At the time, Peres 'was not so enthusiastic about withdrawal from all territories and two states', and so the expectation was that he would react negatively towards the understandings, whereas Rabin would then endorse them.[59]

Rabin never read the document. On 4 November, just days before the understandings were due to be presented to Peres, Yigal Amir, a Jewish religious fundamentalist, assassinated Rabin at a peace rally in Tel Aviv. When Beilin eventually briefed Peres on 11 November, 'he was too overwhelmed by the assassination, and he said this was not the time, so we did not proceed with it'.[60] With a no from Peres, Beilin informed the Palestinians that the document would have to be shelved, and both sides agreed to keep it confidential. Although Pundak believes that Rabin would have adopted the understandings and used them as the basis for final status negotiations, we will never know for certain.[61] Though strong concerns about the substance did exist, the contextual environment was the primary reason for shelving the understandings. Peres feared that such major moves on the Palestinian track would irreparably split an already deeply divided society, and doubted whether adoption of the document would improve his platform in the upcoming Israeli elections.

To this day, Beilin truly laments this decision:

> I was not in a position to put my foot down and insist upon it, maybe it was my mistake not to fight for it enough, but the whole atmosphere then was so crazy that I felt that I could not push Peres more in this situation. He was broken ... It was a *huge* mistake on Peres' side, a *huge* mistake. He could have used it ... After the assassination – when he had an advantage of 25% [in Israeli opinion polls] – at that moment he could have done anything. But he was shocked ... all of us were shocked.[62]

A few years later Agha briefed Dore Gold, Benjamin Netanyahu's advisor and later Israeli ambassador to the UN, on the contents of the Stockholm document. 'His reaction was, very clearly, that if Peres had adopted this document and went to the elections with it, he would have won.'[63] It was rendered a missed opportunity; to the detriment of the peace process, Netanyahu won an extremely narrow victory over Peres.

In a savage twist of irony, the Stockholm document actually contributed to this outcome. In late February 1996, three months prior to the elections, journalist Ze'ev Schiff published an article about the Stockholm talks in *Ha'aretz*. Although Beilin begged Schiff not to publish it before the elections, he could not oblige; apparently another Israeli journalist had also got hold of the scoop, and though he did not want to torpedo the Labour party in any way, Schiff had to publish first.

As with so many other aspects of the Israeli–Palestinian conflict, views on this episode remain divided. While Beilin maintains that Schiff told him the Palestinian team leaked the story, Khalidi strenuously denies this accusation. 'We never ever – all the leaks are from the Israeli side. Every single leak. Neither Hussein, myself, nor Abu Mazen has ever leaked anything on any of the things that we did.'[64] Used by Netanyahu and the Likud to devastating effect in their campaign, the entire endeavour was portrayed as a Labour party 'sell out' of Israel, a further step in a misguided Oslo process that had brought Israel nothing but bloodshed. Right-wing interpretations of the document gave rise to the slogan 'Peres will divide Jerusalem', which proved extremely effective.

What followed was a difficult time for the two sponsors. Beilin did not want to breach his promise of confidentiality to Abu Mazen, but did not feel he could completely dismiss the fruits of his labour as 'nonsense'.[65] In an effort to sell the agreement to the public, reach out to right-wing forces, and highlight the realistic pragmatism of his Palestinian partners, Beilin highlighted some of the significant concessions the Palestinians were willing to make. Unfortunately, his comments were seen by the Palestinians to suggest that they were prepared to accept Abu Dis and outlying municipal areas as a capital instead of East Jerusalem.

This notion, Khalidi explained, did a lot of damage to the channel, to Abu Mazen, and to the document itself, since it robbed it of any credibility on the Palestinian side. Beilin's handling of the situation 'left a bad taste in Abu Mazen's mouth'. He was not happy about being identified with such purported concessions, and – without completely disassociating himself from it – distanced himself from it. Agha remembers that 'the line we agreed with him, that he would take, was that he was aware that some Palestinian academics were involved in this exercise, from time to time they used to inform him, but it has no other status'.[66] Abu Mazen had not signed it, and as such it had no official imprint from the PLO whatsoever. Beilin himself acknowledges that the Stockholm document 'does not bind anyone'.[67]

Khalidi defends Abu Mazen's reasoning thus:

> There's no way that Abu Mazen was going to claim any kind of authorship of a document that had no legal status, had no political status, that he hadn't actually worked on himself, and that the other side hadn't accepted . . . He wasn't going to come out and say, 'Oh this is a great document,' when he had no partner to it! . . . The only thing there was [to reap] would be potential embarrassment for whatever concessions the document contained or seemed to contain. What was he gaining from saying yes to it? Nothing . . . There was nothing which Abu Mazen could wisely, politically, have bit his teeth into.[68]

Furthermore, Abu Mazen did not consider it a finished document but a rolling one, and one that he believed still needed further work and elaboration. Beilin agrees: 'We knew that neither side would agree to adopt the document *as it stood* [emphasis added], and if the two leaderships would accept it as a basis for renewed and accelerated negotiation, this would be the most we could expect to achieve.'[69] Hirschfeld too says the team did not view the document as a finished agreement, but is nonetheless critical of Abu Mazen's stance on the issue: on 31 October, Abu Mazen and Beilin 'both said this is the Beilin–Abu Mazen Understanding . . . Abu Mazen's statement that he had nothing to do with it and that it didn't exist is detached from reality.'[70]

Ultimately, the Stockholm group failed to achieve their objectives on all counts. In this situation, Hirschfeld has suggested that 'the effect of whatever you agree is irrelevant as long as the senior leadership doesn't endorse it', and that public knowledge of any such agreement may harm it: 'you create expectations that you do not fulfil, and you raise those people who don't like it. You give them enough substance to work against it, and you may de-legitimise some of the ideas that you're working on.'[71] Although this is undoubtedly a very real risk, conversely, one should not overlook the wider positive impact of the Understandings on the later peace process. Once new ideas are introduced, they can form a basis to work from, be built on, and developed further in order to advance thinking on a solution. They do not simply disappear into oblivion.

The Stockholm talks were the first real effort to firmly establish principles of final status, and a number of the ideas that originated there remain part of a realistic foundation for any future peace agreement. First, what is Arab in Jerusalem goes to the Palestinians, and what is Jewish goes to Israel. Second, the idea of land swaps. Third, the distinction between the right of return and the actual physical exercising of that right. Fourth, the idea that the Jordan River can be the security border of Israel but not the sovereign border of Israel. These ideas were all expressed there for the first time. Agha has reflected that:

> All the fundamentals of any future deal, until new fundamentals come up, have their genesis in the most comprehensive way in that document. So still, I think that document is the most revolutionary document between the two parties on the issue of final status. And if you look at Geneva, it takes it to more detail, but it does not have any principles of its own away from the principles that we put together in that document. So it is very, very important.[72]

As Agha suggests, the Beilin–Abu Mazen Understandings have been a constant point of reference in any subsequent negotiations. At the Camp David summit in 2000, the Clinton peace team considered putting them on the agenda from the beginning, which would have been to serve their original purpose, but declined to pressure Barak into doing so.[73]

Although they were not an official basis, they nonetheless informed discussion. Beilin remembers that US Secretary of State Madeleine

> Albright told me after Camp David that I was not in Camp David, but my spirit was there because everybody spoke all the time about Beilin-Abu Mazen ... Beilin–Abu Mazen was always there ... in

> the negotiations. From time to time ... they said, 'yes, but this doesn't appear in the map of Beilin-Abu Mazen.' So they did not refer to it officially, but unofficially they referred to it all the time. Why? Because this was the only paper on the agenda.[74]

When Clinton later decided to issue what have become known as the 'Clinton parameters' in late December 2000, these bore the clear fingerprints of the Stockholm document, but neither side were then willing to accept them outright.[75]

Israel–Palestine as a Social Democratic foreign policy priority

In line with their longstanding tradition and in contrast to the Conservatives, the Social Democratic government that returned to power in September 1994 made the Middle East a foreign policy priority.[76] This intention was evident already during the aforementioned meeting between Beilin and Schori on 23 August 1994, when the former made the latter aware of af Ugglas' sponsorship of a secret channel. Beilin encouraged Schori and Sweden to generally increase their political involvement in the Middle East, suggesting additional roles as a channel of communication between Israel and Syria,[77] and as leader of a potential working group for the co-ordination of international aid to the Palestinians (which already existed but was apparently not functioning smoothly). Schori asked him to seek contact with the Foreign Ministry after the election, regardless of who was in power, but assured him that should it be the Social Democrats, they would establish a working group to deal with these issues and co-ordinate future actions with Beilin. Schori ends his memo by saying that the Middle East is one area where Sweden 'could and should be more active'.[78]

The new government took a number of steps to make Schori's pledge a reality. In November, Foreign Minister Hjelm-Wallén and Schori himself, who had been appointed Minister of Development Cooperation, established a working group on the Middle East within the Foreign Ministry, led by Mikael Dahl. Discernable from the circulation of Schori's memo on his meeting with Beilin, Andersson remained very much in the loop in Social Democratic circles, and as noted previously, was on 1 December made an official government envoy on matters pertaining to the Middle East peace process. His relationship with Arafat specifically and the Swedish ties to the PLO generally made Sweden an interesting player, viewed as one of the few nations outside the Arab world that could have an effect on the Palestinian leader and act as a moderating influence. Any Israeli engagement in the wider Middle East would by default be viewed as a conspiracy by the Arab states to dominate the region culturally and economically. As a more objective, trustworthy observer, the Swedes could potentially calm this tendency and be of great use to Israel and the peace process.[79]

The cornerstone of their activities and Swedish Middle East policy as a whole, as outlined by Dahl,[80] was to support the ongoing peace process – this included the implementation of the Israeli–Palestinian Oslo and Cairo agreements, and any efforts to reach peace between Israel and Syria and Israel and Lebanon – in any way they could. The hope was to arrive at a 'fair, lasting, and comprehensive peace that benefits all peoples in the region'. In terms of the Israeli–Palestinian conflict, a durable peace required security for Israel and self-determination for the Palestinians. Of particular concern for the continued viability of the process was: violence by extremists and rejectionists on both sides; the tendency toward authoritarian rule in areas controlled by the PLO; Israeli settlement expansion, efforts to pre-emptively alter the future status of Jerusalem, and border closures.

Within this framework, actively supporting the talks that produced the Stockholm document was just one part of a broader policy. In Dahl's policy outline, this secret sponsorship is surreptitiously referred to within a wider 'readiness to be of service in other ways, should the parties so wish'.[81] This secret support was complemented by a strong outward, very visible public stance. In accordance with tradition, Carlsson invited the Nobel laureates Arafat, Peres and Rabin[82] to visit Stockholm after they had attended the Nobel Peace Prize ceremony in Oslo in mid-December, and took the opportunity to try and intensify bilateral relations, demonstrate support for the peace process and discuss further tangible measures to assist it.[83] The timing of the visit also emphasised a certain level of historical continuity: 12 December, the day of Carlsson's meetings with Arafat and Peres and their addresses to the Riksdag, was just two days before the six-year anniversary of Arafat's historic words in Geneva, which Sweden had helped produce.

In these meetings, foreign aid was a particular focus, an aspect that was very much in line with Social Democratic values and traditions. Here, and on a number of prior occasions, including meetings between Peres and Schori and between Beilin and Andersson, the Israelis emphasised the importance of Swedish aid to the Palestinians.[84] Poverty was a serious problem that threatened the peace process. Peres noted that you could not fight poverty with military means, but that poverty would be a main cause of radicalisation and discontent, ultimately leading to violence against Israel, unless something was done to change this course. This was particularly relevant as around 60 per cent of the population in the Middle East was under 18, and needed to be 'socialised' through improved education, potentially by harnessing the power of computers. Hopes were expressed for a deepening of trade relations with Sweden and the EU, and Swedish participation in the Temporary International Presence (TIP) in Gaza and Jericho, the latter being supported by Israelis and Palestinians alike.[85]

Arafat was frank in his meeting with Carlsson: 'we are in great need of help'. He described his extreme difficulties in Gaza, particularly the need for infrastructure and development, and the pressure he was under from what he described as a great conspiracy of various externally well-funded radical Islamist groups who had militarily attacked the PLO headquarters in Gaza six times. Many saw the leadership as a group of collaborating 'uncle Toms'. The Israelis were making unwieldy demands regarding the upcoming Palestinian elections, of paramount importance, Arafat argued, since they would provide stability and legitimacy. Restrictions and closures made meetings of the PNC impossible, for example to vote on amendments to the PLO Charter, an issue that Carlsson raised. Although the point was not made explicitly, these obstacles were clearly meant to explain the need for a temporary resort to authoritarian measures reminiscent of a police state, widely criticised in previous consultations with other Palestinians like Hanan Ashrawi. Arafat ended by expressing his hope that Andersson would continue to play a significant role in their bilateral relations.[86]

Following this visit, the government announced its decision to allocate an additional 75 million SEK (10 million USD) in bilateral aid to the Palestinians for urgent aid projects, thereby raising the total figure apportioned to them in the 1994–5 fiscal year to roughly 285 million SEK (38 million USD).[87] This aid intended to achieve five basic goals, designed to support the Palestinian people and the peace process, and are still extremely relevant to this day.[88] First, to improve the standard of living in the occupied territories by way of humanitarian aid through UNRWA – effectively the Palestinian local government – which channelled around 146 million of this money. The operative logic was to demonstrate to the Palestinians that peace and reconciliation would improve the quality of their day-to-day lives, and provide an incentive not to resort to violence.

Second, to contribute to the development of government institutions and democratic structures for self-rule. Fifteen million of the additional 75 million were earmarked for the start-up costs of the PA, for example to help pay civil servant and police salaries, and to support the general elections planned for 1995. An additional 24 million was then allocated for these purposes, including 13 million to the Johan Jørgen Holst Peace Fund, named after the late Norwegian Foreign Minister who helped mediate the Oslo Agreement. Another 25 million was allotted to provide health care and future health planning. Also, the government offered PA staff training programmes in organisational management in order to increase professional capabilities.[89]

Third, to contribute to economic development and job creation by developing infrastructure, particularly in the Gaza Strip where unemployment and poverty were the most acute. This was deemed the most urgent short-term measure, and accounted for 40 million of the additional 75 million. This money was to be allocated to 'rapid job creation projects, including the renovation and construction of housing, repairs of roads and streets, the refurbishing of playgrounds and youth centres, and other areas where needs are substantial and the infrastructure neglected'.[90] These were to be overseen by several UN agencies, including UNDP and UNRWA.

The commitment to job creation was further bolstered when, in early 1995, the UN Local Aid Coordination Committee (LACC) to the occupied territories, headed by UN Special Coordinator Terje Rød-Larsen, appointed Sweden the 'shepherd' of one of the 12 'Sectoral Working Groups', that on 'Public Works/Employment Generation'. This appointment had clearly been in the pipeline for some time, since Beilin had mentioned the idea to Schori in August the previous year.

The goal was to increase international aid for this purpose and ensure a more effective use of these funds. In his capacity as Middle East envoy,

Andersson was appointed to take responsibility for these activities.[91] In the longer term, the ambition was to build a viable industrial sector to ensure continued employment in the territories, substantially through a series of 'industrial parks' in the Gaza Strip, an Israeli concept widely favoured by Peres and the international community, but treated with lukewarm interest by Arafat.[92] Other infrastructure projects on the agenda for future consideration included telecommunications, sewage treatment, and additional housing.

Fourth, to encourage the development of a democratic society with increased respect for fundamental human rights. Approximately 12 million was allocated to support some ten human rights organisations, including the Palestinian Independent Commission for Human and Civil Rights led by Hanan Ashrawi. This was in part channelled through Diakonia, a Swedish Christian international development organisation with a focus on human rights, and the Social Democratic Youth League. In cooperation with UNICEF, Schori signed an agreement between Sweden and the PA stating that all Palestinian children had the right to an education.[93]

Fifth, to support the multilateral aspect of the Madrid process by acting as 'shepherd' for issues regarding the welfare of Palestinian children, including refugees in Jordan, Lebanon and Syria. In the 12 December meeting between Carlsson and Peres, Beilin had expressed the desire for the Swedes to play a leading role in the multilateral working group on water issues, but this was very much secondary to the former. Ambassador Thomas Hammarberg, former Secretary General of Amnesty International, was commissioned by the Foreign Ministry to manage Sweden's shepherdship of the childrens project. He had been working throughout 1994 to identify, analyse, and mobilise international support to benefit these needy children. This included more immediate programmes drawn up and coordinated with UNICEF, and the more long-term development of a National Programme of Action for the protection of children and children's rights within the PA. In a report to the Foreign Ministry and the Swedish International Development Agency (SIDA) dated 4 October 1994, Hammarberg outlined the work, initiatives, and planning proposals the group had spearheaded to date. He notes that they were widely very well received internationally, and emphasised the need for continued political support and further funds.[94]

Aid continued to be motivated by these objectives throughout the Oslo process. Direct Swedish aid to the Palestinians during the fiscal year 1995–6 amounted to approximately 180 million SEK. This figure does not take into account the additional contributions from the industrial and commercial sectors looking to cooperate with the Palestinians, or the value of credits and loan guarantees.[95]

Throughout this period, Swedish aid to the Palestinians was 'distinctly *political*'. It was not primarily about building 'normal' long-term development cooperation with a state, but rather to provide political support to a fragile peace process of historical importance. Rather than working together with an already established political administrative structure, they had to help build a government. Unlike aid from many Arab states, Swedish aid was 'aid in kind', that is to say in the form of specific projects and services rather than mere cash transfers.

As a result of the difficult circumstances, aid to the Palestinians did not adhere to orthodox aid practices.[96] Processes of accountability and transparency, for example, were difficult since the local bureaucracy to satisfy such requirements did not exist. Demands for such practices were thus less stringent than would otherwise normally be expected. Due to the need for immediacy, a premium was put on speed and flexibility, amid a general atmosphere among donors to 'throw money at anything that moved'. The technical status of Gaza and Jericho further complicated matters. The European development bank EBRD had approved loans to the Palestinians, but could not make payments without loan guarantees from a sovereign state, something the Palestinians could not give. Similarly, it was unclear who would sign and underwrite loans from the World Bank.

With the benefit of hindsight, this type of aid clearly carried with it an enormous element of risk. At the time, however, the nascent peace process was widely considered irreversible, and the two-state solution was the only option on the table. It was therefore an investment in peace. Willingness to contribute to the cause actually created substantial problems on the donor side. Competition existed between the United States, the World Bank, Norway, and the EU, which harmed co-ordination within the donor structure. Originally, the former three were the primary donors, with Norway single-handedly shouldering huge financial responsibilities, partly due to the inadequacy of the EU at that time.

By February 1995, a Foreign Ministry report noted the increased importance of the EU, which later emerged as the biggest donor. 'The Palestinians speak very appreciatively of EU aid. It is substantial, it is delivered, it is flexible, it is planned with responsiveness and little paternalism.'[97] For political purposes, ownership of the process needed to be in the hands of the PA. Bolstering their position vis-à-vis rejectionists was a priority to show that the decision to engage with Israel was yielding tangible benefits, ultimately funded by international donors but provided thanks to the actions of the PA.

Towards the end of January 1995, Eliasson and Schori travelled to Israel and the occupied territories to be updated on the development of the interim negotiations, the general mood towards the peace process, and follow up on certain issues raised in Stockholm a month previously. It was clear that the Israeli government was struggling domestically after a recent terror attack in Beit Lid that killed 21 people. Peres had since made it clear to Arafat that he had to take visible measures against terrorist groups in the Gaza Strip. In their meeting with Shaath – Arafat was not in Gaza at the time – the Swedes stressed that they had conveyed concerns over settlement expansion and security closures, but that the Palestinians had to act against terror, verbally and on the ground. They could not merely arrest and then release Hamas or Islamic Jihad operatives, as the Israelis complained, but had to hold them accountable somehow.[98] Shaath complained of a very delicate political situation, between being called collaborators and accused of not doing enough by the Israelis.[99] This would prove to be a recurring problem raised regularly.

The main consequence of this trip was the signing of a Memorandum of Understanding between Israel and Sweden on trilateral foreign aid cooperation with Africa in the field of arid agriculture. It was the first such agreement between the nations, and constituted the 'turning over of a new leaf' in Swedish–Israeli relations.[100] These had improved during the Conservative government, but were now on the rise even with the Social Democrats since the Israeli Labour party now officially shared their stance vis-à-vis the PLO as a legitimate partner, which had previously been a sticking point between them. Peres noted that relations were 'excellent' and was very pleased that they had intensified in this way.[101]

The Swedes appeared keen to maintain this improved relationship, but not at the cost of their policy toward the conflict. In mid-May,

Deputy Prime Minister Mona Sahlin was on a visit to Israel to attend a memorial ceremony for the murdered Count Folke Bernadotte. Afterwards, she had planned to meet Faisal Husseini and other Palestinian leaders at Orient House in East Jerusalem, but was requested not to do so by the Israelis. They insisted the meeting should take place in Gaza or Jericho, since an official visit to Orient House could be taken to imply Palestinian diplomatic status and rights of ownership in East Jerusalem, something the Israelis were adamantly opposed to. An angry Sahlin reluctantly heeded the request, but in protest simultaneously cancelled her scheduled meeting with Rabin and cut short her stay in Israel. Upon returning to Stockholm, she announced her intention to return to Israel later in the year and meet with Husseini at Orient House. The Israeli embassy in Stockholm warned that such a trip would cause 'political turmoil', and that if she insisted on visiting Orient House, 'it would be better if her visit was cancelled entirely'.[102] Sahlin relented once again, and the matter was put on hold.

Karin Roxman, the Consul General in Jerusalem, was perturbed by this series of events. In a letter to Schori, dated 9 October 1995, she highlighted a number of concerns which needed to be addressed. Despite policy statements attesting to a prioritised involvement in the peace process, there had been a lack of high profile diplomatic visits to the Palestinian territories since Schori's own trips at the beginning of the year. Roxman noted the substantial number of other international leaders who had recently been, many more than once, and complained that Sweden was trailing behind in its support. After the disappointment of Sahlin's two cancelled trips, Roxman and the Palestinians were eager to receive Swedish officials. She suggested that either Schori himself or Hjelm-Wallén visit as soon as possible, and that in-depth cooperation with the PA on political, economic, and personnel issues was required. This was especially necessary given the signing of the interim agreement, which meant 'something new in the Middle East' and had to be visibly supported.[103]

The Middle East working group led by Dahl shared this opinion, and high-level exchanges with the Palestinians soon took place. Schori travelled to Gaza in December to sign development agreements with Finance Minister Muhammad Nashashibi. After winning the Palestinian elections, Arafat came to Stockholm and met with Prime Minister Carlsson, Hjelm-Wallén, Schori and Andersson on 30 January 1996, where he pleaded for help to get the final status negotiations underway. Specifically, Arafat requested that the Swedes quietly raise the issue of Jerusalem with the Israelis, and work on an initiative to make it a shared capital, pointing to Rome, shared between Italy and the Vatican, as an example. Arafat also sought expertise from Swedish engineering firm ABB for a proposed elevated bridge and rail link between the West Bank and the Gaza Strip. The Swedes agreed to help in any way they could, but continued to emphasise the need for changes to the PLO Charter, a concern constantly flagged by the Israelis. Arafat and the Palestinians argued that the contents of the Oslo Agreement had addressed Israeli concerns and rendered their arguments defunct.[104]

A week later, 5–10 February, Hjelm-Wallén was on an official visit to the area. The Orient House issue came to the fore once again, but this time the Swedes were persistent. During her meeting with Foreign Minister Ehud Barak, he asked that she refrain from meeting Palestinian leaders at Orient House. She replied that the EU Council of Ministers had agreed on this policy, and that she, as one of 15, was in no position to change this. Peres told Hjelm-Wallén that he did not understand the EU insistence on visiting Orient House. Jerusalem was in terms of religious practice an open, free city, but not politically. The Israelis considered the creation of a Palestinian political centre there to be an unacceptable prejudicing of the outcome of a final status issue to be negotiated. Beilin further noted that the issue was embarrassing for the Labour government, particularly difficult with the election approaching.[105]

Israeli complaints notwithstanding, acknowledgement of the Palestinian presence in Jerusalem was important at such a crucial political juncture, and also in light of continued Israeli settlement expansion around the city which was establishing 'facts on the ground'. Sweden had, after all, never accepted the Israeli annexation of East Jerusalem. Swedish policy had consistently advocated a two-state solution, where Jerusalem was to be the shared capital of Israel and a future Palestinian state, a dual centre of political power. If the Sahlin episode had sowed any doubts, Hjelm-Wallén dispelled them and marked the continuance of policy by meeting Husseini, Ashrawi and others at Orient House a few days later. They stressed the importance of continued visits there, the legitimacy of the Palestinian historical narrative, and their claim to Jerusalem.[106] In response to questions from *Ha'aretz* as to why she had refused Israeli pleas, Hjelm-Wallén replied that 'she had met Palestinians wherever they are to be found, including also in Jerusalem'.[107]

Interest in Orient House was not just the exclusive preserve of the government, but also at the top of the OPIC priority list. The Centre sponsored a number of projects, including Social Democratic cooperation with Israeli and Palestinian youth organisations such as Young Guard and Fatah Youth, other youth exchange programmes, plus the development of and exchange with Palestinian trade unions like PGFTU. Additionally, it had contacts with the Arab Studies Society, the Jerusalem Institute for Israeli Studies, and the Israeli–Palestinian Centre for Research and Information.[108]

In support of the Arab Studies Society, 'the backbone of Orient House', SIDA and the OPIC funded the independent Jerusalem Research Department, intended to prepare the Palestinians for the inevitable final status discussions on Jerusalem by providing judicial teams to advise on the issue, and conducting research on local demography, geography, planning, housing, sociology, economy, and infrastructure.[109] Research and original historical documents would then be made publicly accessible through an Arab Studies Society Library or Document & Information Centre. Other assistance included the provision of satellite imagery to produce accurate maps. Since the Swedes possessed little political clout with the Israelis on the issue, helping the Palestinians in their negotiations was an attempt to level the marked asymmetry between the parties somewhat.

Contrary to Israeli warnings, there was no diplomatic fallout or turmoil following the earlier Orient House episode. In remarks to *Svenska Dagbladet*, Hjelm-Wallén noted that there was a palpable improvement in Swedish–Israeli relations, together with an increased Swedish profile and interest in the region. Part of this new relationship was to express concerns over policy with tact and discretion, as any trusted friend would, and had been done with the Palestinians for many years.[110] In this instance, the focus was on human rights, specifically the proposed Israeli law allowing the use of 'moderate physical pressure' during interrogation of prisoners. Hjelm-Wallén made it absolutely clear that the Swedish government deplored any and all forms of physical violence in such scenarios and discouraged Israel from adopting the law, but to no avail. An editorial in *The Jerusalem Post* stated that

Hjelm-Wallén's public opposition to the proposed legislation was 'typical of her government's patronising interventionist attitude'.[111]

Similar concerns were raised with Arafat about the International Committee of the Red Cross (ICRC) not being allowed to visit prisoners in Palestinian jails, despite a Memorandum of Understanding with the PLO. Arafat assured her that the Understanding was in the process of being signed by the PA, which would apparently solve the issue. Arafat was characteristically evasive on the main issue of adjustments to the PLO Charter, once again arguing that it was *'caduc'* (obsolete) following the two-state declaration in Algiers from 1988. Still, the PNC was looking to convene in Gaza in order to vote on the changes, he said, but many members remained abroad, awaiting Israeli permission to enter the territory. Moreover, Israeli closures meant severe losses for the Palestinian economy, and Arafat also expressed concern over the confiscation of land and construction of new settlements.[112]

A spate of suicide bombings carried out by Palestinian terrorists in Ashkelon, Jerusalem, and Tel Aviv between 25 February and 4 March 1996, left 59 Israelis dead.[113] Facing serious rebuke from Israel and the international community, Arafat convened the PNC in Gaza in April, where they voted 504 to 54 to annul parts of the Charter referring to Israel's destruction.[114] This did little to reassure the Israelis, however. For many of them, this intense period of Palestinian terrorism was the straw that broke the camel's back.[115] Far from increasing their security, as the leftist peace camp argument ran, the peace process was costing Israeli lives. In the six years of the first *intifada*, 172 Israelis were killed; between 1993 and 1996, suicide bombings claimed the lives of almost 300 Israelis.[116] As has long been the case in Israeli politics, the security dimension reigned supreme; Netanyahu's image as 'Mr Security' was instrumental to his narrow victory over Peres in the 1996 elections.

The Netanyahu years: swimming against the current

With a campaign based on a stringent anti-Oslo platform, Netanyahu's premiership was a regression to the obstinate politics of the previous Likud government led by Shamir. While Rabin was in Washington announcing a historic new path, Netanyahu railed that 'Israel faces an unprecedented threat to its security. The government is allowing the PLO to carry out its plan to destroy Israel.'[117] In his three years in power, he dealt a devastating blow to a peace process he fundamentally did not believe in. Although he claimed he would continue the process on his own terms, it became clear what this meant in reality: as little implementation of the interim agreement as possible, pointing to 'security' and 'reciprocity' as the most crucial factors, and even refusal to abide by past agreements. The withdrawal from most of Hebron, for example, which Rabin and Peres had agreed to, had to be renegotiated. Netanyahu voiced unequivocal opposition to a Palestinian state, any negotiation of the future of Jerusalem, and withdrawal from the West Bank and Gaza, while favouring tougher security measures there to counter terrorism and protect illegal settlements, the expansion of which continued apace. In such an atmosphere, final status negotiations were impossible to conduct in the timeframe stipulated by the Oslo agreement.

This development caused great consternation at the Swedish Foreign Ministry. Immediately following the elections, an analysis by Hammarberg identified the dangers inherent in Netanyahu's politics:

> It is plainly obvious that the peace process will slow down, if not worse. A 'freeze' of a few years may not sound so threatening, but is practically an impossibility. The Oslo Agreement was not in itself a peace agreement but an understanding on a process. When this process was embarked upon, it was important that it was constantly advanced; it has always been clear that any deadlock would begin to undermine that which had already been achieved. The situation now is completely untenable for the Palestinians, [with blockades and closures limiting movement, hampering economic development, and increasing anger and bitterness.]

Arafat had already lost a great deal of face through concessions to the Israelis which yielded little in return, and the prospect of renegotiation rather than implementation made his weak standing even more precarious.[118]

In light of these developments, Andersson and the 'Stockholm group' were evaluating how best to further their work on the Stockholm document. The advent of Netanyahu's leadership created a new, more difficult political environment, but they were determined to continue. Agha and Khalidi 'had a very clear mandate from Abu Mazen to finish the document', and particularly wanted to work on the sections covering Jerusalem and the refugees. 'We continued meeting for some time in the expectation, or the hope perhaps, that the Netanyahu era would soon be over, and that at some stage they would ... launch formal final status talks.'[119]

A third party environment outside the conflict zone became all the more important given the increased tension on the ground, and the four academics received guarantees from the Swedish government that their sponsorship of the project would continue. In a report from June 1996, they were highly appreciative of the Swedish commitment:

> The team wishes to record its unqualified appreciation for the unique role played by the Swedish government and its representatives, and in particular the Foreign Minister, and for its unstinting support for the project's work. This work represents an invaluable contribution towards a final peace between the Israeli and Palestinian peoples and stands as a historical effort of the first magnitude.[120]

Traditionally, the Social Democrats had excellent contacts with their friends in the Israeli Labour party, but few contacts within the Likud. This would inevitably make relations with the Israelis more difficult, and reduce what little influence the Swedes had in Jerusalem and Tel Aviv. Hammarberg noted that 'it is difficult to overestimate the importance of the fact that Yossi Beilin and other key Israeli figures will now disappear'. It also prompted a strategic re-evaluation of the Swedish role in the peace process. The Middle East would remain a foreign policy priority, with a focus on foreign aid, political support, international law, and human rights, but were the Swedes to continue to prioritise communication facilitation and mediation, or increasingly try to shape international opinion by adopting a more outspoken public profile?

Actually, the two were not mutually exclusive, as the nature of Swedish mediation meant that one did not negate the other. The continuing work of Andersson and the 'Stockholm group' was secret, and not conducted with any members of the Israeli government. All the members of the 'Stockholm group' were ideologically oceans apart from Netanyahu and the Likud. Indeed, the differences between the Israeli and Swedish governments were well known. The same *Jerusalem Post* editorial that had criticised Hjelm-Wallén earlier in the year was entitled 'Sweden's Unsuitability', and concluded that it would be 'a grave error indeed to invite Sweden's mediation on Jerusalem or any other issue. No government has proved itself less suitable for the job.'[121]

Consequently, an outspoken public profile was hardly a new innovation but par for the course, a mere continuation of traditional Swedish policy. Hammarberg suggested that Sweden could continue as ever to be an interesting partner for the Israelis (and even the Americans) in their contacts with the Palestinians, and they could simultaneously criticise shortcomings on all sides when warranted.[122] Roxman believed that Sweden must continue to adhere to the well-established principles of international law that had guided its policy for decades, particularly in forums such as the UN and EU, and advocate unified policy on these grounds. This was all the more important as Sweden held a temporary seat on the UN Security Council. Any easing or softening of these could potentially be justified in certain public mediator roles, but hardly for the particular behind-the-scenes supportive stance that Sweden continued to assume.[123]

Developments on the ground rendered Swedish silence impossible. The new Israeli cabinet lifted the previous ban on new settlement construction and sought to limit Palestinian activity in East Jerusalem. On 23 September, in a particularly provocative gesture to signify their control of the Old City, Israel opened an old Hasmonean tunnel under the religiously extremely sensitive Temple Mount. The act precipitated a week of Palestinian protests, riots, and armed clashes in the West Bank, causing the deaths of 80 Palestinians and 15 Israeli soldiers.[124]

In the Riksdag, Hjelm-Wallén and Schori criticised Israeli actions and highlighted their continued opposition to settlement activity, which they had repeatedly expressed to the new Israeli government. The tunnel incident acted as a trigger, but protests and riots were primarily manifestations of Palestinian frustration at the wider lack of progress in the peace process, they said. 'The mood among the Palestinians was provoked by Israeli government policy on settlements, Hebron, and Jerusalem', and 'the Israeli government can only stem the escalation of violence by living up to its commitments under the interim agreement'. Schori noted that in addition to failing to implement previous agreements and expanding settlement activity, the Israelis had revoked the ID cards of many Palestinian Jerusalemites and demolished a Palestinian orphanage in the Old City, which had been partly financed by the Swedish Church Mission. He urged Israel to close the tunnel, quoting from written pleas by Christian leaders in Jerusalem.[125]

Towards the end of February 1997, Netanyahu announced plans to build 6,500 new housing units in Har Homa, an Israeli-occupied area on the south-eastern outskirts of Jerusalem known to Palestinians as Jabal Abu Ghneim. This decision, necessary to appease the more right wing parties in his coalition after perceived concessions in the renegotiated Hebron Agreement, soured relations with the United States and the international community, and exacerbated the serious tensions that existed with the Palestinians. In a statement to the Security Council, the Swedish representative said 'the construction of settlements is a grave obstacle to peace, incompatible with the DoP, and in contravention of international law, notably the Fourth Geneva Convention'.[126] A resolution critical of Israeli settlement activity was supported by among others France, Great Britain, Portugal, and Sweden, but vetoed by the United States. In another Security Council statement on 21 March, ambassador Anders Lidén expressed strong regret that the Council could not agree on either a resolution or a presidential statement.[127] Israeli UN ambassador David Peleg accused these European nations of contributing to an atmosphere that strengthened the Palestinian negotiating position, and could encourage a resort to terrorism, the latter position described on Swedish radio by Jan Eliasson, State Secretary for Foreign Affairs at the time, as perplexing.[128]

Though Eliasson expressed the hope that relations with Israel would not suffer as a result of this episode, the cumulative effect of this and other Swedish statements made this improbable. On 24 March, David Granit of the Israeli Foreign Ministry contacted the Swedish embassy in Tel Aviv and delivered a 'strong demarche' over two other Swedish statements. Firstly, in conversation with the Israeli ambassador to Stockholm about recent bombing raids in Lebanon, the head of the Middle East and North Africa desk had described Hezbollah as a 'resistance movement' and not a terrorist organisation.

Secondly, on a recent trip to the region, Andersson had apparently said that the international response to Israeli actions was muted because of sympathy for Jewish suffering during the Holocaust. He had also said that Netanyahu's statements that Arafat was encouraging violence were pure lies. Granit, who was 'annoyed' and 'upset', considered these signs of a negative development in the Swedish attitude towards Israel, a relationship that had until then been marked by 'regular and constructive dialogue' between the two Foreign Ministries.[129]

It is evident from a report written on 19 April by Roxman in Jerusalem that this annoyance was mutual. Netanyahu had suggested that the parties skip any implementation of the interim agreement and go straight to final status in six to nine months, but with trust between the parties at its lowest ever ebb, such an idea seemed completely unrealistic and bound to end in failure. The Palestinians, however, as Erekat admitted to Roxman, would have little choice but to accept any official offers along those lines. Despite all its flaws and weaknesses, Oslo and the interim process was the only game in town, and should try to be implemented. The power asymmetry between the parties had become particularly marked of late and was deeply problematic. Roxman observed that 'Netanyahu's arrogance and oppressive attitude toward his partner in the process, whose rights he seems to completely circumvent, has contributed to the Palestinians feeling even more marginalised. Netanyahu's goodwill is considered spent, as is his trustworthiness.'[130]

Roxman advised that the best way to shore up the peace process in its current impasse was to continue to support the Palestinians in a number of ways, in addition to substantial existing Swedish aid. Confidence-building measures were of the essence to try to restore some measure of trust. Whatever truth there was in Netanyahu's assertion that Arafat had given a 'green light' for terror against Israel, she said, the Israeli public believed it wholeheartedly and, since there was no peace process without Arafat, his image needed to be improved. Andersson could be instrumental to convince Arafat to make an appearance in the Israeli media, unequivocally denouncing terrorism and acknowledging Israel's right to exist. This message needed to be oft repeated, regardless of criticism from Palestinians.[131]

Immediately following Netanyahu's election the previous summer, Arafat approved an idea from Andersson to try and get a leading group of American or European Jews to endorse his leadership and the peace process in general, but nothing appears to have come of it. Just over a year later, a similar confidence-building measure was presented during a meeting of the Stockholm group in London. Hirschfeld and Pundak had put together an initiative to improve the peace profile in the United States, which involved Erekat and Nimrod Novik meeting with prominent groups of American Jews to legitimise and 'de-demonise' the Palestinians. At the time of their meeting, it was being floated in the United States.

Parallel to their work in the Stockholm group, Hirschfeld and Pundak were actively supporting bridge-building people-to-people activities, the promotion of contacts, both political and academic, and cooperation between the two sides, which the peace process was in dire need of. The concept of people-to-people activities had originally been at the heart of Hirschfeld's conception of the Oslo agreement. Annexes III and IV embodied this spirit, outlining cooperation in the economic and development spheres.[132] Further grassroots cooperation was detailed in Annex VI of the interim agreement, particularly Articles VII and VIII.[133]

Like so many other aspects of Oslo, implementation of these did not live up to expectations. Hirschfeld has wistfully recalled that

> the terrible thing about Annex III and Annex IV was that I wrote it and Rabin said it was fine and didn't correct one word, but he wasn't committed to it. And it was never implemented. And Uri Savir might have wanted to implement it, but he had other things on his mind and he didn't do anything.[134]

Pundak is similarly critical when he observes that 'the two governments did almost nothing to promote and realise ... the dialogue which is so important between the two communities on either side of the Green Line'.[135] Thus, the peace process remained solely a top-down affair.[136]

With the benefit of hindsight, Savir honestly acknowledges this failure:

> The greatest weakness of the three-year negotiation effort was that its messages did not filter down enough to the people. The decision makers often had to respond to internal criticism by claiming that the peace process was the best way to achieve traditional aims: security for Israel, statehood for the Palestinians. There was little talk of reconciliation, even less of the other side's predicaments. While the key decisions were motivated by values, such as a desire to end the occupation and replace rejection

with cooperation, these were often obscured in favour of pragmatic arguments.[137]

While the Norwegians bore the brunt of the costs, Sweden and many other nations, including the Austria, Finland, and the United States, also contributed funds for people-to-people activities.[138] Hirschfeld argues that from the very beginning, these activities were too donor-oriented and patronising without taking into account the views of Israeli and Palestinian peace activists on the ground, an error only rectified later on in the process, by which time the violence of the second *intifada* brought what positive development there was to a halt.[139] People-to-people sessions were predominantly only preaching to the converted, those already committed or sympathetic to the notion of compromise and two-state co-existence. Those outside the peace movement, such as religious groups, were not part of these sessions. Steinberg considers this a major failure, rendering the sessions ineffective because there was little to no 'spillover', a term for the dissemination of the message to the wider community, obviating the point of the enterprise.[140] Liel notes that the failure of people-to-people was a regrettable reality that Norwegian donors found it very difficult to accept.[141]

Throughout the interim period, violations of agreements – in both letter and spirit – and violence marred what cooperation and people-to-people initiatives were underway. Hirschfeld has reflected that for these to stand any chance of success, the security situation is paramount: 'If there's not a commitment to non-violence, it doesn't help.' An additional precondition is the cessation of settlement expansion, since Palestinians who cooperate with the Israelis complained that they became de-legitimised among their own people in such an environment.[142] Salem corroborates the latter problem, observing that a majority of Palestinians do not favour cooperation or normalisation with Israel while they are still under occupation, and resent the patronising overtones sometimes employed in dialogue with them.[143]

Accordingly, as Steinberg argues, the Palestinians were by and large not interested in conciliatory dialogue during that stage of the peace process. Instead, institutional opposition to it existed. Palestinian participants were generally restricted to Fatah members approved by the leadership, who had specific political goals.[144] Nasser-Najab notes that these were largely to

> attempt to influence Israeli public opinion and convince Israelis of the legitimacy of the Palestinian national struggle against occupation. Therefore, the Palestinian objective was no different in the post-Oslo period than it was in pre-Oslo, despite the fact that the objective of people-to-people was cooperation and coexistence.[145]

As Rynhold and Steinberg argue, the wider ripeness required for reconciliation and conflict resolution did not exist.[146] The cooperative and peacebuilding initiatives pursued were not nearly on a wide enough scale to produce this atmosphere on a grassroots level, and thus had little effect when they were most needed.[147] It reflected a difficult paradox: conflict transformation and reconciliation initiatives, though necessary to overcome violence in the longer term, require an immediate atmosphere of non-violence. The occupation complicated this further with a chicken or egg dilemma: no Palestinian normalisation with Israel until there is an agreement and an end to the occupation, an ultimate goal that requires a level of genuine mutual recognition normally achieved by normalisation. Ultimately, bottom-up encouragement was acutely necessary to complement, facilitate, and support the top-down political process, but the capacity of third parties to affect this change was extremely limited.

After Netanyahu had formed his government, Eitan Ben Sur, the newly appointed director general of the Israeli Foreign Ministry, requested and received all the information about the work of the Stockholm group from Yossi Beilin. Although it did not initially appear to have been of much interest, suggestions of moving to final status talks had put the Stockholm document back on the radar. Ann Dismorr had understood that Netanyahu's advisors were highly interested in it, and whether or not it provided any insights into 'how to clinch a deal'. The document had not yet been presented to the Israeli Prime Minister, which Agha expressed a desire to do personally.[148] He did not get a chance to do so, but instead presented the document to Dore Gold, Netanyahu's advisor, who 'found it very interesting, but that's as far as it went'.[149]

Since the beginning of 1997, the group had met six times, thrice in Stockholm, twice in Israel and once in London. At these meetings, they redrafted, expanded, and developed parts of the document, particularly on the issues of Jerusalem, settlements and security. On 19–20 July, in London at their seventh meeting, they continued this process and debated whether or not to make Barak, the new Labour party leader, aware of the Stockholm document. The Palestinians were adamantly in favour of this, and though the Israelis, Pundak in particular, initially disagreed, they eventually desisted. The group thus agreed to show it to Barak by October, and hopefully get him to endorse it or, at the very least, not oppose the exercise.[150] They had to settle for the latter. In a debate with Beilin while they were vying for the Labour party leadership, Barak said 'he will not send people secretly to the forest of Scandinavia, as if this was a sin'.[151] Although he would later change his position on using the forests of Scandinavia, his stance on the document and the involvement of academics would vary between hesitancy and negativity.

In a September 1997 memo on the peace process, Mossberg frankly acknowledged that despite their efforts, the Swedes had not played a particularly prominent role in the last few years in either the operative or normative political planes, nor had the EU. His analysis was a sobering dose of realism. EU attempts to adopt an operative role in the peace process had 'long been an almost embarrassing affair to observe'; the nomination of a Special Representative for the peace process, Miguel Moratinos, served primarily to convince the EU that they played any political role whatsoever. It had become increasingly apparent, he observed, that the EU lacked the necessary prerequisites, both political and organisational, to play an effective role. They were paying for much of the stuttering process, but could do little to control or affect it. While it could in theory bring its economic position as the major donor to the Palestinians and as a trading partner with the Israelis to bear, making aid and trade conditional on behaviour was problematic. Unity on any notion of sanctions against Israel would be difficult to achieve, and punitive financial measures against Palestinians would harm the moderate forces they sought to encourage and undermine the entire peace process.

Others, like the Norwegians, had adopted more operative roles. While the Swedish government regularly condemned both Israeli settlement construction and Palestinian terrorism, and the EU had in July that year outlined the foundational principles of its vision for peace in Annex III of the Amsterdam treaty, Mossberg believed that this could be articulated 'clearer, more prominently, and in a sharper tone'. This was the primary option afforded to them given the current deadlock in the region, and could be pursued both as Swedish policy and within the EU framework. Still, he himself admits that no amount of noise would have had much effect on Israeli policy. The only third-party who could conceivably exert significant influence was the United States.[152]

As Hjelm-Wallén pointed out in a Riksdag debate on 29 January 1998, attempts to formalise international condemnation of settlement expansion in the Security Council had fallen on the American veto. As for the EU, they were trying to prevent the import of products and materials emanating from illegal Israeli settlements, but without specified origins on labels and, given existing trade agreements, this was difficult. Sweden was actively working for a more unified and consequential EU position in line with her foreign policy, and Hjelm-Wallén maintained that progress was being made, however slowly. In the words of the Foreign Minister, 'The EU has a role. The USA has another role. We complement each other.'[153] This begs the obvious question, what was the American role during the Netanyahu period?

From facilitator to coercive mediator

The Swedes were certainly not the only ones frustrated with the right-wing Israeli government. For President Clinton, Netanyahu was a world apart from Rabin, a man whom he greatly admired and considered a very close friend. He had also established a fine relationship with Peres and had gone to great lengths to help him in his election campaign by organising an international summit at Sharm el-Sheikh to show support for the Oslo process, and co-ordinating his public statements with Peres' campaign needs, all of which infuriated Netanyahu.[154] After their first meeting in Washington, where Netanyahu had apparently lectured him on history and security, Clinton privately railed against him, exclaiming, 'Who the fuck does he think he is? Who's the fucking superpower here?'[155]

Previously preferring to act as a facilitator and reluctant to become involved in the substance of negotiations, the Clinton administration – which had begun its second term after its re-election in November – upgraded its role as a mediator in the peace process in order to keep it from collapsing entirely. With the onset of violence after the opening of the Hasmonean Tunnel, Special Middle East Co-ordinator Dennis Ross slowly came to realise that 'with Netanyahu in the Prime Minister's office, I was to become a full-time mediator ... negotiating with each side, finding out what they could do, drafting for them, and brokering the compromises'.[156]

This was an absolute necessity. Given the evident stagnation of the peace process, the American observation that the parties were doing it on their own was clearly no longer valid. Facilitation by small states can be extremely useful for parties genuinely motivated to reach an agreement or transform a conflict, but not for the intransigent who need to be dragged in kicking and screaming. In such a situation, as became evident, even the odds of a superpower succeeding are extremely limited. For both Israelis and Palestinians, the primary concern became avoiding being blamed for failure and thus losing credibility with the United States, but this was not enough.

Nonetheless, the Americans did not use their coercive power available at all effectively to improve things. While pressure on the Palestinians to act on their security obligations had some effect – partly because it was from time to time in Arafat's political interest to limit his Hamas rivals – Aaron Miller, Clinton's deputy Special Middle East Co-ordinator, cannot 'recall a single tough, honest, conversation in which we said to the Israelis, "Look, settlements may not violate the letter of Oslo, but they're wreaking havoc with its spirit and compromising on the logic of a gradual process of building trust and confidence."'[157]

Indeed, the commitment, personal relationships, and building of trust so central to the gradualist process had been completely ruptured. Netanyahu had decried Rabin and Peres for shaking hands with Arafat, and his personal enmity towards the elected PA President was apparent. While Rabin's distaste for Arafat was patent and their handshake on the White House lawn in 1993 was visibly extremely difficult for him, Indyk notes that the two had developed a working relationship and a certain element of trust, particularly over the Hebron issue where both gradually came to acknowledge the domestic difficulties of the other.[158] No such relationship ever stood a chance of developing between Netanyahu and Arafat. Andersson had raised the idea of a joint address by the two leaders before the EU to try to initiate a dialogue between them, which Arafat agreed to, but it did not materialise.[159]

After months of difficult negotiations mediated by Ross and his team, Israel and the PA initialled the Hebron agreement on 15 January 1997.

It reconfirmed the basic elements of the interim agreement that concerned Hebron, but with certain security arrangements strengthened in Israel's favour. Although Netanyahu refused to sign anything committing Israel to further redeployments from the West Bank as delineated in the interim agreement, a 'Note for the Record' was written by Ross as an appendix to the agreement, which stated that Israel remained committed to the interim agreement 'on the basis of reciprocity', but did not specify any amount of territory.

An additional part of the agreement was a letter from Secretary of State Warren Christopher to Netanyahu spelling out four American understandings, the second of which concerned the three-stage withdrawal plan of Oslo II. It stated Christopher's 'belief' that Netanyahu would proceed with the plan under the stipulated conditions, but it crucially did not constitute an Israeli commitment. The Palestinians thus gained little in concrete terms, but kept the process alive. More than anything else, it showed that maybe progress could be made with Netanyahu after all. However, it was also evidence of the centrality of the American role, which would only increase as spoilers on both sides definitively crippled a limping process.[160]

Israeli settlement expansion at Har Homa was met with suicide bombings in Tel Aviv on 21 March and Jerusalem on 30 July. The Americans had been planning an initiative to restart negotiations, but the second attack put it on hold and obviated any pressure being put on Netanyahu. With the peace process at a standstill, implementation persistently falling behind schedule, and trust at an unprecedented low level, new Secretary of State Madeleine Albright made her first speech on the subject on 6 August, where fighting terror was the key message, and 'refraining from unhelpful unilateral acts', i.e. settlement construction, came second: 'Let me be clear. There is no moral equivalency between suicide bombers and bulldozers, between killing innocent people and building houses. It is simply not possible to address political issues seriously in a climate of intimidation and terror.'

A comprehensive peace had been a 'top priority', she said, and outlined how the US had supported the peace process politically and economically, recently by trying to get negotiations back on track. These efforts would continue, but suggesting a heightened American role, Albright said they had to 'prepare to do more' to move towards final status. They had 'at times even gone beyond the traditional role of facilitator and played the role of mediator', but made it clear that the United States 'cannot, should not, and will not impose solutions'. The Clinton administration remained 'committed to doing everything possible to help the parties succeed':

> We will continue to play our role as a full partner. In this partnership, only the parties must make the decisions, but we can support them. In this partnership, only the parties must conduct the negotiations, but we can be with them at the table. In this partnership, only the parties must determine the shape of peace, but we can work with them to facilitate, protect and broaden that peace. Let there be no doubt, the United States will continue to do all it can to promote peace between Israelis and Palestinians and throughout the Middle East.[161]

On 10 September, Albright made her first visit to the region. Her agenda had been pre-determined by events six days earlier, when Palestinian suicide bombers had once again targeted Jerusalem with devastating effect. According to Ross, 'everywhere she went, she heard the same refrain: the US must do more. Her answer was there was little we could do if the suicide bombings continued. She could, and to some extent did, speak about Israeli actions that also must stop', but the onus was on Arafat to crack down on Hamas.[162]

On 28 September, Andersson met with Shaath in New York, who was pessimistic about their chances of success and said that Arafat was more 'disheartened' than ever before. He expressed serious doubts as to whether Clinton stood behind Albright or not.[163] Albright and Ross met with Arafat and Netanyahu to try to reach understandings on security cooperation and the extent of Israeli withdrawals. Quandt notes that 'her irritation with the Israeli prime minister was noticeable' as he kept trying to insist on an extremely low second further redeployment and dropping the third completely.[164]

The two leaders came separately to Washington in January 1998 for talks with Clinton. Beilin and Schori observed that each leader appeared pleased, albeit for different reasons: Arafat because he was treated with respect, as an equal; Netanyahu because he got the impression he would not have to implement the second and third further redeployments of the interim agreement. Beilin felt that it was generally a catastrophe; Washington wanted to give the impression that there was a healthy process and that progress was being made, but in actual fact nothing was happening at all.[165]

In April, after months of work, the Americans finally presented the parties with a more or less complete proposal to improve security, enact Israeli withdrawal from 13 per cent of the West Bank and Gaza, and begin permanent status negotiations in Washington on 11 May. Arafat accepted 'in principle', while Netanyahu did not. Albright's announcement had the effect of setting a deadline for the Israeli leader, warning that non-acceptance would force the United States to 're-examine its approach to the peace process', and that 'there is no point in talking about permanent status ... if we have not agreed on these other issues'.[166] 11 May passed without immediate consequences, as they continued to try and find a formula Netanyahu could accept.

Quandt believes that Clinton decided to avoid confrontation over the issue and opt for quiet diplomacy on the advice of National Security Advisor Sandy Berger and Vice President Al Gore.[167] Miller and Ross observe that Clinton was generally not keen to have a confrontation with anybody, and though the Israeli–Palestinian conflict would provoke anger in him, he would never channel that emotion into sustained toughness. Miller does not accept that domestic political pressure from the Jewish-American lobby was the cause of this. Rather, he suggests that Clinton's unwillingness to push back against any Israeli Prime Minister stemmed from a 'concern that if he pushed too hard, he might not succeed in Arab–Israeli peacemaking'. Progress, no matter how little, required Netanyahu's cooperation.[168]

Albright, on the other hand, appears to have shared the Swedish view of Netanyahu as intransigent and she repeatedly advocated getting tough with him, particularly after he had sent a team to lobby Congressmen and American-Jewish leaders that double-digit percentage redeployments were a mortal threat to Israel. Her announcement reflected her feeling that they had been too accommodating towards the Israelis, that the Prime Minister had to 'put up or shut up' rather than continue to dodge their proposals.[169]

In a push to break the standstill, Clinton brought Arafat and Netanyahu to the Wye River Plantation in Maryland for talks that began on 15 October 1998. Albright had made numerous trips to the region, and this continued diplomatic pressure was necessary to make the Israelis attend. Prior to the summit, Clinton hosted a private dinner party in the White House for junior members of the Jordanian royal family, to whom he offered his view on Netanyahu. He said, 'I am the most pro-Israeli president since Truman . . . But the problem with Bibi is that he cannot recognise the humanity of the Palestinians.'[170] This thought appeared to resonate with the President and his team during the negotiations, where friction with the Israeli prime minister ran high.

In his narrative of the summit, the head Palestinian negotiator Abu Ala describes it as the Palestinians and the Americans on the same page, struggling with an intransigent and evasive Israeli leader. Netanyahu's initial strategy 'had been to play for time and avoid substantive issues' – by 'play[ing] games with all present and flood[ing] the negotiations with unrealistic demands' – until his Foreign Minister, Ariel Sharon, arrived to provide political cover against the inevitable recriminations of his extreme right-wing government partners and the settler movement. According to Abu Ala, Netanyahu's behaviour during this initial period was described by one of the Americans there as 'pathetic', a sentiment apparently shared by some of the Israeli delegation. The Palestinian team perceived Netanyahu to be 'plagued by his fear of the consequences of taking any definite step. His indecision prevented him from making a positive response to the pressure the Americans brought to bear. He ran away from difficult confrontations.'[171]

By all accounts, it was Clinton who truly shone as the key to the Wye River Memorandum, signed on 23 October. Originally planned over only four days, the Americans made it clear that they were staying the course and would do everything in their power to arrive at an agreement. Miller views it as an achievement but ultimately a hollow one:

> It was a summit about nothing, not because the issues weren't important – 'land for security' was essentially the core Oslo trade-off [though then expressed as 'land for peace'] – but because a year had been spent on this agreement, and eight days of the president's time brokering an accord between two leaders who could never implement it, all against a backdrop of a peace process that had been kept on life support by the US.[172]

This verdict is an accurate reflection of the entire period. With both the Hebron and Wye agreements, the process was kept alive, but seemingly only for the sake of keeping it alive. The Americans were 'holding the whole process together like some modern day Dutch boy with his finger in the dike', and built up a false sense of confidence that if they just kept the process going, momentum would build up and everything would get back on track.[173] Each agreement eventually struck later had to be renegotiated with each new Israeli Prime Minister, and very little was done to ensure their implementation, the glaring and recurring failure of the Oslo process.

Indeed, the Wye River Memorandum was only partially implemented. Amid great protest at home from part of his coalition, Netanyahu withdrew from around 500 km^2 of the West Bank – 2 per cent from Area C to Area B; 7.1 per cent of Area B to Area A – but suspended further implementation, since he deemed the Palestinians were not living up to their end of the bargain. While Netanyahu was suffering, Clinton was making good on his promise at Wye to visit Gaza in December when the PNC finally revoked the controversial parts of their Charter. This first official visit was an important symbol of the improved US–Palestinian relationship, one of Arafat's more important achievements during this otherwise rocky period. In a meeting with Swedish General Consul Roxman in February 1999, Arafat emphasised how crucial the American role was, and he was very pleased that Clinton promised to do more to further peace.[174]

Trying to balance the complex set of domestic and international challenges that he faced, Netanyahu effectively managed to alienate everyone. The more right wing elements of his coalition abandoned him over his concessions to the Palestinians; the United States, the EU (exemplified by states like Sweden), Egypt and Jordan[175] were all exasperated by his arrogance and his inflexible approach towards the Palestinians; moderate Israelis were alarmed at Israel's worsening international standing – particularly with the United States, who appeared to be moving closer to the Palestinians – after the significant political and economic openings that characterised the years immediately following Oslo. This was reflected in Barak's election victory on 17 May 1999, a significant development that re-instilled hope among those working for a peaceful solution to the conflict, not least the Swedish government.

CHAPTER 5

THE 'STOCKHOLM CHANNEL' AND BEYOND: 'A BIT OF A CON'[1] AND A 'TRAGEDY OF ERRORS'[2]

It was amateur hour.

– Anonymous former official, describing American mediation[3]

When I think back on those days I really now understand how incredibly dysfunctional this whole thing was, and how it never could have worked . . . I knew this was going to be a catastrophe. One way or another, it was going to be a catastrophe. I watched the nature of the preparations, but I got sucked into it all.

– Aaron Miller[4]

We did not understand that the whole exercise was doomed to fail. There was objectively no prospect that this could ever succeed.

– Mathias Mossberg[5]

On 18 August 1995, Ingvar Carlsson announced his decision to resign as Social Democratic party leader and Prime Minister. After leading frontrunners Mona Sahlin and Jan Nygren dropped out, both positions fell to Göran Persson, the Minister of Finance, who was elected party leader at a special party congress on 16 May 1996, and then became Prime Minister five days later on 21 May.

Persson came from a different background to most of his predecessors. He was not personally acquainted with the previous generation of Social

Democratic leaders. Unlike Sten Andersson, Ingvar Carlsson, Jan Eliasson, or Pierre Schori, Persson had not known or worked with Olof Palme, and did not entirely share his political tradition. Like Palme, Persson was staunchly opposed to totalitarian political systems of any persuasion, whether fascist or communist, but Persson put a particular premium on democratic governance, and was critical of Palme's politics towards the developing world. He thought that Palme

> did not always understand the foundational principle of social democracy, that democracy always, always comes first ... Secondarily, you can focus on creating a socialist society. Palme often prioritised things differently. He had a soft spot for socialist dictators.[6]

In his analysis of the Israeli–Palestinian conflict, Persson differed markedly from Palme and Andersson. The latter two were both fundamentally pro-Israeli socialists who, like Persson, saw the Israeli *kibbutz* as the highest form of socialism, an exemplary experiment that deserved support. They then came to object strongly to the occupation of the West Bank and Gaza Strip, which they viewed as a serious threat to Israeli democracy. Persson, on the other hand, remained focused on the fact that Israel was the only democracy in the region, 'an open and vital democracy that has been threatened since its inception' by hostile Arab states who, bent on its destruction, have maintained a perpetual state of war. In this respect, he argued, it was unique. Persson admitted that, like all democracies, it was not without its faults, but it was far ahead of its neighbours.[7]

Persson has recounted a conversation he had with Andersson on the subject, who told him, 'Eventually, you will also come to understand the Israeli's guilt. I myself have been down that same road.'[8] But Persson never went through that metamorphosis. He remained true to the more traditional socialist pro-Israeli mould, steadfast in his solidarity. He described the last few decades of Social Democratic politics on the subject as 'propagandist', a completely one-sided approach in favour of the Palestinian national cause which placed responsibility for the conflict squarely at Israel's feet.[9]

Persson's attitude was also heavily influenced by the suffering and persecution of the Jewish people during the Holocaust, a tragedy that Persson has said he could never fully intellectually comprehend.

> I have never understood how it could happen in our time, in our proximity, by people who actually could have been our parents. It is, after all, not longer ago than that. I read about it when I was seven or eight years old – I read a lot about the Second World War generally while growing up – and the images of the Holocaust have always stayed with me in the back of my mind, I have never been able to free myself from them. I have never understood it, and it has plagued me.[10]

In response to an alarming article in *Dagens Nyheter* that suggested that a third of Swedish youth were unsure whether the Holocaust was historical fact or not,[11] Persson announced a new government initiative during a Riksdag debate on 12 June 1997. The following autumn, the government began offering free information to all Swedish children about the Holocaust and the manner in which European Jewry and other '*untermenschen*' were persecuted and systematically murdered. Persson saw this period as a powerful example of the danger posed by undemocratic societies. 'What you saw was the result of a system of politics and ideology which trampled on universal human worth and considered some better than others, to the point where one had a right to kill, the right to kill a people ... Have we sufficiently emphatically made it clear that this must never happen again?'[12] Through education, the world would keep memory alive and learn from history in order to prevent similar atrocities from happening again.

The Living History Project, as it came to be called, produced a book entitled *Tell ye your children...*[13] with almost two million copies distributed to date in Sweden alone. Following on from its domestic success, the Task Force for International Cooperation on Holocaust Education, Remembrance, and Research (ITF) was founded at a meeting in Stockholm on 7 May 1998, and decided that the book was to be translated into a number of other languages and distributed internationally.

A series of four conferences were held between 2000 and 2004 known as the Stockholm International Forum (SIF). The first, held in January 2000, dealt specifically with the Holocaust and was attended by delegations from 47 countries, including 22 heads of state. The following three conferences were centred on the theme of 'Conscience and Humanity', and explored aspects of genocide and its prevention from a contemporary perspective.

Prior to mid-1998, Persson had not substantially altered Swedish–Israeli relations, despite his personal views. They had, after all, been steadily improving under the previous government, and the absence of a ruling Labour government in Israel – Likud leader Benjamin Netanyahu took office only weeks after Persson – no doubt also contributed to this decision. Moreover, his foreign policy experience was limited. Thus, Foreign Minister Lena Hjelm-Wallén was free to continue her existing policy, and Andersson and his entourage continued the secret work of the 'Stockholm group'. Persson sanctioned the group's activities, but viewed them with considerable scepticism. He would soon change the rules of the game and frustrate their efforts.

On 26 April 1998, at the celebrations marking Israel's fiftieth anniversary in Stockholm, Persson was the keynote speaker. He saw this as an excellent opportunity to express his strong admiration for Israel, re-emphasise the need for the continued work of the Living History Project, and thank those in the audience who had helped make it so successful. In his speech he referred to Auschwitz and the Holocaust, the need to ensure that it never happened again, and the importance of a secure Jewish state.[14] Per Ahlmark of the Liberal party, arguably the most fiercely pro-Israeli Swedish politician, had also given a speech where he praised Israel without reservation and lambasted her Arab neighbours. Persson approached him where he sat next to the Israeli ambassador, shook his hand, and said, 'Thank you. I agree with every word you said. I could not have said it better myself.'[15]

Persson's speech caused consternation within the Foreign Ministry. In his limitless praise of Israel, the Prime Minister had ignored many fundamental tenets of Swedish foreign policy towards the Israeli–Palestinian conflict, for example by neglecting to mention the Palestinians or the occupation even once. It differed wildly from recent speeches by Hjelm-Wallén and the Minister for Development Cooperation, Pierre Schori, not to mention the iconic speeches given by Palme.

Concern mounted that the government did not appear to be speaking with one voice. The Foreign Ministry had produced multiple drafts of the speech, but they were rejected by the Prime Minister's office. In a Foreign Ministry memo, Peter Weidenrud complained that his last attempt to 'fit a ceremonial speech within the frame of our policy' had been rejected outright in favour of extremely one-sided romanticism. The essence of his formulation acknowledging legitimate criticism of Israel – 'A true friend's duty can never be solely to present the message that is easiest on the ears', a message reminiscent of Palme and Andersson – was not included anywhere in the speech, but dropped in favour of what Weidenrud considered unnecessary political flattery likely to cause problems.[16]

A different political agenda was clearly at work within the Prime Minister's office: to promulgate the Living History Project prior to its international meeting in Stockholm at the expense of making clear how Israel fit into wider regional policy and how the government believed her future was best guaranteed. In a document seemingly emanating from her office, the Foreign Minister provided Persson with some succinct answers to potential questions about policy discrepancies on the Israeli–Palestinian conflict. These dismissed any suggestion that there had been a change in policy, and emphasised that it continued to be based upon principles of international law, as it had been for many years.[17] It was clear that Persson's fundamentally pro-Israeli attitude did not always square with the line taken by Hjelm-Wallén, a situation that she felt made things difficult for her.[18]

This difference between the Prime Minister's office and the Foreign Ministry became even more pronounced in the new government assembled after the Social Democratic victory in the September 1998 elections. Persson embarked upon a clear recalibration of Swedish relations with Israel akin to the older Social Democratic perspective from the 1950s and 1960s, prior to the onset of the occupation. The new Foreign Minister Anna Lindh had been the first female president of the Swedish Social Democratic Youth League, and her six years in the position were marked by a strong commitment to international affairs, specifically issues like South Africa and the Israeli–Palestinian conflict. An adherent of the Palme tradition, she deferred a lot of responsibility for the Middle East to the experienced Andersson, who was kept on as an envoy. Their influence on the subject became increasingly marginalised.

Foreign policy was no longer the exclusive domain of the Foreign Ministry, as had been the case with the erstwhile Carlsson government, but was heavily influenced by the Prime Minister's office. Persson believed that both had to form foreign policy together, but that a Prime Minister's role was increasingly significant in a world of instant communication and rapidly accessible information. Leaders 'are so integrated into the international political process that it is unavoidable. To imagine that a situation would arise where we receive lines to say from the Foreign Ministry on Swedish foreign policy, those days are behind us.'[19] One can thus imagine what he thought of Hjelm-Wallén's Q&A advice.

Not since Palme had a Social Democratic Prime Minister paid such attention to foreign affairs. Still, Persson went about it in a very different way. Palme was an orator, an agitator, a 'placard politician'; Persson maintained a lower profile, and operated with more discretion. The ITF and the SIF series, for example, opened up a number of doors for Sweden in Israel and the United States, two countries very close to Persson's heart and central to his foreign policy.[20] Without being overt foreign policy gestures, they served as the government's ticket to the international stage.

Persson's representative to these was State Secretary Pär Nuder, his chief of staff, closest advisor, and trusted operator. Together, they spearheaded the new official approach to the Israeli–Palestinian conflict. Nuder shared Persson's affection for Israel and his belief that Swedish policy was far too one-sided in favour of the Palestinians. His was a very personal interest. He had grown up across the street from Cordelia Edvardson, a Swedish journalist covering the Middle East, and was best friends with her son, Simon. Originally a German Jew, Edvardson was rescued from Auschwitz as a teenager and settled in Sweden. Following the 1973 Arab–Israeli War, she and Simon made *aliyah* to Israel but remained close friends with Nuder, who visited them there.[21]

Although it clearly had positive spin-offs, Nuder denies that the Living History Project and everything that followed it was done specifically to improve relations with Israel or to enable Sweden to play a more substantial role in the peace process.[22] Gradually in 1999, as the Israeli political mood shifted away from Netanyahu, an idea lingered in the back of their minds: that a strengthened relationship with Israel and the Labour party could provide opportunities for Sweden to assist the peace process in some way, should Labour return to power. A fellow Labour party committed to working for peace with the Palestinians was without a doubt worthy of strong Swedish support.

High-level political contacts with Israel began in earnest in early 1999, when Nuder travelled to Israel in order to meet the new Labour leader Ehud Barak and try to establish a rapport with him. Persson and Nuder reasoned that while Barak had outstanding security credentials from his distinguished military career, he was relatively new to politics, and did not have a firm political tradition or an intimate knowledge of social democracy. Nuder says he saw a Labour leader thirsting for and seeking contact with international Labour affiliates, looking for ideas with which to strengthen his domestic political agenda. He presented Barak with a paper on the Swedish view of trends in Labour politics at that time, particularly Tony Blair's Third Way, which was very much in focus. Nuder considered the meeting a success.[23]

After Barak's emphatic victory in the 17 May elections, this initially speculative outreach proved to be the beginning of a meaningful political dialogue. In early October 1999, Persson became the first Swedish Prime Minister to officially visit Israel since Erlander had done so in 1962. It had an additional personal significance for him, in that it was his first time in Israel. In his youth he had twice planned to visit the country and work at a *kibbutz*, but 'trivial personal reasons' prevented him from following through on his dream.[24] Ahlmark was delighted at this development, and noted that 'Persson's visit to Israel represents a dramatic change in Swedish politics, sidelining Olof Palme and Sten Andersson ... We have in Persson a Prime Minister who is more sensitive to and knowledgeable about Jewish issues than any of his predecessors.'[25]

Persson was only the second international leader to visit Israel under Barak's tenure as Prime Minister, which suggests a mutually valued bilateral relationship. Barak warmly praised the Living History Project, expressed appreciation for all that Persson had done in this regard, and described Sweden as a model for other states to follow. The two leaders agreed to establish cooperative projects in the field of IT, and Barak inquired how Sweden had recovered from the serious economic recession it endured in the early 1990s.[26] Naturally, Persson also visited *Yad Vashem*, the Israeli Holocaust memorial museum in Jerusalem.

It was also the first time a Swedish Prime Minister visited the occupied and PA controlled territories. He met with Arafat and the Palestinian leadership, including a meeting with Faisal Husseini – significantly not at Orient House, but at the Swedish consulate in East Jerusalem. During the course of his meetings he introduced the idea of establishing several new bilateral cooperation committees to help develop PA institutions, which the Palestinians to responded very positively.

In the months that followed, contacts with Israel were intensified. Barak paid an official visit to Stockholm, a number of political visits were exchanged at ministerial level, and the agreed upon IT cooperation was initiated. A good personal relationship had developed between the two leaders, visible already during Persson's visit to Israel, which was only their second meeting. They spoke regularly on the phone, and Barak briefed Persson on developments in his negotiations with the Syrians and Palestinians.[27] This particular aspect of their relationship would now come into focus.

A stumbling peace strategy

Soon after becoming Prime Minister, Barak explained his intentions to Terje Rød-Larsen. He likened the conflict to a dog with an ugly tail: 'If we take the tail away, the dog would be beautiful. You Oslo people would chop the tail off like salami. I will chop it off.'[28] Barak 'wanted to open up *all* tracks and to have an end of conflict agreement' in 'a grand architecture' which was 'completely contrary to the stone by stone approach of Oslo'. Larsen repeatedly warned everyone, Americans and Israelis alike, of the dangers of this totalist strategy, but to no avail. At lunch with the American peace team, Larsen remembers, 'I was very agitated, and I basically said, "This is too risky and it is going to fail, and it's going to lead to terrible bloodshed."'[29] His grim prognosis proved to be correct.

Barak's first speech to the Knesset as Prime Minister clearly identified peace as a priority. On the campaign trail, Barak had pledged to get Israel out of southern Lebanon within one year, and the key to a peaceful withdrawal, he reasoned, was a peace agreement with the Syrians who exercised *de facto* control over Lebanon. Like Rabin, Clinton, and many members of the American peace team, Barak considered a Syria-first strategy preferable.[30] Unlike the Palestinians, Syria posed a strategic threat to Israel, and the issues of contention between the two states were much simpler. As with Egypt a few decades earlier, peace with the Syrians involved a fairly straightforward trade-off free of existential identity issues: full withdrawal from the Golan Heights in exchange for full recognition, peace, and security.

As for the Palestinians, in a move reminiscent of Netanyahu, Barak wanted to defer the implementation of the Wye River Agreement while working toward a Framework Agreement on Permanent Status (FAPS). Ross saw a 'conceptual divide' between the parties which persisted: 'the

Palestinians wanted to see the Israelis deliver on their Wye [and Oslo II] commitments before addressing the permanent status issues; Barak wanted to see if he really had a partner', which he defined by engagement on permanent status issues.[31] Still, on 4 September 1999, the parties signed the Sharm el-Sheikh Agreement. It stipulated: that permanent status negotiations were to resume on 13 September, to be completed in one year; that a FAPS was to be concluded by the end of January; a new timeline for a phased implementation of the Wye further redeployments by 20 January; and that 350 Palestinian prisoners were to be released.

Barak told the Knesset that 'the Sharm Memorandum ... creates the initial conditions that are best suited for permanent status negotiations', and argued that implementation of Wye as stipulated in its original timetable 'would have compromised the political and security interests of the State of Israel'. The agreement would rebuild trust between the two sides, while upholding Israeli interests, particularly security concerns.[32] Trust, however, was a commodity in short supply, and Barak did little to inspire even a modicum of it. Barak proceeded to focus all his energy on the Syrian track, a move which Clinton and his peace team generally supported.

This decision was unpopular among many in Barak's coalition government. Ami Ayalon, the head of Shin Bet, and later also Shaul Mofaz, Chief of Staff of the IDF, pushed Barak to focus on the Palestinians amid concerns that Palestinian frustrations over the failure of Oslo would boil over. They warned of the consequences of extensive delays: 'we will lose the ability to do the deal with the Palestinians and a historic opportunity will be lost'.[33] Barak's negotiator Gilead Sher also shared this view.[34]

On the US side, Aaron Miller, Ross's deputy, similarly advocated a continued focus on the Palestinian track. He laments that 'with our full backing Barak went off to pursue Syria in a way I thought was doomed to fail. I'd seen this movie at least twice before, and I was convinced we were wasting time we didn't have.' When Clinton publicly invited Israel and Syria to hold talks in Washington in December at Blair House, Miller was with the Palestinians in Ramallah. Arafat squeezed his hand and told him, 'Barak shouldn't take me for granted.'[35] Arafat considered Barak's decision to negotiate with Syria first an instrument of pressure designed to isolate the Palestinians, a public humiliation to put them in their place. This affront was aggravated by the fact that Assad had made no overtures whatsoever, while the PLO had recognised Israel, conducted bilateral negotiations and cooperated on security issues.[36]

Although Barak had a grand regional strategy, actions toward the Palestinians appeared to be based on very short-term thinking. It was fire fighting, dealing with crises and problems as and when they arose. Ross starkly acknowledges that Barak 'did not have a strategy toward the Palestinians; he had one toward Syria and it did not work.'[37] While the Syrians were in focus, the Palestinians were placated when necessary to avoid problems, sometimes at the behest of the Americans who sporadically conditioned the Syrian track on it.

Miller reflects that 'Barak had it all gamed out, it's just that no one else cooperated.'[38] Former chief of staff of the IDF and then Minister for Tourism Amnon Lipkin-Shahak too notes that Barak's plan had a certain logic to it, but 'the problem was that his logic worked only for him.'[39] Gilead Sher and Ephraim Sneh, Barak's deputy Defence Minister, further corroborate this view of a man convinced that his logic would subsume everyone else's and prevail over everything.[40] Though bold and confident, Barak's plan became completely unrealistic as time went on.

The Palestinians became a sideshow, as the ambitious timetables and deadlines of Sharm el-Sheikh consistently went unfulfilled. Nearly two months behind schedule, Israel carried out another redeployment in January 2000. As the revised deadline for the next redeployment neared on 15 February, Barak was noncommittal on its implementation. After direct negotiations between the two failed to resolve the matter, Arafat suspended all negotiations with the Israelis. The situation was resolved through a package of understandings finalised in early March which the Americans helped negotiate between the two parties. Barak was eager for Clinton to meet with Assad, but the Americans had made it clear that this would not happen without movement on the Palestinian track.

This leverage appears to have impelled Barak to agree to transfer three villages surrounding East Jerusalem to the Palestinians, two on 23 April and the third on 23 May, although this aspect was not made public. The latter date was also the new target for the FAPS. The third and final redeployment stipulated in the Interim Agreement was to be carried out on 23 June, with further releases of Palestinian prisoners as provided for by Sharm el-Sheikh still to be discussed. Clinton confirmed the contents of the package with Arafat, and provided his assurance that it would be implemented.[41] It was not.

This failure further eroded trust and American accountability. The last Wye redeployment from 6.1 per cent of the West Bank was carried out on 21 March, and proved to be the last substantial act of implementation. In early May, Arafat met Barak and agreed to a new proposal: the transfer of Abu Dis, al-Azariya and al-Sawahra to full Palestinian control if the third redeployment was suspended until after a FAPS had been reached. This was the polar opposite of all previous agreements between the two, which had specified that the lack of a FAPS should not affect implementation of other commitments.

While negotiations on a FAPS were to have begun ten days after Sharm el-Sheikh, it took Barak two months to even nominate a head negotiator. In part, this was due to internal disagreement about Gilead Sher's role within Barak's government as a consultant rather than a full-time civil servant, but this needs to be considered within the context of Barak's broader strategic plans.[42] A tripartite meeting between Arafat, Barak, and Clinton was held in Oslo on 2 November to mark the sixth anniversary of the Declaration of Principles (DoP) and to try to create some momentum on this faltering track. In addition to finally inaugurating the official final status negotiations, the leaders agreed to set up a secret back channel.

Abu Ala and Abu Mazen, both present in Oslo, were to represent the Palestinians, while Shlomo Ben-Ami, Israel's Internal Security Minister, and Lipkin-Shahak would represent Israel. But Abu Mazen did not think that such secret formal negotiations were the best way to proceed. In fact, he thought it was the worst way of doing it. He far preferred the resumption of the secret Track II format that had previously been used in Stockholm, a notion that had long been popular among Americans, Palestinians, and Swedes.

In December 1998, Arafat came to Stockholm at the invitation of the Swedish government and the Olof Palme International Centre (OPIC) to mark the tenth anniversary of his 1988 Stockholm meeting which helped initiate a US–PLO dialogue. In front of representatives from the UN, EU, United States, Egypt, Jordan and Norway, Arafat gave a very positive speech – written by Agha and Khalidi – outlining the key principles of peace and mutual coexistence. Initiated and organised by the Stockholm group, it was a serious attempt to reinvigorate final status negotiations, and attracted the attention of the American peace team who were very positive about this opening.

In February 1999, Aaron Miller travelled to Stockholm and met with Andersson, Anders Bjurner, and Mathias Mossberg, all veterans of the US–PLO mediation in 1988. He believed that a secret channel was necessary, and thought that Sweden and the Stockholm group could make a valuable contribution in this regard.[43] Khalidi thought that this 'was a big deal for the Swedes, because it was the first time that the Americans had shown any direct interest in this particular channel'.[44]

In October, Arafat and Abu Mazen told the Americans that they wanted a secret channel with Barak in order to work on the FAPS. Abu Mazen sent Agha and Khalidi to Washington to brief the American peace team on the fundamentals of a final status agreement and to make them fully aware of the contents of the revised Stockholm document. Rob Malley, President Clinton's special assistant for Arab–Israeli affairs, remembers that

> most of us I think on the [American] peace team ... had a certain bias in favour of the secret unofficial talks that we thought might be more conducive to breakthroughs and to out of the box thinking, including with the very people who negotiated [the] Beilin-Abu Mazen [Understandings], at least on the Palestinian side.[45]

Thus, Ross thought it would be fruitful for them to make contact with the man he believed stood closest to Barak, negotiator Gilead Sher, and arranged a meeting between the three of them. A few weeks later, Sher travelled to London to secretly discuss final status issues with Agha and Khalidi. Sher describes it as a positive meeting, one that constituted grounds for further discussion of such a secret channel, which could make progress and then become the basis for the official channel.[46] Khalidi recalls, however, that at the end of their day together, 'Gilead in so many words said, "No way will we ever think of the Abu Mazen–Beilin document. Forget it, it's not going to happen. No way."'[47] While this document was considered detailed and useful, Barak wanted to start with a clean slate rather than use a pre-existing framework for the discussion.[48]

News of their meeting soon appeared in *Ha'aretz* and damaged this potentially promising connection. The source of the leak is as yet unknown. Weary of leaks and further negative publicity, Abu Mazen immediately rang Agha and told him to stop everything. He explained that Egyptian ambassador Osama al-Baz had been 'on his back already', accusing him of being 'up to his old tricks again'.[49] Khalidi has explained that Abu Mazen

> really became very sensitive to the notion that he was going behind people's backs, or doing things secretly ... One of the biggest criticisms of the Oslo process, echoed everywhere even until this day, was this notion that it was secret. You know, 'Abu Mazen hatched a secret plot in Oslo.' The Arab world has kind of latched onto this. Criticism of Abu Mazen – of his style or approach – has been directed against this notion that he kind of plots in secret. So post-Oslo, and then Abu Mazen–Beilin, I think he became doubly sensitive to these kind of criticisms.[50]

On 3–4 November 1999, Maen Rashid Areikat, Director General of the PLO Negotiations Affairs Department (NAD) was in Stockholm to discuss Swedish support for his department, which was substantial in terms of both monetary aid and professional expertise. Areikat welcomed continued Swedish involvement in the peace process during a meeting with Bjurner, who explained that Persson's recent visit to the region had for some reason been misinterpreted by the press to suggest that Sweden did not wish to play a role anymore. This was not the case. Rather, Sweden did not wish to play a role that the parties themselves did not specifically request, a point which Bjurner emphasised. Potential forms of support mentioned included 'confidence building measures, support for ideas, contributing to ad hoc solutions, and to organise meetings', the details of which would be discussed with Abu Mazen.[51]

Abu Mazen had hoped to visit Stockholm together with Areikat for precisely this purpose, but had been unable to come for 'practical reasons'. Instead, Areikat carried with him a confidential letter from Abu Mazen to Lindh.[52] Although its contents are as yet unknown, it is likely to have concerned a renewed Swedish role in the peace process.

In mid-December, Andersson and Mossberg were invited to Ramallah for a meeting with Abu Mazen and Areikat. In private, while Areikat was out of the room getting some refreshments, Abu Mazen raised the idea of re-establishing a secret Swedish channel for negotiations. He sought to replicate the original Stockholm group formula which had worked so well and, above all, remained secret for the duration of their original work. Moreover, he saw Sweden's improved relations with Israel as a positive development in this regard, since Barak would be more comfortable working with a government he trusted.[53] They assured him that they would forward his request to the Prime Minister.[54]

Upon his return on 19 December, Andersson rang the Prime Minister's assistant to request an urgent meeting regarding this important development. He did not get to see Persson until 29 February 2000, and only then at the funeral of a former Social Democratic government minister, which was 'not the right environment to discuss sensitive foreign policy problems'. Although he felt snubbed, Andersson also felt that he had conveyed the import and urgency of the matter.[55]

Meanwhile, innumerable meetings were held between a number of influential Israelis and Palestinians on a variety of different tracks. Official front channel talks began between Oded Eran and Yasser Abed Rabbo, the heads of the delegations for permanent status, but they remained unproductive, largely because Eran was not given the necessary mandate to seriously discuss the final status issues.[56] From December to January, Abu Ala met five times with Eran, and in February, while negotiations were officially suspended, he met three times with Ben-Ami. As they primarily dealt with permanent status, most of these meetings were conducted secretly.[57]

After having participated in a number of back-channel meetings with Abu Ala and Abu Mazen, Lipkin-Shahak got the impression that Abu Mazen was not enthusiastic about continuing their talks. This was not because he did not want to engage with the Israelis, but because he found their arrangements unsuitable. Lipkin-Shahak has admitted that he shared Abu Mazen's assessment of the situation, but his reservations focused on a different aspect. He thought that 'talking simultaneously through different channels on the same issues means that something is wrong. This is not the way to do it.' He informed Barak of his impressions and ceased participating in the back channel, as did Abu Mazen.[58]

Abu Mazen finally came to Stockholm in early March 2000 in order to officially follow up on his request for Swedish assistance to set up a different secret channel. On the 7th, he was scheduled to meet separately with Lindh and Persson. His itinerary specifies a private 15-minute meeting with Lindh where they discussed his proposal. However, no such private meeting was scheduled with the Prime Minister.[59]

Of their hour-long meeting, Sven-Eric Söder felt that 'they sat and waited for each other ... Abu Mazen was waiting for Persson to raise the issue, Persson was waiting for Abu Mazen to raise the issue, and everyone knew it was a sensitive subject.'[60] Andersson claims he made it clear that Abu Mazen wanted Persson to do this. Mossberg remembers that the two had been supposed to go aside at some point and discuss the matter privately, but never did. Whether a deliberate omission, procedural error, or misunderstanding, a private discussion between the two did not take place, much to Abu Mazen's annoyance and disappointment. He left Sweden, unsure whether they would prove a suitable host.[61]

Still, he had discussed it with Lindh, and the proposal had been known to the government for many months. At Andersson's insistence, Lindh suggested to Persson and Nuder that they use their newfound friendship with Barak to convince him to commit to Abu Mazen's secret channel.[62] On 12 March, Andersson spoke briefly to Persson at an extra Party congress, where Persson said he would speak to Nuder about it. It was around this time that Persson's interest truly peaked. It was clear from the outset that he was to make this endeavour his own. In line with his views on certain foreign policy responsibilities, the process was not to be run by Lindh, Andersson, or the Foreign Ministry, but by the Prime Minister's office. This was characteristic of Persson's leadership style; he was sometimes commonly referred to as 'HSB', a Swedish acronym for *han som bestämmer* (he who decides).

Nuder arrived secretly in Israel on 1 April 2000, to personally deliver a letter from Persson to Barak. In Jerusalem, Nuder met with Barak's Chief of Staff, General Danny Yatom, who conveyed the letter. It read:

> The chances of what we all dream of – a just and lasting peace in the region – look better than ever, largely thanks to your personal and dynamic contribution to the process ... the Palestinians are very worried that the current process is not working fast enough to produce results on time. They see a need for better options for secret talks, for more informal contacts between the sides, and for ways and means that will allow free and completely secret discussions on the core issues, together with you. To this end,

> Abu Mazen has asked us to help promote the creation of such contacts. He specifically asked that I contact you personally on this issue ...[63]

A few days later, Nuder received a phone call from Barak's office to arrange a meeting with Sher at the King David Hotel at midnight. Sher asked Nuder several questions about Abu Mazen's proposal and eventually gave a conditional response. Barak agreed to the idea of a secret channel in Sweden, but explicitly rejected the participation of Agha and Khalidi, whom Abu Mazen had nominated to represent him. Barak insisted on high-level representation from officials such as Abu Mazen himself, Abu Ala, or Muhammad Dahlan; these were to be 'real negotiations, not a seminar'.[64]

Nuder traveled to Tunis to break the news to Abu Mazen, who was disappointed with this response. It was precisely the official approach that he sought to avoid. Nuder tried to convince the Israelis that Abu Mazen's overture was serious and in good faith, but Yatom and Sher maintained that Barak would settle for nothing less than official interaction. At this point, unsatisfied with the Israeli response, Abu Mazen absolved himself of the enterprise and basically said, 'Let them do whatever they want.'[65] Similarly disappointed, Nuder returned to Stockholm believing that his mission had come to nothing, unaware that it would take on a life of its own.

Public front channel permanent status negotiations had restarted in March between Eran and Israel Hasson on the Israeli side, and Abed Rabbo and Saeb Erekat on the Palestinian. The latter two were getting increasingly exasperated during the course of their talks. Eran was 'a good guy, but not authorised' to discuss any of the crucial final status issues – borders, settlements, territory, refugees, security, or Jerusalem – which were in theory the reserve of the secret talks. The front channel dealt with functional issues, such as water, economic relations, legal questions, day-to-day security co-ordination, etc.[66]

Barak thought Abed Rabbo and Erekat were 'compulsive leakers', so he insisted on this arrangement, and while Arafat had agreed to this with Barak and Ross, he had not made this division of labour clear to his negotiators.[67] Erekat and Abed Rabbo were repeatedly expressing their disappointment with the talks in public, referring to them as a 'sham' and a 'charade'. Ross worked hard with the Israelis to give the front channel a sense of credibility, important since it acted as a smokescreen for the back channel. Barak eventually allowed Eran to present a map on territory and borders, which – though its contents infuriated the Palestinians – kept the talks going.[68] Apart from the element of camouflage, these talks were 'meaningless',[69] or, as Erekat described them, merely 'games we Israelis and Palestinians like to play'.[70]

In late March 2000, the final incarnation of the secret back channel had begun to meet. It was this group of negotiators who would eventually travel to Stockholm. For the Israelis, Ben-Ami and Sher; for the Palestinians, Abu Ala and Hassan Asfour. Abu Mazen attended a more informal meeting with Abu Ala and Ben-Ami, but had long since taken a step back and was not a regular fixture in these talks.[71] It is unclear whether Abu Ala found out about the Swedish option from the Israelis or his Palestinian colleagues, but, either way, he became the head of the future Stockholm delegation. After a series of meetings, Abu Ala told Ross that Ben-Ami 'was a good man, and he is determined to do a deal. I can work with him.' He said that he was 'working hard on' Abu Mazen to get him to actively support the channel, and that he was considering including Agha or Khalidi in the group bound for Stockholm to give him a stake in it.[72]

In early May, Agha and Khalidi received phone calls from Abu Mazen, who told them to expect a phone call from Abu Ala, asking them to come to Stockholm. Agha wondered what had happened, and asked Abu Mazen what to do. Abu Mazen replied, 'It's up to you', which Agha knew meant, 'Don't go.'[73] Khalidi too could tell that Abu Mazen did not think it was a good idea. Moreover, he was convinced that there was no functional use whatsoever in Agha or himself going as part of an official secret delegation to Stockholm, particularly when Abu Ala was leading it. 'You have to maintain some kind of party discipline, which we're very bad at. Our job is not to maintain a party line or party discipline whatsoever, [and] you can't sit there and disagree with the head of your formal delegation, so there was no point in us going.'[74]

At the beginning of May, while he was with Persson in Washington, Nuder received a call from Yatom. If the Swedes could still guarantee total seclusion and secrecy, the parties would send a small, high-level group to negotiate there. After consulting Persson, Nuder replied in the affirmative and the Stockholm Channel, as it has become known, was born.

Harpsund

The negotiations were held at Harpsund, the Prime Minister's official countryside residence located about an hour and a half outside Stockholm. In their personal accounts of the proceedings, practically every participant comments on the natural beauty of their surroundings. With its serene, picturesque lakeside location, it seemed a world removed from the political turbulence and violence that characterised their region. The Swedish secret service, SÄPO, was in charge of security. They discreetly transported all delegations to and from the site, and unobtrusively ensured a secure environment. In addition to Nuder, Mossberg had been included in the inner circle to monitor the negotiations, together with John Hagard, the head of the Middle East desk at the Foreign Ministry and a former Swedish ambassador to Israel. These three constituted the Swedish team present at Harpsund.

Late on the evening of 11 May 2000, Nuder landed at Ben Gurion airport in Persson's official government plane to pick up the two delegations. The next morning, work began in the central hall at Harpsund. The extent of Swedish involvement was made clear in Nuder's opening remarks at the first meeting: 'It is you who will decide if Sweden has a role – as a friend to both sides – and if so, what such a role would be ... From this point on, we will be here, around, at your service.'[75] This was the essence of the Swedish mission. They had convened the two parties, given them a secure physical environment for negotiations, and would involve themselves only when they were called upon to do so. The Swedes were 'offering a venue. No more, no less.'[76] Once again, though their role was limited to facilitation, this still constitutes an important facet of mediation.

Part of this facilitative role was also to communicate with Ross and the American peace team. The night before he flew to pick up the delegations, Nuder rang Ross to let him know the immediate timetable, and offered to make logistical arrangements for the Americans once they let him know when they would be arriving. He also kept him informed about the mood of the talks as they went on. Harpsund was the ninth meeting of this particular back channel. Discussions focused on borders and settlements, both issues that they had begun to address in their Jerusalem meetings. While the initial chemistry was very good and extremely promising, Nuder reported that the atmosphere soon deteriorated somewhat amid difficult discussions.[77]

The mood rapidly got a lot worse. Only hours into their first meeting, Sher received a call on his mobile from Raviv Druker, political correspondent for the Israeli military radio station Galei Tzahal, asking him to confirm that meetings were taking place in 'a European capital' between Abu Ala, Asfour, Ben-Ami, and himself.[78] The following day, the Swedes informed the parties that an AP story from Palestinian sources had said there were secret negotiations going on in Europe, and Galei Tzahal had broadcast a detailed story identifying Stockholm as the site.[79]

This left the negotiators demoralised and dismayed. Nuder recalls that 'Ben-Ami feared for his political life, and Abu Ala for his earthly life, absolutely. They were very, very worried, and accused each other of this and that. Then they pulled themselves together and continued, but it was very sensitive for a while.'[80] While the negotiations continued, the atmosphere was 'undeniably soured'.[81] Still, the American peace team arrived on 14 May, and despite the leak, saw some positive movement from both sides on important principles and encouraged them to build on it. The next day, 15 May, was *Nakba* day. Palestinian prisoners were on hunger strike, rioting had erupted as a show of solidarity with them, and armed clashes between Palestinian security forces and the IDF ensued. In protest, Barak recalled his team, and so the parties returned home to brief their leaders. By the end of the day, five Palestinians had been killed and hundreds wounded, while a dozen Israeli soldiers had been injured.[82]

On 18 May, despite no longer enjoying the benefit of secrecy, the parties returned to Harpsund to begin drafting an unofficial FAPS, or a 'non-paper'. Sher's assistant Gidi Grinstein and Palestinian attorney Hiba Husseini joined their respective teams for this purpose. Prime Minister Persson came one evening to hear separate reports from the teams and urged them to continue. Mounting tension, however, was making this increasingly difficult, as two Palestinian 'days of rage' continued on 19–20 May.

Abu Ala acknowledges that 'the demonstrations began to overshadow the talks and placed great responsibility on the shoulders of the Palestinian delegation. We felt we had to tread ever more carefully.'[83] He was chain smoking 'with both hands' while constantly on the phone to associates in the West Bank and Gaza. Ben-Ami described the effect of it all on Abu Ala as 'devastating . . . It meant that he was being criticized. He couldn't bear it . . . Now he needed to go back to the fundamental positions ... Basically that was the end of it. He was a different man.'[84]

In this latest round of rioting, five Israeli soldiers were injured and over 100 Palestinians were wounded. In protest at the deteriorating security situation, Barak once again withdrew his negotiators from Sweden. The teams continued to meet in Tel Aviv in the first few days of June, but these additional sessions yielded little more. The Stockholm channel had stopped producing and was therefore over.

Assessments of this transitory episode vary wildly. Abu Ala and Ben-Ami both agree that the channel yielded positive results – the former describes it as 'a brief but meaningful contribution', while the latter says that 'enormous progress' was made.[85] Sher has gone even further, suggesting that 'we reached the point where the leaders had to decide. The summit is prepared as far as we were concerned, as negotiators ...'[86]

These positive evaluations are in a sense understandable. For the first time in formal negotiations, the Palestinians did not plainly reject an Israeli demand for a modification of the 1967 border to incorporate the larger West Bank settlement blocs such as Ariel, Gush Etzion and Ramot, though Asfour specified that he would publicly deny he had ever accepted that. Israeli maps showing percentages of proposed Palestinian territory, although still unrealistically low, were at least an improvement on previous efforts.[87] After meeting with the Israeli and Palestinian teams at Harpsund and reviewing what they had produced, Ross confided to Nuder that he had not 'seen anything as good as this'.[88] Finally, official negotiators were at least discussing the taboo final status issues.

With the benefit of hindsight, many of the Americans have observed that Harpsund 'gave a false sense of confidence to the Israelis'.[89] Given the faltering nature of Israeli–Palestinian negotiations up to that point, discussions there had been relatively productive, but the effort had not brought about any substantial breakthroughs.[90] Gamal Helal, the State Department's Arabic translator and Middle East advisor, believed that 'the Israelis completely misinterpreted [Harpsund]. They came up with an interpretation that was so rosy ... which had nothing to do with reality, especially with regard to the right-of-return issues'.[91]

This erroneous view was espoused by Persson, no doubt keen to emphasise the success of his contribution. In August 2000 he suggested that the issues of borders and refugees were practically settled there, while in January 2001 he reflected that the parties had been 'this close' to a finished agreement.[92]

Miller recalls that 'I couldn't figure out what actually occurred [at Harpsund]. And nor could I figure out why everyone was so excited. I remember talking to Gamal [Helal], we couldn't figure it out.' When Helal asked Abu Ala what kind of movement there had been on the Palestinian side, Abu Ala just laughed. 'Abu Ala got it, which is why I think there was a ... bit of a con here.' He goes on:

> I remember leaving persuaded on one hand that Israelis and Palestinians had achieved such remarkable success, but not really understanding why. We believed that the Israelis and Palestinians had gone farther on several of the issues than they had gone before, [but] I'm not sure anybody really believed that there was enough substantive closure on any of these issues to warrant going to the next stage ... This was no basis on which to go to a conflict ending solution. It was all over the place![93]

Huge gaps still existed between the parties. Palestinians still saw Israeli positions on territory as unacceptable annexation and continued occupation under the guise of security needs. On refugees, Abu Ala notes that 'division was deeper than on any other issue'.[94] Jerusalem, one of the thorniest issues, was not even officially up for discussion; Barak had not authorised his negotiators to bring it up. Ben-Ami and Sher overstepped their mandate by doing so, and any drafting on it was out of the question. Though these discussions led Barak to claim that 'everything about Jerusalem was discussed at length in Stockholm and in other meetings', this assessment is not widely shared.[95]

Israeli and Palestinian shortcomings

Significant shortcomings on both sides contributed to the demise of the Stockholm channel.

Primarily, the immediate cause of failure was the leak, which rendered the dynamic of give and take in a secluded environment impossible. As with every leak in such a context, it is difficult to definitively discern who was responsible for it, but one must ask '*cui bono*'? The peace process was moving into a higher gear, and there were those on both sides with an interest in thwarting progress on ideological, personal, or political grounds. Multiple theories exist, but there is as yet no proof for any of them.

Among Israeli and Western observers, the orthodoxy is that Abu Mazen leaked the talks. Having initially approached the Swedes with the idea, he and his associates were then excluded from the channel in favour of other political rivals, prompting someone from his entourage to leak the talks and torpedo them.[96] This line of thinking has received particular currency due to the fact that Abu Mazen had a very acrimonious relationship with Asfour over the implementation of Wye.[97] Muhammad Rashid, a PA account manager who stood close to Asfour and Dahlan, convinced Arafat not to send Agha or Khalidi to Stockholm.[98]

From his negotiations with them, Lipkin-Shahak observed that 'when Abu Mazen and Abu Ala were both together, it made each one of them more stubborn and less flexible. Because the one who has to give, exposes himself in front of the other one, who might use it against him. There was always tension between these two guys.'[99] At the debriefing with Arafat and Abu Mazen after returning from the first round of the Stockholm talks, Abu Ala remembers,

> In retrospect, Abu Mazen expressed some irritation at the inclusion of Hassan Asfour in the Stockholm delegation. After some recrimination over the leakage of the 'Swedish track', we agreed on the need to put a stop to the internal rivalry between members of the Palestinian leadership that was rampant at the time and was having detrimental effects on our ability to negotiate.[100]

An anonymous interviewee observed that 'we – the Palestinians – sometimes overlook our national interest, and it becomes a personal interest. Who is leading what, as opposed to what the nation needs.'[101] According to Agha, this damaging dynamic was institutionalised:

> Arafat was very aware of the conflicts between them [his subordinates], and more often than not he made use of these conflicts to further his own personal influence and position. Which is legitimate in politics ... That was Abu Ammar [Arafat's *nom de guerre*], that's how he used to operate. He would send you on a mission, and he would send somebody else on exactly the

opposite of that mission and whoever succeeds and brings him back something, that's all he cares about. He might send you on a mission and send three other people on the same mission, and sit and wait to see who would bring him back the goodies.[102]

The divisiveness of these personal power struggles was demonstrated quite clearly by Abed Rabbo, who resigned from his position as head negotiator on 14 May after learning about the Stockholm channel. Slighted by Arafat, left to work on an official track which was merely a smokescreen, Abed Rabbo – in the words of Erekat – 'was personally touched ... He was so angry, so so angry, when he heard the news of Stockholm.'[103] This could possibly have driven him to leak them.

Erekat has comprehensively dismissed any notion of Abu Mazen leaking the talks as 'bullshit ... Abu Mazen is not like this ... he doesn't think this way'.[104] Khalidi shares this belief: 'I don't think it was Abu Mazen. It's not his style.' Abu Mazen clearly knew about the upcoming Stockholm channel, as evidenced by his calls to Agha and Khalidi, who deny that Arafat excluded Abu Mazen from the channel:

> He wasn't excluded from it, he excluded himself from it. He didn't want to be part of it, because he didn't think it would succeed, and because he didn't think this was the right way to proceed. He wanted to go the other Track II way, and that's why he went all the way to Sweden to talk about it, what he went to set up. And when it switched to being a secret formal channel, he thought this wasn't the right way of doing it ... He didn't intervene to spoil the process, but he did nothing to facilitate it or support it either. But he knew that there will be a meeting in Stockholm, and that this would include Abu Ala.[105]

Secondly, in addition to the leak, violence on the ground marred the atmosphere. When Americans and Israelis called upon Arafat to control his people, he replied that he would do what he could but could 'not guarantee anything', which according to Ross meant in 'Arafatspeak' that he would do nothing to stop it. Arafat believed violence served his cause at a time when Palestinian anger was mounting and he was under pressure domestically. It released pent-up frustration on the street against the Israelis rather than against himself, and showed that the

Palestinians could not be ignored. In his calculus, it was also a way to put pressure on the Israelis to be more forthcoming.[106] Violence, however, made Barak less willing to offer any concessions or goodwill measures to the Palestinians.

Although extremely harmful to the negotiations, it was an understandable expression of Palestinian frustration. Since Wye, the Palestinians had seriously acted on their security obligations, cracked down on terrorist groups, and received little in return. Barak had repeatedly re-negotiated the Sharm el-Sheikh timetables and consistently failed to implement them, when Sharm was itself a re-negotiation of a previously agreed implementation agreement of a previous agreement.

He sought to keep the Palestinians committed to the peace process while making as few concessions as possible. He did not wish to erode the Israeli negotiating position before sitting down to do a permanent status deal, where he would inevitably have to give up more,[107] nor did he wish to precipitate fractures in his coalition. Israeli society and the Knesset were not as cohesive as Barak's election victory in 1999 might suggest.[108] His coalition included right wing parties like Shas, the Sephardic religious party, and the National Religious Party (NRP), who objected to concessions on Jerusalem.

This difficulty became clear around mid-April when Barak publicly announced his intention to transfer the three villages outside East Jerusalem to the Palestinians. Yitzhak Levy of the NRP declared that his party would leave the coalition if this happened, and did so when the Knesset narrowly approved the transfer on 15 May. Throughout that period, Shas exploited their crucial coalition position as holders of 17 seats, and used the villages as leverage to further their own concerns. Minister of Education Yossi Sarid, leader of the secular Meretz Party, was arguing against funding for separate religious schools, and so Shas dug their heels in: 'no money for their educational system, no support for the villages and no support for the Barak government'.[109]

There is no doubt that Barak's fears over his government were genuine and valid. If his government collapsed, he would no longer have been able to pursue peace the way that he had planned. These constraints severely limited his ability to deliver on his promises to the Palestinians, which discouraged them from continuing. They had consistently been flexible to meet Barak's needs, and were getting little in return. If he could not even transfer the three villages as agreed, they reasoned, how on earth would he be able to deliver on all the necessary final status issues? Unable to see this point of view, Barak resented having to explain delays on the village transfers to Arafat, and wondered why he should have to take steps that may bring down the very government that could go so far to respond to Palestinian needs.[110]

Previously happy to make the Palestinians wait, his coalition problems propelled Barak to quickly proceed towards the end game. When Arafat noticed Barak was in a hurry, he started dragging his feet, looking to use Israeli desperation to his advantage and extract more from them. Barak had long envisioned a tripartite leaders summit in Washington to close a final status deal. The groundwork for such a summit, however, did not exist. Stockholm had failed, and subsequent negotiations in the region had similarly failed to yield anything even approaching a FAPS. Khalidi reflects that 'without Abu Mazen onboard, and you've got Abed Rabbo publicly denouncing the track, one of the essential pre-Camp David processes was completely screwed'.[111]

After a meeting in Nablus on 25 June 2000, Abu Ala got the impression that Ben-Ami was trying to revitalise Israeli positions but 'working under difficulties generated by his own side . . . dragging Barak forward one small step at a time'.[112] Crucially, Jerusalem had only been discussed with the Palestinians in general terms. Barak thought this was an obvious necessity 'because such a discussion before the moment of decision could blow up the whole negotiation', and had resisted moves from both the Americans and his own negotiators to address the issue seriously.[113] At the Nablus meeting, Erekat remembers that Arafat wanted 'to give Shlomo Ben-Ami the message that he knows Jerusalem, and Jerusalem is the most important thing, and that if you haven't even opened the file of Jerusalem in Stockholm, how can you take me to a summit. . .[?]'[114]

Barak reasoned, 'We can't break this impasse without a leaders' summit and we'll never know if we could pass this impasse without such a meeting.'[115] Lipkin-Shahak is critical of this summitry strategy:

> If there was a real interest to prepare everything before Camp David, it means that all the issues should have been raised in Stockholm. Once not all the issues were raised, and not real agreements have been achieved in Stockholm, we went to Camp David without any real and serious understanding on the main

issues. So what was the meaning of paving the road if there is no road and no pavement?[116]

The failure of American and Swedish mediators

By all accounts, the entire American peace team had serious misgivings about the Camp David summit but argued that it was a risk worth taking. Not doing so would invite accusations of a failure to grasp an historic opportunity, and violence would in all likelihood erupt among the Palestinians anyway. Clinton did not need much convincing that the cost of a summit would be far less than the cost of not doing so and watching everything fall to pieces.[117]

This particular instance is representative of a wider American failure. At the expense of their own strategy, they made themselves subordinate to Barak's priorities and tactics, convening a summit at his behest without accurately gauging the basic bottom lines of each party. 'If Barak said he can go this far, we can't push him beyond it. If Barak wants us to jump, we ask him how high', and 'the net result of these decisions was to cede effective control over US policy to the Israelis'.[118] As Albright has admitted, the Americans 'went to Camp David on Barak's word'.[119]

Fundamentally, the negotiating scenario was erroneously configured. Miller has correctly suggested that 'those who argue that Camp David wasn't well prepared miss the point. Israeli and Palestinian redlines, the lack of trust, and the explosiveness of the issues made conventional preparation impossible.'[120] Malley has explained that due to

> the format that existed then – a format which ultimately both Arafat and Barak were leaning towards – which was these negotiations between their formal envoys ... it didn't matter how much time you would spend. These conversations ... whether in Stockholm or Eilat or elsewhere, were not yielding anything because both leaders were holding their cards too close to their chest and neither side was going to be prepared to divulge any more wiggle room until they reach what they thought was the moment of truth. That was the logic, and it may have been wrong headed, but that was the logic, and that's what Barak was telling us, and that's what in the end I think the peace team felt and the administration felt.[121]

On 8 July, just a few days prior to Camp David, the peace team placed the Beilin–Abu Mazen Understandings on Clinton's desk, who said, 'This is it. This is simply the whole framework agreement. It is exactly this paper that has to be signed.'[122] Beilin was told that 'Clinton's people wanted to put Beilin–Abu Mazen on the agenda on the first day and see the reactions . . . on the two sides, but their commitment was to co-ordinate everything with us' – under the 'no-surprise rule' – 'which was crazy'. Barak threatened to walk out if any such framework was tabled as a basis for the summit.[123] In internal Israeli consultations, the possibility of making the Beilin–Abu Mazen Understandings the point of reference for the summit agenda had been raised, but clearly not viewed with favour.[124]

Yair Hirschfeld views this as a serious error:

> You know, part of the trouble with the way Barak led the negotiations was that he said from the beginning, 'I will not go on Beilin-Abu Mazen,' which I believe was a major mistake. It destroyed a lot of goodwill and a lot of time. And afterwards, Barak went far beyond Beilin–Abu Mazen. Barak was at the beginning saying I never will go there, and then he went far beyond what we had agreed upon.[125]

This suggests that flaws in strategy were a substantial reason for failure. Barak was willing to make serious concessions, but was unwilling to look like a *freier* – Yiddish for something akin to a 'sucker' – who was ready to concede things up front.[126] Ben-Ami argues that Barak's failure to be more forthcoming about his red lines was his 'major tactical blunder', since they kept changing and only encouraged Arafat to persist and await more concessions.[127]

On the whole, the Americans did not take control of the summit, but let themselves be subordinate to Barak, his plan, and his wishes. In his analysis, Malley identifies the withdrawal of the initial American paper at Camp David as

> the moment where we lost our nerve. We made a mistake. And it was hard to recover from that, because not only did it take away a tool which was critical if you wanted to succeed, but sent the exact wrong message to both sides, who felt that an objection was enough to get us to shift course.[128]

In line with critical American self-assessments, Beilin observes that 'they did it in a really amateurish way'.[129]

Following the outbreak of the *intifada*, Barak again convinced the Americans not to put a plan on the table.[130] When, at the end of December, Clinton finally decided to issue his parameters, they were heavily based on the Beilin–Abu Mazen Understandings. But by this point, the Palestinians saw it as positive progress resulting from the use of violence. Multiple interviewees criticised this move, suggesting that the parameters should have been in place far earlier.[131] Presented when they were, 'the learning curve for Arafat was, I can fight and shoot, and it's OK with the Americans'.[132] When both parties expressed reservations, they were once again removed from the table rather than negotiated and adapted.

Like the Americans, the Swedes too subscribed wholeheartedly to Barak's approach. Commenting on Swedish strategy, Abu Ala writes that 'the Swedes were very cautious, and perhaps felt insufficiently prepared to intervene in highly intricate situations', offering the added observation that the Swedes 'refrained from playing a part comparable to the creative role taken by their Norwegian neighbours'.[133] From the moment he left Israel disheartened in April to the moment he received Yatom's call in May, Nuder had not had any contact whatsoever with the parties. The Swedes were not privy to any of the discussions that led to this new arrangement, nor did they seek any information on the matter. Nuder was determined that the Swedish role was not to extend beyond facilitation, and argued that a more active role would in fact have been counterproductive.[134]

He also extended this reasoning to other third parties. Nuder thought that the Americans were altogether too 'pushy': 'I think it would have been better if the Americans had let Israelis and Palestinians sit on their own in peace and quiet.'[135] Though the government clearly believed that bilateral talks were preferable, they subscribed to Barak's logic and not to the approach espoused by Abu Mazen.

Persson had always been very sceptical of the Stockholm group, the prior Track II efforts sponsored by Sweden. He did not feel that Sweden was making an important contribution to the peace process by sponsoring their work, whose results he deemed peripheral and did not hold in particularly high regard.[136] Nuder has expressed himself more diplomatically and honestly acknowledged Andersson's important contributions, but the basic message remained the same: 'Göran and I thought that the work done in the "Stockholm group" certainly had its merits, but it was always very far from the ruling powers on the Israeli side. There was a bit of wishful thinking about the whole thing.' Yossi Beilin, the Israeli sponsor of the group, was seen as an outstanding and admirable intellectual, but not an 'electable' politician who could assume the highest office.[137]

Together with the Swedish ambassador to Israel, Anders Lidén, they believed that any negotiations had to be elevated to the top political level. The more academic Track II exercise had previously been tried, they reasoned, and it had failed.[138] Rather than spending time producing something that would prove unacceptable to either leader, official negotiators would obviate that risk.

Indeed, Agha believes that

> genuinely, Persson and his team did not understand the Track II significance of this. They looked at it as secret diplomacy. They looked at it as a secret meeting between both officials, between both parties, which is a completely different thing than having a Track II exercise.[139]

Official interaction by its very nature severely limits the flexibility and creativity of discussions when trying to move negotiations forward.

Khalidi points out that

> when you have Shlomo Ben-Ami and Gilead Sher, of course they have to be careful. Whether it's secret or public, it doesn't make any difference. Because after all, you don't actually know what happens in the public talks anyway. So the difference between formal public talks and formal secret talks is very marginal as far as I'm concerned.[140]

Agha also shares this perception, observing that 'officials are officials even if they meet secretly'.[141] Though officials inevitably have to negotiate at a later stage, that point was a distant prospect at the time.

Mossberg laments the fact that the Swedes lent their name, reputation, and resources to a construct that was fatally altered. When he learned how different the channel would be from Abu Mazen's original conception, Mossberg immediately expressed reservations. Both Ross and himself were concerned that Abu Mazen would oppose it, or at least would not help to insulate it or pressure Arafat to take it seriously and protect the fruits of its labour.[142] Mossberg urged Nuder to contact Abu Mazen and inform him of these developments, but Nuder refused.[143] To clear up this uncertainty, Nuder got Persson to ring Arafat, who said that he supported the channel and that Abu Ala would report directly to him.[144]

Mossberg is critical of the government for allowing Abu Mazen's initiative to be turned on its head. He argues that they violated a primary rule in any negotiation, which is that each side must be allowed to nominate its own participants without one side dictating terms to the other. In effect, like the Americans, they allowed their sympathies for Barak to cloud their judgement and unquestioningly subscribed to his demands of the Palestinian side.[145] Though the Palestinians did in fact eventually nominate their own participants, this can legitimately be viewed as a reaction to Barak's diktat when few alternatives existed.

Though they enjoyed excellent relations, the Swedes certainly did not have the requisite influence over Barak to change his mind. When the parties had agreed among themselves to send negotiators, who were the Swedes to tell them, 'No'? As Khalidi admits, 'to be fair to the Swedes, it's true there were mixed signals coming out of the Palestinian side.'[146] Still, the Swedes could have thought a bit more creatively about how to set up the kind of channel that Abu Mazen had in mind. As for the Israelis, Barak could have sent his chosen officials to interface with Agha and Khalidi in an inverse reincarnation of the origins of the Oslo channel. Since Arafat had years earlier accepted the Stockholm document as a basis for further negotiations, the two academics clearly represented positions well aligned with the Palestinian leadership.

As it happened, Abu Mazen became completely disenfranchised, an error that suggests that both the Israelis and Swedes appeared to be operating on a faulty analysis of the power structures within the PLO. Abu Mazen was number two after Arafat within the hierarchy, and Mossberg was convinced that 'he had to be involved in one way or another, but we created a channel that did not involve him, and that was not good'.[147] Agha remembers that when he was contacted by Abu Ala to participate in the Stockholm channel,

> that was the moment when I knew that Camp David had no chance of success, because people did not realise – the Israelis, I don't know how they didn't realise – that the whole file of final status issues and resolution of final status issues has been in the hands of Abu Mazen since the mid-70's ... When other people were imposed on him, he went cold, which means that you cannot resolve it, because Abu Ammar is not well versed in the final status issues ... He relies on Abu Mazen, and if Abu Mazen is out of the picture, then you cannot have a final deal with the Palestinians. You really just cannot. It's like knocking on the wrong door, reaching for the wrong address.[148]

As feared, from thereon, Abu Mazen did not seem particularly interested or engaged in the negotiations.[149] Khalidi explains that this unenthusiastic posture 'was very very crucial, because Arafat was not going to do anything at Camp David or anywhere else without a clear sense that he was backed, supported, and fully embraced by Abu Mazen'.[150]

Mossberg's criticism reflects the vast schism within the Social Democratic party. Sten Andersson, the Swedish head of the Stockholm group, had a very antagonistic relationship with Persson, mainly due to their serious disagreement on Middle East policy. He considered Persson a cynical, self-serving politician who had no place in the party.[151] Nuder observes that Persson inspired a blend of fear and admiration; he was respected but not particularly popular, and for many 'a necessary evil but no more than that'.[152] Many within the party had always questioned his leadership, and there was a strong sense that he had usurped a position meant for Nygren or Sahlin. From the many conversations they had throughout this period, Khalidi recalls that Andersson thought Persson was leading the party down a reactionary line. 'Sten was a progressive in the old sense, and I think he felt this was a real betrayal of the Labour party and social democracy as he understood it, and the heritage that he had fought for' from the Palme era.[153]

In preparation for a meeting of the Stockholm group in December 2000, Andersson made a few pages of notes that are illuminating. He wrote,

> I tried to use everything I had learnt as the Secretary General of the Party to convince the Prime Minister to accept what Abu Mazen

> suggested in December 1999 to revive the peace process. It took more than four months. And then the Prime Minister put me and the Foreign Office aside – so eager to please Barak and the Americans ...

He argues that the decision not to act on Abu Mazen's offer sooner was one of the reasons for the collapse and failure of Camp David: 'There was a need for more time and a slower process, giving the Palestinian leadership a chance to stick together behind compromises' rather than sow division among each other as they did during the negotiating process.

Andersson was also convinced that Persson's refusal to include him in any aspect of the initiative, 'to have all the game in his own hand', was because he wanted 'all the [lime]light and all the honour'. He believed Persson looked upon the Stockholm group 'as some sort of competitor, despite the fact that we are all playing on the same team'.[154] Given their basic disagreement with Abu Mazen's original strategy, not to mention Agha and Khalidi's status as 'Sten's Palestinians', it is difficult to imagine that the Prime Minister's office effectively lobbied Barak for their inclusion. Agha certainly got the impression that Persson 'did not want to include Sten's crowd in it, and we were associated with Sten, so we fell by the by because of that'.[155] Andersson also suggested that Mossberg had been forbidden to attend meetings of the Stockholm group, as he was working with Persson at the time.

Apart from Mossberg, Persson excluded Andersson and his likeminded associates from his policy-making circle. This was a fundamental error, which meant that the traditional trust Sweden enjoyed with the Palestinians was mismanaged and, to a certain degree, squandered. Andersson's experience was unparalleled. Through decades of work, he had built a repository of trust, respect and friendship with Arafat unlike any other European. The government appears to have misunderstood that while the Social Democratic party certainly had a great deal of credit with the Palestinians, Andersson in particular was the key to this. In addition to Andersson, Sweden had an abundance of other diplomats and Social Democrats with extensive experience in the Middle East. Rather than using them, Persson relied on envoys who were not ideal interlocutors. Though thankful for the continued contacts, the Palestinians did not feel that they had particularly good rapport with Persson's government.[156]

Differences felt by the two Swedish diplomatic missions in Jerusalem and Tel Aviv also mirror this discrepancy. Lidén says that in Tel Aviv he was kept well informed of his government's plans throughout this period, and that he 'had absolutely nothing to complain about' in this regard.[157] Consul General Catharina Kipp in Jerusalem, on the other hand, did not feel that the government kept her in the loop.[158] Contacts with Tel Aviv generally appear to have been greater than those with Jerusalem, and reflected the recalibration of Swedish relations in the Middle East.

During the UN Millennium Assembly in New York held on 7–8 September 2000, Persson met first with Arafat and then Barak to ascertain where the peace process stood. These were very illustrative of the Swedish approach to the two sides. Pierre Schori, then the Swedish ambassador to the UN and an adherent to the Palme tradition, thought that the meeting with Arafat was 'a big failure'. He thought Persson's discussion with Arafat showed poor knowledge of the issues and a lack of finesse in communicating with the Arab world.[159] Schori's report to Stockholm suggests that they mainly spoke about Jerusalem and the Palestinian view on the progress made at Camp David, with Persson finally emphasising to Arafat that this was a 'golden opportunity which might not last much longer'.[160] Though Schori certainly has a point, more important to note is the fact that this meeting was completely redundant. Nabil Shaath had already presented these views to Foreign Minister Lindh and John Hagard in Sweden on 12 August.[161]

Unlike Arafat, Barak was embraced warmly. Persson shared his impressions of Arafat from the day before. Although Arafat and Shaath repeatedly said the Palestinians were willing to restart negotiations under American mediation within a few days, Persson treated them with scepticism and judged that they were nevertheless not in a hurry to proceed. He said that Arafat and Shaath had been on an international public relations trip immediately after Camp David that had been 'successful', and had spread their version more effectively than the Israelis. Persson advised Barak that 'Israel should look to intensify its diplomatic efforts and better convey its position.' Towards the end of their exchange, Barak highlighted the importance of imbuing Arafat, Abu Mazen, and Abu Ala with a sense of responsibility for the negotiations and the future. The fear was that some European countries, upset at having been kept out of the process, may not adequately pressure Arafat to continue, but send him mixed signals.[162]

Andersson had sent a letter to Arafat on 9 August, where he congratulated the Palestinian leader on his 'political success' at Camp David. Although many had criticised Arafat's behaviour, it was Andersson's 'conviction that you have strengthened the Palestinian negotiating position and thereby paved the way for a continued negotiation ...' It was no doubt this type of language that Barak and Persson sought to avoid. Still, Andersson clearly emphasised that Israeli concessions constituted 'a very big step' and that time was short, with the favourable political conditions for a just settlement due to 'evaporate or even disappear' over the next few months. He urged Arafat to prepare for further talks, reminded him that a successful conclusion was 'in your hands', and empowered him with references to confidence in his 'wise statesmanship'.[163] Andersson thus tried to appeal to Arafat's particular mindset. Khalidi notes that 'not every Western leader managed to find the right chemistry with him, and I think Sten did. He kind of understood him.'[164]

Unhappy with Persson's meeting with Arafat, Schori raised the matter with Nuder, and urged him to speak with the Prime Minister about the possibility of sending Andersson to Gaza to meet with Arafat. On the Swedish side, he was the only one who could affect Arafat's thinking. In November, instead of sending Andersson, Persson dispatched Nuder and Hans Dahlgren, State Secretary for Foreign Affairs, two men who had no particular standing among the Palestinians. This trip prompted certain unnamed Palestinians to call Mossberg and plead, 'Can't you stop this amateurish bungling? They are causing us a hell of a lot of problems!'[165]

At a meeting of the Stockholm group in December, Israeli participants Yair Hirschfeld and Ron Pundak mentioned that their government – in all likelihood Minister of Justice Beilin – had also contacted Nuder and requested that Andersson be sent to speak with Arafat. Nuder apparently answered positively, but this Israeli request was seemingly never conveyed to Andersson.[166] In the words of Schori, Persson 'did not want to bet on horses that he himself did not own', and at a crucial juncture, this detracted from the potential effectiveness of the Swedish message of moderation to the Palestinians.[167]

On his travels with Arafat following Camp David, Shaath got the impression that 'among the Europeans there is a sense of frustration that the United States will not let them do anything and so there is a feeling of impotence. They are not very confident that they can do much.'[168] This was certainly reflected by the French, who then held the rotating presidency of the EU. On 4 October, Albright and the Americans were in Paris trying to curb the violence of the second *intifada* and agree a common basis for negotiations. Albright recognised that 'there was a risk in having it in France ... because the question was what was the French role in all of this'.[169]

Contrary to an agreement with Albright, French President Jacques Chirac got involved in the substance of the talks, backed Arafat's demand for an international commission of inquiry into the beginning of the second *intifada*, and insisted on hosting a private meeting with Arafat. As far as Albright was concerned, this let Arafat off the hook:

> I said to Chirac ... we are about to initial this document [later signed at Sharm el-Sheikh on 18 October], can you make sure that Arafat comes back to do this, that he doesn't use [the meeting] as a way not to come back, and he said, 'Yes, yes, I will do that,' and then of course clearly he didn't.[170]

Sweden stood next in line to take over the rotating EU presidency on 1 January 2000, and this responsibility had informed the government's long-term thinking ever since their initial dialogue with Barak in early 1999. Cognisant of this, and appreciative of their modified stance, following Camp David Ben-Ami told a Swedish diplomat in Tel Aviv that 'we very much want you to remain in the picture', while Palestinians too continued to regularly stress that Sweden and the EU could play an important role.[171]

It became clear, however, that the Swedes would be more attuned to the American and Israeli line than the French. On 20 October, the General Assembly voted on a resolution that condemned the disproportionate force used by the IDF against Palestinian civilians. While France and eight other EU member states voted in favour, Sweden and five others, including the United Kingdom, chose to abstain. Schori was not present for the vote, so the deputy chief of mission Per Norström rang the Prime Minister's office in Stockholm, where state secretary Lars Danielsson told him to abstain. Norström expressed regret that the EU had not been able to agree, and explained that Sweden did not consider the resolution a constructive addition to the peace process.[172] This was a concrete example of Persson's conviction that Sweden should cease to isolate Israel internationally, which he thought they had been doing for far too long.[173]

With the Clinton administration a thing of the past, the EU was free to adopt a more prominent position. At the last-ditch Taba talks in January, EU special envoy Miguel Moratinos was the most senior foreign representative, but most of his discussions with the parties were unofficial and, unlike his American colleagues, he was not present in the negotiating room. The EU still lacked the political clout to play any other role, certainly one unpalatable to Israel.

The sponsoring of bilateral talks was entirely in line with Swedish facilitative policy, but at such a late stage, the context was immensely unfavourable and success unlikely. Although he considers it an honest and serious attempt, Nuder acknowledges that Taba was more or less doomed to fail.[174] Lipkin-Shahak, Sher and others 'realised that there was no realistic chance of reaching an agreement at Taba, but felt that there was no reason not to pursue dialogue right up to the elections'.[175] Sher confided to Erekat that an agreement was not possible given the upcoming Israeli elections and the status of Barak's minority government, and that a mutual declaration by Arafat and Barak was the best they could hope for.[176]

Stockholm was the planned site of a crowning ceremony for any agreement reached at Taba – scheduled for 30 January/1 February – a natural choice as the capital of the EU presidency and a prominent history of prior involvement in the peace process. Lindh expressed reservations about holding the summit for fear of being seen to interfere in the upcoming Israeli elections, but the matter soon became purely academic. After Arafat's controversial speech at the World Economic Forum in Davos where he railed against Israel's 'barbaric', 'ugly', and 'fascist' aggression against the Palestinians,[177] it became clear that no such summit would take place. Still, Sweden had been ready to serve and made the necessary preparations should it have been needed.[178]

Though Persson denies fundamentally altering Swedish policy on the conflict, the UN vote did exactly that. Ultimately, Persson was the elected head of state with a mandate to depart from previously accepted policy if he so wished. Still, without specifically referring to the UN vote, he has since admitted that he may sometimes have gone too far in his defence of Israel.[179] This was certainly the feeling among the

Andersson camp. Andersson wrote in a letter to Arafat dated 14 December that he felt 'ashamed' of the Swedish failure to condemn the 'insane' Israeli violence in the UN. He did not consider it compliant with long-established Swedish policy or the tenets of international law upon which it is based.[180] Mossberg remembers that he met Lindh in the lobby of the Foreign Ministry one evening soon after the vote: 'We saw each other, and we didn't say anything. She stopped, and I stopped ... We stood there for five, ten seconds almost, and then finally she said, "Yes, it's fucking outrageous." And then she left.' Although she had very strong personal views on the subject, Lindh vocalised them selectively. She valued her future political ambitions too highly to jeopardise them, and chose not to make an issue of the matter.[181]

Andersson was similarly incensed, but did not hold back. In a thinly veiled jab at the Persson government during a speech at the OPIC in November, he emphasised that mediation needed to take account of history, and that it required a convergence of diplomatic competence – 'abundant at the Foreign Ministry' – and political intelligence and experience – 'a somewhat rarer commodity'.[182] In 2001, the situation escalated dramatically as the conflict between Andersson and Persson became increasingly public. On 28 May, Persson and a number of other EU heads of state were due to meet Arafat at the Hilton in Copenhagen. As they went to meet Arafat they bumped into Andersson in the lobby, who had already had a long meeting with the Palestinian leader himself without informing the government. Arafat had invited him, an invitation that Andersson said he would have declined had Beilin not requested his help in an urgent but as yet unknown matter.[183]

Persson was furious, and understandably so. Although Andersson's status as envoy had not been formally revoked, a number of restrictions on information led him to understand that his mission had more or less ended shortly before the Harpsund meetings, as the Prime Minister's office assumed control of the process. In July Andersson wrote a scathing eight-page letter to the Social Democratic Party executive where he attacked Persson's Middle East policy and conduct in the peace process. Continued silence on the matter, he concluded, was no longer an expression of loyalty but cowardice.[184] 'I am even prepared', he later said, 'to go so far as to say that had Swedish actions been different, there could have been peace in the region by now. That is why I am so upset.'[185]

To suggest that Swedish policy constituted the difference between peace and continued conflict is a gross exaggeration of Swedish capacity and influence.[186] However, the strategy favoured by Abu Mazen and the Stockholm group constitutes an interesting alternative, which could have produced better results. It could have averted many of the crucial difficulties, particularly on the Palestinian side. A framework agreement guiding permanent status, like the Beilin–Abu Mazen Understandings, would have made Abu Mazen a key strategic partner with the political strength to unite the Palestinian elite, as he had done during Oslo.[187] As it was executed, the Stockholm channel only contributed to what Miller describes as the 'mad rush towards disaster'.[188]

Rejected by Barak and certainly not favoured by Persson, this alternative strategy has not been accorded the significance it ought to. The short time frame which resulted from American, Israeli and Swedish errors did not lend itself to the longer term process that a Track II initiative normally requires. An alternative time frame posited by Khalidi would have been preferable:

> if you had six months or so from December 1999 – say January 2000 until June 2000 – of serious back track engagement, building on the first Stockholm channel, with proper inputs into the leadership on both sides, with sponsorship by Abu Mazen and someone equivalent on the Israeli side, I think things would have been completely different at Camp David.[189]

When Camp David failed and the parties tried to salvage the process, the inclusion of Andersson in the proceedings could have encouraged a more moderate and compromising stance from Arafat. There is of course no guarantee that Andersson would have affected Arafat's behaviour, but Persson refused even to try to capitalise on that relationship. It is likely that personal differences factored strongly, and that 'Persson didn't want to give Sten space for any kind of political victory.'[190]

Moreover, Persson criticised Andersson for previously having used Middle East diplomacy for domestic political purposes,[191] which he certainly had done; but Persson was no different. Not only did he exaggerate the success of Harpsund, but he invited Abu Ala and Shimon Peres to speak at the Social Democratic Party congress in November 2001, where they both heaped praise upon the government's most recent sponsorship of negotiations.[192] Both Andersson and Persson were full-blooded career politicians, interested in building prestige, and as their dispute became public in mid-2001, they each sought to score points at the others expense.

The schism that emerged between Persson and Andersson, and more widely between the Prime Minister's office and the Foreign Ministry, had a detrimental effect on the Swedish contribution to the peace process. Had these two Social Democratic camps been able to work together, the Swedish role could potentially have been much more responsive to the needs of both sides and found an alternative workable strategy. A facilitative or even formulative strategy was appropriate, but the formal format was not.

CONCLUSIONS

Sometimes diplomatic talks, like mushrooms, grow better in the dark.
– Madeleine Albright[1]

In an interview with journalist Eric Fichtelius in 2004, Swedish Prime Minister Göran Persson clearly stated his belief that Sweden had not played a role in the peace process prior to the talks held at Harpsund in May 2000.[2] This assertion is completely disconnected from reality, and evinces a truly meagre historical knowledge of the peace process and Swedish diplomacy. He also suggests that the Norwegian Social Democrats maintained 'a more balanced position' on the conflict, and that this was why a peace accord was struck in Oslo. Sweden could not play this role because it was perceived as biased in favour of the Palestinians.[3] Although the latter point has some merit, the overall analysis of events is fundamentally misguided. The hollowness of Persson's argument only gives credence to charges of foreign policy amateurism and cynical political opportunism levelled against him by former Foreign Minister Sten Andersson and substantial segments of the Social Democratic party.

First, Persson completely ignores the history of Swedish involvement. The Social Democrats, spearheaded by Olof Palme, had for two decades prior to the Oslo Agreement argued in favour of dialogue to advance peace. They championed a normative approach to the conflict and its resolution in the form of a two-state solution, which undeniably helped set the tone for the future peace process. Palme's legacy was then carried on by Andersson and his 'quiet diplomacy'.

As this book has shown, the Oslo Agreement was made possible because of this 'quiet diplomacy', which helped moderate the PLO and brought Arafat into the legitimate international fold. The Swedes had thus already played a significant and unique role in the peace process, which they then tried to build on, but despite their efforts, they could not initiate relations between Israel and the PLO. Though Sweden had long been out of favour with the right-wing Likud leadership, Israeli attitudes were nowhere near as uniformly negative as Persson suggests. Contact was maintained with the Israeli left-wing opposition who saw value in a continued Swedish role. It was then rendered impossible in late 1991 by the new conservative coalition government whose foreign policy was focused on Europe, not the Middle East.

Second, Persson's analysis and understanding of the Oslo channel is extremely simplistic, if not completely mistaken. The key to the success of Oslo is not to be found in nuances of Norwegian foreign policy, but in Terje Rød-Larsen. Larsen's analysis of the conflict context in 1992 and the weaknesses of the official negotiations was exactly right, and he was in a position to offer a superior alternative. Though each party's perception of the government probably became more of a factor as Foreign Minister Johan Jørgen Holst became increasingly involved, Larsen was the initiator of the channel and the linchpin throughout the negotiations. The initial choice of facilitative strategy was both necessary and highly successful, which then developed into a more formulative approach. Moreover, Israel and the PLO were each facing their own internal pressures, which made an agreement necessary for them.

Third, Persson fails to appreciate the importance of the Stockholm group formed in late 1994. Their efforts built on the well-established Swedish principle concerning the importance of dialogue and the successful model of negotiation developed in Norway. They adapted it to create a pure Track II scenario, a strategy that was highly suitable for the stipulated task, which was to get the parties to explore creative solutions to sensitive final status issues and prepare the ground for official negotiations. Though the onset of Swedish sponsorship was fortuitous, they proved to be perfect for the role. This important contribution fell victim to political pressure when Peres felt unable to adopt the fruits of their labour.[4]

In his dismissal of the work of Andersson and the Stockholm group, Persson approaches the notion of success in highly absolute terms. In a conflict where the ultimate failure of mediation has become the norm, this is a dangerous perspective. Though a failure in the sense that the Beilin–Abu Mazen Understandings – or the Stockholm document, as its Palestinian authors prefer to call it – have never been formally adopted, they have constituted the benchmark for thinking about final status and have informed all negotiations on the matter since. Contrary to the old adage, the devil is not in the detail but in the principles.[5] This pragmatic thinking on the main principles and parameters of a durable permanent status agreement was ground-breaking. To dub the entire enterprise a complete failure would be to deny progress made and to ignore a significant intellectual development.[6]

In fact, contrary to Persson's analysis, of all the instances of Swedish involvement, the two meetings of the 'Stockholm channel' at Harpsund probably had the least positive impact on the peace process. Modest progress was achieved, but the channel fell prey to the conflict context and was part of Barak's erroneous strategy, which the Swedish government subscribed to. Although the Swedish facilitative strategy appears sound at first glance, a Track II approach akin to that of the Stockholm group a few years earlier would have been preferable. One can even go so far as to say that the Stockholm channel had an overtly negative impact in that it exacerbated fragmentation within the Palestinian political elite and disenfranchised Abu Mazen. There is no doubt that Arafat's leadership style was central to this problem, but Israeli sensitivity to the domestic politics of their negotiating partners would have been beneficial. By the time Barak grasped the centrality of Abu Mazen and the need to help foster unity within the PLO leadership, it was too late.

As this book has demonstrated, Track II strategies and secret back channels have been a very important element of the Israeli–Palestinian peace process, but this reality underlines an inherent and problematic catch-22. Secrecy is vital to negotiations, since specific information about planned concessions can open the door for spoilers to sabotage any chances of success. Simultaneously, the general populace must be supportive of the compromises necessary for peace. Any permanent status agreement will need public support on both sides in order to stand the test of time, because while politicians can sit down and forge agreements, the citizens they represent are the ones who must make it work.

Hassassian notes the importance of this aspect, observing that 'what is required is the establishment in parallel to the ongoing political negotiations of a process of mutual conversion of interests based on the dramatic changes of stereotyped images which have been built up cumulatively in this deep historical conflict ...'[7] Mutual satisfaction with any agreement is crucial, but divergent notions of a 'fair' and 'just' peace are extremely difficult to reconcile.[8] Each society must be ready to make the concessions that a permanent peace requires, work to minimise the effect of spoilers, and honour agreed understandings in spirit and practice, something that has been glaringly absent thus far. Neither side has adequately prepared their people for peace, nor realistically addressed the requisite compromises.

Dennis Ross summarises the attitude rather well: 'For Arab leaders ... peace with Israel is a favour, not a necessity; peace is the absence of war, not reconciliation with a former enemy.'[9] However, this arguably also applies to Israeli leaders who seem confident maintaining the harmful status quo of occupation. For Israelis and Palestinians to live in peace, their two exclusivist identities must be replaced with transcendent identities based on co-existence. They must recognise not only the legitimacy of the other, but that the only way for each party to survive, feel secure, develop, and prosper as a people is for the other to do the same.[10] Unless these societies start reflecting such a mutual understanding, genuine peace is a distant hope.

Extended dialogue between the parties, not only at a political level but particularly at a sub-elite and grassroots level, is thus vital. Kriesberg argues that mediation of such dialogue 'can help in preparing the adversaries for taking de-escalating steps, making agreements, and implementing them', particularly in such a protracted conflict context.[11] A multitude of small states, including Norway and Sweden, sponsored such activities during the Oslo process, but they had a very limited impact.[12] Ultimately, it is difficult to maintain such dialogue while violence is ongoing, as familiar patterns of conflict are easily reverted to.

As the case studies examined in this book demonstrate, the success or failure of mediation is about much more than just a negative conflict context. Mediators are often undone by their own errors of judgement, particularly in the realm of strategy. The process begun at Madrid was eventually rescued by Oslo where the United States was not involved. At the official Washington talks parallel to Oslo, the 'problem for the

Americans was that while their power and influence had been essential to persuading, and even strong-arming, the parties to the table, that very power and influence stood in the way of settling the dispute'.[13]

The facilitative strategy traditionally adopted by Norway and Sweden, however, was generally sound, particularly given the nature of the conflict. Mutual acceptance and understanding is not something that can be obtained through the carrot and stick approach or forms of coercion.[14] Fundamental identity elements cannot be reduced to bargaining chips, nor can outsiders force these decisions upon them; consensus must develop largely from within. A facilitative strategy, as practised by small states and that can operate on multiple levels, seeks to enhance the ability to do so.[15]

By contrast, a powerful state like the United States has a different role to play. Haass suggests that 'as a rule the United States would be wise to lower its sights and work to build confidence between the parties, so that with time more ambitious diplomacy might succeed and in the meantime conflicts not erupt'.[16] This confidence building should not, however, translate into a more limited facilitative US role at the negotiating table. As Princen observes, 'the degree to which the United States can foster communication and trust – between itself and each of the parties and between the two parties – is highly constrained by the structural relationship between the third party and the disputants'.[17] Their presence at the negotiating table has the potential to negatively affect dynamics and distract from the task at hand. In the context of Israel's negotiations with Syria, Israeli negotiator Uri Savir argued in favour of bilateral rather than trilateral talks:

> To help make my case, I told him a story that I had heard from [Israeli Prime Minister Shimon] Peres. A young man, it went, fell hopelessly in love with a young lady but was too shy to profess his passion to her directly. So every day he sent her a love letter. The result was that, after a year, the woman married the mailman. [Syrian Foreign Minister Walid al-] Moualem laughed, and I asked him to tell the story to Assad. I doubt that he did or that he thought it was necessary, for Damascus was truly less interested in its Israeli 'suitor' than in the American 'mailman'.[18]

At Israel's request, the United States stayed out of the implementation process. Aaron Miller observes that they let themselves be 'relegated to an important but derivative role as caterer, cash man, and crisis manager', and that they were 'not in a position to change the contours of the Israeli–Palestinian peacemaking process'.[19] The Oslo process was not their breakthrough, and they were reluctant to impose themselves on the process. Eventually, the United States adopted the role of an active mediator to keep the negotiations alive, but though they successfully negotiated the Hebron, Wye River, and Sharm el-Sheikh agreements, they remained unable to effectively wield their unique coercive power. As a guarantor, US credibility was severely dented when these agreements were not fully implemented. Crucial to the building of accountability, confidence, and trust is the implementation and enforcement of agreements reached. As the world superpower, this is where the United States has a significant role to play. With the benefit of hindsight, accountability and implementation should have been the main focus, even if it meant taking issue with the Israeli Prime Minister.

Together with the international community, they will also be required to contribute billions of dollars to the implementation process – loans, security guarantees, refugee compensation, and so on. Their presence at the negotiating table, however, should be minimal. Yossi Beilin shares this view:

> We don't need a third party to suggest ideas to us, what we need is facilities, what we need is money, what we need is the big money for the solution, for the refugees, for the settlers ... so we cannot dismiss the importance of a third party. But not in the point of finding solutions for us.[20]

The cases examined here suggest that in accordance with Beardsley's statistical analysis of mediation strategies and the arguments of multiple other scholars,[21] a variety of third party mediators will be required to play a number of different roles if an agreement is to be reached. Small states can discreetly work with representatives of each party and support the negotiating process. Additionally, they can finance and sponsor grassroots, bottom-up peacebuilding initiatives. Anything above and beyond that is likely to fall beyond their remit.

When the time comes to close on a final agreement, a manipulative mediator who uses their political and economic leverage effectively will be required. Currently, only the United States – supported by rest of the Quartet – can realistically fulfil this role of midwife. Arab states like Egypt, Jordan and Saudi Arabia can also play an important role by politically supporting the negotiating Palestinian leadership, and incentivising peace for Israel through regional normalisation as envisaged in the neglected Arab Peace Initiative of 2002.[22] The marginalisation of these regional actors by the Americans at Camp David in 2000 was a significant error, and one that should not be repeated.[23]

A division of labour along those lines can be very promising, but everyone still needs to be singing from the same hymn sheet. The rifts and personal prestige issues in the Norwegian and Swedish teams during their respective secret channels are smaller scale examples of this dynamic. These tensions only become more loaded when raised onto an international level. The more mediators you have, the greater the likelihood of conflicting interests, perceptions, positions, and objectives, and the more complex the interconnections among all the parties concerned.[24] Crocker *et al.* observe that

> when more than one mediator is involved in a conflict, there is clearly a need to not only time and sequence interventions so that the right mix of skills and resources is being brought to bear on the parties to the conflict, but also to ensure that interventions by different parties are pursued consistently and coherently over time in order to move the parties to an agreement.[25]

Rob Malley also warns that any future American administration is going to want to have a degree of control, ownership and influence over the process, but it is unclear how this will manifest itself.[26] Dan Kurtzer observes that it will naturally depend on the individuals involved, but both seem positive about the idea despite the challenges involved. 'My view has always been that the tent is big enough for everybody who wants to make it work. And there's certainly enough to do.'[27]

APPENDICES

Appendix I. The Stockholm Document, Prepared on 23 November 1988[1]

The Swedish Foreign Minister Mr. Sten Andersson invited to Stockholm the following representatives of the PLO as well as the following American Jewish personalities, who met together on 21 November, 1988:

Mr. Khaled al-Hassan
Mr. Hisham Mustapha
Mr. Afif Safieh
Mr. Eugene Makhlouf
Mrs. Rita E. Hauser
Mr. Stanley K. Sheinbaum
Ms. Drora Kass

The first meeting was opened by Mr. Sten Andersson and all meetings were attended by Swedish Foreign Ministry officials.

The Palestinian National Council met in Algiers from November 12 to 15, 1988, and announced the Declaration of Independence which proclaimed the State of Palestine and issued a Political Statement.

The following explanation was given by the representatives of the PLO of certain important points in the Palestinian Declaration of Independence and the Political Statement adopted by the PNC in Algiers. The PNC:

1. Agree to enter into peace negotiations at an international conference under the auspices of the UN with the participation of the permanent members of the Security Council and the PLO as the sole legitimate representative of the Palestinian people, on an equal footing with the other parties to the conflict; such an international conference is to be held on the basis of UN resolutions 242 and 338 and the right of the Palestinian people to self-determination, without external interference, as provided in the UN Charter, including the right to an independent state, which conference should resolve the Palestinian problem in all its aspects;
2. Accepted the existence of Israel as a state in the region;
3. Declared its rejection and condemnation of terrorism in all its forms, including state terrorism;
4. Called for a solution to the Palestinian refugee problem in accordance with international law and practices and relevant UN resolutions (including right of return or compensation).

The American personalities strongly supported and applauded the Palestinian Declaration of Independence and the Political Statement adopted in Algiers and felt there was no further impediment to a direct dialogue between the United States Government and the PLO.

Appendix II. Annexes III and IV of the Declaration of Principles (DoP), the Oslo Agreement, signed on 13 September 1993

Annex III. Protocol on Israeli–Palestinian Cooperation in Economic and Development Programs

The two sides agree to establish an Israeli–Palestinian continuing Committee for Economic Cooperation, focusing, among other things, on the following:

1. Cooperation in the field of water, including a Water Development Program prepared by experts from both sides, which will also specify the mode of cooperation in the management of water resources in the West Bank and Gaza Strip, and will include proposals for studies and plans on water rights of each party, as well as on the equitable utilization of joint water resources for implementation in and beyond the interim period.
2. Cooperation in the field of electricity, including an Electricity Development Program, which will also specify the mode of cooperation for the production, maintenance, purchase and sale of electricity resources.
3. Cooperation in the field of energy, including an Energy Development Program, which will provide for the exploitation of oil and gas for industrial purposes, particularly in the Gaza Strip and in the Negev, and will encourage further joint exploitation of other energy resources. This Program may also provide for the construction of a Petrochemical industrial complex in the Gaza Strip and the construction of oil and gas pipelines.
4. Cooperation in the field of finance, including a Financial Development and Action Program for the encouragement of international investment in the West Bank and the Gaza Strip, and in Israel, as well as the establishment of a Palestinian Development Bank.
5. Cooperation in the field of transport and communications, including a Program, which will define guidelines for the establishment of a Gaza Sea Port Area, and will provide for the establishing of transport and communications lines to and from the West Bank and the Gaza Strip to Israel and to other countries.

In addition, this Program will provide for carrying out the necessary construction of roads, railways, communications lines, etc.

6. Cooperation in the field of trade, including studies, and Trade Promotion Programs, which will encourage local, regional and inter-regional trade, as well as a feasibility study of creating free trade zones in the Gaza Strip and in Israel, mutual access to these zones, and cooperation in other areas related to trade and commerce.
7. Cooperation in the field of industry, including Industrial Development Programs, which will provide for the establishment of joint Israeli–Palestinian Industrial Research and Development Centers, will promote Palestinian–Israeli joint ventures, and provide guidelines for cooperation in the textile, food, pharmaceutical, electronics, diamonds, computer and science-based industries.
8. A program for cooperation in, and regulation of, labor relations and cooperation in social welfare issues.
9. A Human Resources Development and Cooperation Plan, providing for joint Israeli–Palestinian workshops and seminars, and for the establishment of joint vocational training centers, research institutes and data banks.
10. An Environmental Protection Plan, providing for joint and/or coordinated measures in this sphere.
11. A program for developing coordination and cooperation in the field of communication and media.
12. Any other programs of mutual interest.

Annex IV. Protocol on Israeli–Palestinian Cooperation Concerning Regional Development Programs

1. The two sides will cooperate in the context of the multilateral peace efforts in promoting a Development Program for the region, including the West Bank and the Gaza Strip, to be initiated by the G-7. The parties will request the G-7 to seek the participation in this program of other interested states, such as members of the Organisation for Economic Cooperation and Development, regional Arab states and institutions, as well as members of the private sector.
2. The Development Program will consist of two elements:
   a. an Economic Development Program for the West Bank and the Gaza Strip.

b. a Regional Economic Development Program.

c. The Economic Development Program for the West Bank and the Gaza strip will consist of the following elements:

    1. A Social Rehabilitation Program, including a Housing and Construction Program.
    2. A Small and Medium Business Development Plan.
    3. An Infrastructure Development Program (water, electricity, transportation and communications, etc.)
    4. A Human Resources Plan.
    5. Other programs.

d. The Regional Economic Development Program may consist of the following elements:

    1. The establishment of a Middle East Development Fund, as a first step, and a Middle East Development Bank, as a second step.
    2. The development of a joint Israeli–Palestinian–Jordanian Plan for coordinated exploitation of the Dead Sea area.
    3. The Mediterranean Sea (Gaza) – Dead Sea Canal.
    4. Regional Desalinization and other water development projects.
    5. A regional plan for agricultural development, including a coordinated regional effort for the prevention of desertification.
    6. Interconnection of electricity grids.
    7. Regional cooperation for the transfer, distribution and industrial exploitation of gas, oil and other energy resources.
    8. A Regional Tourism, Transportation and Telecommunications Development Plan.
    9. Regional cooperation in other spheres.

3. The two sides will encourage the multilateral working groups, and will coordinate towards their success. The two parties will encourage intersessional activities, as well as pre-feasibility and feasibility studies, within the various multilateral working groups.

Appendix III. Articles VII and VIII of Annex VI – the Protocol Concerning Israeli–Palestinian Co-operation Programs – of the Interim Agreement, 28 September 1995

Article VII. Cultural and Educational Cooperation

1. Cultural Cooperation
   The two sides shall promote cultural cooperation and encourage the development of cooperation between their institutions or organizations in the fields of art, music, theater, literature, literary translations, publishing, cinema and film-making.
2. Media and Communication
   The two sides shall promote and encourage direct cooperation between news agencies, newspapers, and radio and television stations. In addition, the two sides will cooperate with third countries in order to promote the exposure of the benefits of the peace process to the respective societies.
3. Educational Cooperation
   a. The two sides shall promote cooperation by encouraging and facilitating exchanges in the field of education and by providing appropriate conditions for direct contacts between schools and educational institutions of both sides.
   b. The two sides shall cooperate with the aim of raising the level of general education and professional training of their respective populations taking into consideration priorities to be determined by each side.
   c. The cooperation shall focus, in particular, on the following areas:
      1. cooperation among educational/training institutions;
      2. exchanges of information between universities;
      3. language training; and
      4. other ways of promoting better mutual understanding of their respective cultures.
4. Sports and Youth
   a. The two sides shall encourage cooperation in sports and physical culture, especially through the exchange of sports delegations and teams, as well as through the organizing of sports meetings and games.

b. The two sides shall encourage contacts and exchanges between youth organizations and shall promote exchanges of high school and university students.

Article VIII. The People-To-People Program

1. The two sides shall cooperate in enhancing the dialogue and relations between their peoples in accordance with the concepts developed in cooperation with the Kingdom of Norway.
2. The two sides shall cooperate in enhancing dialogue and relations between their peoples, as well as in gaining a wider exposure of the two publics to the peace process, its current situation and predicted results.
3. The two sides shall take steps to foster public debate and involvement, to remove barriers to interaction, and to increase the people to people exchange and interaction within all areas of cooperation described in this Annex and in accordance with the overall objectives and principles set out in this Annex.

Appendix IV. 'The Beilin-Abu Mazen Understandings' or 'The Stockholm Document', 31 October 1995[2]

Framework for the conclusion of a final status agreement between Israel and the Palestine Liberation Organization.

THE ATTAINMENT OF PEACE BETWEEN THE ISRAELI AND THE PALESTINIAN PEOPLES RESOLVES THE CORE PROBLEM AT THE HEART OF THE ISRAELI–ARAB CONFLICT AND COMMENCES AN ERA OF COMPREHENSIVE PEACE CONTRIBUTING THEREBY TO THE STABILITY, SECURITY, AND PROSPERITY OF THE ENTIRE MIDDLE EAST.

The Government of the State of Israel and the Palestine Liberation Organization (hereafter "the P.L.O."), the representative of the Palestinian people;

WITHIN the framework of the Middle East peace process initiated at Madrid in October 1991;

AIMING at the achievement of a just, lasting and comprehensive peace in the Middle East based on the implementation of UN Security Council Resolutions 242 and 338 in all their aspects;

REAFFIRMING their adherence to the commitments expressed in the Declaration of Principles (hereinafter 'the DOP') signed in Washington D.C. on September 13th 1993, the Cairo Agreement of May 4th 1994, and the Interim-Agreement of September 28th, 1995;

REAFFIRMING their determination to live in peaceful coexistence, mutual dignity and security;

DECLARING as null and void any agreement, declaration, document or statement which contradicts this Framework Agreement;

DESIROUS of reaching a full agreement on all outstanding final status issues as soon as possible, not later than May 5th 1999, as stipulated in the DOP;

HEREBY AGREE on the following Framework for a Final Status Agreement;

Article I: The Establishment of the Palestinian State and its Relations with the State of Israel

1. As an integral part of this Framework Agreement and the full Final Status Agreement:

a. The Government of Israel shall extend its recognition to the independent State of Palestine within agreed and secure borders with its capital al-Quds upon its coming into being not later than May 5th 1999.
b. Simultaneously, the State of Palestine shall extend its recognition to the State of Israel within agreed and secure borders with its capital Yerushalayim.
c. Both sides continue to look favorably at the possibility of establishing a Jordanian–Palestinian confederation, to be agreed upon by the State of Palestine and the Hashemite Kingdom of Jordan.

2. The State of Israel and the State of Palestine (hereinafter: 'the parties') will thereby extend mutual recognition of their right to live in peace and security within mutually agreed borders as defined in Article II of this agreement and in the Final Status Agreement. In particular, the Parties shall:
   a. Recognize and respect each other's sovereignty, territorial integrity and political andeconomic independence.
   b. Renounce the use of force, and the threat of force as an instrument of policy and commit themselves to a peaceful resolution of all disputes between them.
   c. Refrain from organizing, instigating, inciting, assisting or participating in acts of violence, subversion or terrorism against the other party.
   d. Take effective measures to ensure that acts of or threats of violence do not originate from or through their respective territories, including their airspace and territorial waters, and take appropriate measures against those who perpetrate such acts.
   e. Undertake not to join, assist, or cooperate with any military or security coalition, organization, or alliance hostile to either party.
   f. Exchange and ratify the instruments of peace between them as shall be defined in the full Final Status Agreement.

Article II: The Delineation of Secure and Recognized Borders

1. The secure and recognized borders between the State of Israel and the future State of Palestine are described in the attached Maps and in Annex One of the Final Status Agreement. The Parties recognize

that these borders, including their respective subsoil, airspace and territorial waters shall be inviolable.

2. The parties shall define the route and mode of implementation of, as well as the extent of, territory to be yielded by Israel for the agreed extra-territorial passage between the Gaza Strip and the West Bank (as described in Annex One of the Final Status Agreement).
3. The border in the Jerusalem area is to be delineated in accordance with the provisions of Article VI of this Framework Agreement.
4. The Parties shall recognize the final borders between the two states as permanent and irrevocable.

Article III: The Creation of Normal and Stable Inter-State Relations

1. Upon the exchange of the instruments of ratification of the peace treaty, the Parties agree to establish full diplomatic and consular relations between them and to promote economic and cultural relations including the free movement of people, goods, capital and services across their borders.
2. The Parties shall continue to cooperate in all areas of mutual interest and will seek to promote jointly and separately similar regional cooperation with other states in the area and the international community.
3. The Parties shall seek to promote mutual cultural relations and will encourage mutual programs for the dissemination of their respective national customs, folklore and traditions between them.
4. The Parties shall secure freedom of access to places of religious, and historical significance on a non-discriminatory basis. Access to, worship in, and protection of all holy places and sites shall be guaranteed by both Parties.

Article IV: Schedule of Israeli Military Withdrawal and Security Arrangements

1. In implementing UN Security Council Resolutions 242 and 338, the parties agree that the withdrawal of Israeli Military and Security Forces shall be carried out in three stages:

a. Withdrawal from the Central areas of the West Bank and the entire Gaza Strip, (as defined in Annex Two to the Final Status Agreement and attached Map/s), to commence not later than May 5th 1999 and be completed not later than September 4th, 1999;
b. Withdrawal from the Eastern areas of the West Bank (as defined in Annex Two to the Final Status Agreement), to commence not later than September 5th 1999 and be completed not later than January 4th, 2000;
c. Withdrawal from the Western areas of the West Bank (as defined in Annex Two to the Final Status Agreement) to commence not later than January 5th 2000 and be completed not later than May 4th 2000.

2. Thereafter Israel shall maintain a minimal residual force within agreed military compounds and in specified locations. This residual force will comprise:
a. Three reinforced battalions, two existing Military Emergency Stores, and integral logistical forces (their location and terms of lease, duration, mode of deployment, function and numerical strength, are detailed in Annex Two to the Final Status Agreement).
b. Three Early Warning stations and three Air Defense Units as defined and agreed in Annex Two to the Final Status Agreement will be maintained until May 5th 2007 or until peace agreements and bilateral security arrangements between Israel and the relevant Arab parties are attained, whichever comes last.

3. The Parties agree to the formation of an Israeli–Palestinian Coordinating Security Commission (hereinafter 'the CSC') to oversee the implementation of Israel's military withdrawal, to establish the modalities governing its residual military presence, and to coordinate all other security matters (its structure and authorities are detailed in Annex Two to the Final Status Agreement). The CSC shall also implement an agreed schedule for the introduction of Palestinian Security Forces (hereinafter 'PSF') into Palestinian territories commensurate with and parallel to the withdrawal of Israeli forces. The Parties agree that the CSC shall commence its deliberations not later than May 5th, 1998 (see

Annex Two to the Final Status Agreement).

4. Joint Israeli–Palestinian patrols will be held along the Jordan River as well as along both sides of the Israeli–Palestinian border, in order to deter, prevent and combat the infiltration or organization of cross-border terrorism and other forms of violent activities. The mandate and duration of these patrols shall be determined by the CSC, as detailed in Annex Two to the Final Status Agreement.
5. The Parties agree that the State of Palestine shall be demilitarized. The PSF shall remain subject to agreed limitations as defined in Annex Two to the Final Status Agreement. By mutual agreement, and not before May 5th 2007, Palestinian self-defense capabilities shall be negotiated by the Parties.
6. The Parties agree that the co-sponsors and other parties agreed upon, shall be invited to guarantee the arrangements for Israel's military withdrawal and other bilateral security agreements as stipulated in this Framework Agreement. In their capacity as guarantors, the said third-parties shall also be invited to participate in observation, verification and other technical duties to be agreed in the CSC. The said third parties shall accordingly be requested to establish and finance a permanent International Observer Force (hereafter the IOF) whose mandate and functions are described in Annex Two of the Final Status Agreement.

Article V: Israeli Settlements

1. Subsequent to the establishment of the Independent State of Palestine and its recognition by the State of Israel as described in Articles I and III of this agreement:
   a. There will be no exclusive civilian residential areas for Israelis in the State of Palestine.
   b. Individual Israelis remaining within the borders of the Palestinian State shall be subject to Palestinian sovereignty and Palestinian rule of law.
   c. Individual Israelis who have their permanent domicile within the Palestinian State as of May 5th 1999, shall be offered Palestinian citizenship or choose to remain as alien residents, all

without prejudice to their Israeli citizenship.

d. Within the agreed schedule for the withdrawal of Israeli forces from Palestinian territories as described in Article IV and Annex Two to the Final Status Agreement, the Israeli Government and its security forces shall maintain responsibility for the safety and security of Israeli settlements outside the areas of Palestinian security jurisdiction, pending the transfer of said areas to full Palestinian rule.

e. The CSC shall establish the mechanism for dealing with security issues relating to Israeli citizens in Palestine and Palestinian citizens in Israel.

Article VI: Jerusalem

1. Jerusalem shall remain an open and undivided city with free and unimpeded access for people of all faiths and nationalities.
2. The Parties further agree that a reform of the current Jerusalem Municipal System and its boundaries shall be introduced not later than May 5th 1999, and shall not be subject to further change by law or otherwise, unless by mutual consent, prior to the fulfillment of the provisions of paragraph 9 below. This reform shall expand the present municipal boundaries of Jerusalem and shall define the city limits of the 'City of Jerusalem', to include: Abu Dis, Eyzariya, ar-Ram, Az-zaim, Ma'ale Adumim, Givat Ze'ev, Givon, and adjacent areas in the attached map/s.
3. Within the 'City of Jerusalem', neighborhoods inhabited by Palestinians will be defined as 'Palestinian boroughs' The exact borders of the 'City of Jerusalem' and of the Israeli and Palestinian boroughs are delineated and described in Annex Three to the Final Status Agreement and attached Map/s. The number of Israeli boroughs and of Palestinian boroughs will reflect the present demographic balance of 2:1. This proportion will be updated in accordance with the modalities, criteria and schedule as described in Annex Three to this Final Status Agreement.
4. The Parties agree to maintain one Municipality for the 'City of Jerusalem' in the form of a Joint Higher Municipal Council, formed by representatives of the boroughs. These representatives will elect the Mayor of the 'City of Jerusalem'. In all matters related

to the areas of the 'City of Jerusalem' under Palestinian sovereignty, the Joint Higher Municipal Council shall seek the consent of the Government of Palestine. In all matters related to the areas of the 'City of Jerusalem' under Israeli sovereignty, the Joint Higher Municipal Council shall seek the consent of the Government of Israel.

5. The 'City of Jerusalem' shall consist of the Joint Higher Municipal Council, two sub-municipalities – an Israeli sub-municipality, elected by the inhabitants of the Israeli boroughs, and a Palestinian sub-municipality, elected by the inhabitants of the Palestinian boroughs – as well as a Joint Parity Committee for the Old City Area as described in paragraph 12 below.
6. The Parties further agree that the municipality of the 'City of Jerusalem' shall:
   a. Delegate strong local powers to the sub-municipalities including the right to local taxation, local services, an independent education system, separate religious authorities, and housing planning and zoning, as detailed in Annex Three to the Final Status Agreement;
   b. Develop a twenty-five year Master Plan for the 'City of Jerusalem' with agreed modalities for its balanced implementation, including safeguards for the interests of both communities.
   c. Provide for Israeli and Palestinian citizens resident within the jurisdiction of the City of Jerusalem Municipality and sub-municipalities to vote and seek election for all elected posts as shall be specified in the Jerusalem Municipal bylaws.
7. Within the 'City of Jerusalem' both parties recognize the Western part of the city, to be 'Yerushalayim' and the Arab Eastern part of the city, under Palestinian sovereignty, to be 'al-Quds' (see attached Map/s).
8. Upon the exchange of the instruments of ratification of the peace treaty between them:
   a. The Government of the State of Palestine shall recognize Yerushalayim, as defined under Article VI, paragraph 7 and Annex Three to the Final Status Agreement, as the sovereign Capital of the State of Israel.
   b. The Government of the State of Israel shall recognize al-Quds, as defined under Article VI, paragraph 7 and Annex Three to

the Final Status Agreement, as the sovereign Capital of the State of Palestine.

9. The ultimate sovereignty of the area outside Yerushalayim and al-Quds, but inside the present municipal boundaries of Jerusalem, shall be determined by the parties as soon as possible. Each party maintains its position regarding the sovereign status of this area. A joint Israeli–Palestinian committee for determining the final status of this area shall be established not later than May 5th, 1999 and shall commence its deliberations immediately thereafter. Without prejudice to the determination of the final status of this area:
   a. Palestinian citizenship shall be extended to Palestinian residence of this area.
   b. In certain matters Palestinian citizens residing in this area shall resort to Palestinian law (as detailed in Annex Three to the Final Status Agreement).
   c. The Parties will enjoy free access to and use of the Qalandia Airport in this area. A new designated Palestinian terminal shall be constructed, to commence operation concurrent with the signing of the Treaty of Peace (for the modalities of operation, see Annex Three to the Final Status Agreement).
10. The Parties acknowledge Jerusalem's unique spiritual and religious role for all three great monotheistic religions. Wishing to promote interfaith relations and harmony among the three great religions, the Parties accordingly agree to guarantee freedom of worship and access to all Holy Sites for members of all faiths and religions without impediment or restriction.
11. In recognition of the special status and significance of the Old City Area (see map/s) for members of the Christian, Jewish, and Muslim faiths, the parties agree to grant this area a special status.
12. The Parties further agree that:
   a. The Palestinian sub-municipality shall be responsible for the municipal concerns of the Palestinian citizens residing in the Old City Area and their local property.
   b. The Israeli sub-municipalies shall be responsible for the municipal concerns of the Israeli citizens residing in the Old City Area and their local property.
   c. The two sub-municipalities shall appoint a Joint Party Committee to manage all mattersrelated to the preservation of the unique

character of the Old City Area (its structureand modalities are detailed in Annex Three to the Final Status Agreement).

d. In case of a dispute between the two sub-municipalities on matters related to the Old City Area, the issue shall be referred for a decision to the Joint Parity Committee.

13. The State of Palestine shall be granted extra-territorial sovereignty over the Haram ash-Sharif under the administration of the al-Quds Awqaf. The present status quo regarding the right of access and prayer for all, will be secured.
14. The Church of the Holy Sepulchre shall be managed by the Palestinian sub-Municipality. The Joint Parity Committee, shall examine the possibility of assigning extra-territorial status to the Church of the Holy Sepulchre.
15. Supervision of persons and goods transiting through the 'City of Jerusalem' shall take place at the exit points. Other security matters related to persons, vehicles and goods suspected of involvement in hostile activity are dealt with in Annex Two to the Final Status Agreement.

Article VII: Palestinian Refugees

1. Whereas the Palestinian side considers that the right of the Palestinian refugees to return to their homes is enshrined in international law and natural justice, it recognizes that the prerequisites of the new era of peace and coexistence, as well as the realities that have been created on the ground since 1948, have rendered the implementation of this right impracticable. The Palestinian side, thus, declares its readiness to accept and implement policies and measures that will ensure, insofar as this is possible, the welfare and well-being of these refugees.
2. Whereas the Israeli side acknowledges the moral and material suffering caused to the Palestinian people as a result of the war of 1947–1949. It further acknowledges the Palestinian refugees' right of return to the Palestinian state and their right to compensation and rehabilitation for moral and material losses.
3. The parties agree on the establishment of an International Commisssion for Palestinian Refugees (hereinafter 'the ICPR') for the final settlement of all aspects of the refugee issue as follows:

a. The Parties extend invitations to donor countries to join them in the formation of the ICPR.
b. The Parties welcome the intention of the Government of Sweden to lead the ICPR and to contribute financially to its activities.
c. The Government of Israel shall establish a fund for its contribution, along with others, to the activities of the ICPR.
d. The ICPR shall conduct all fundraising activities and coordinate donors' involvement in the program.
e. The ICPR shall define the criteria for compensation accounting for:
   1. moral loss;
   2. immovable property;
   3. financial and economic support enabling resettlement and rehabilitation of Palestinians residing in refugee camps.
f. The ICPR shall further:
   1. adjudicate claims for material loss;
   2. prepare and develop rehabilitation and absorption programs;
   3. establish the mechanisms and venues for disbursing payments and compensation;
   4. oversee rehabilitation programs;
   5. explore the intentions of Palestinian refugees on the one hand and of Arab and other countries on the other, concerning wishes for emigration and the possibilities thereof;
   6. explore with Arab governments hosting refugee populations, as well as with these refugees, venues for absorption in these countries whenever mutually desired.
g. The ICPR shall implement all the above according to the agreed schedule defined in Annex Four to the Final Status Agreement.

4. The ICPR shall be guided by the following principles in dealing with the 'refugees of 1948' and their descendants as defined in Annex Four to the Final Status Agreement:
   a. Each refugee family shall be entitled to compensation for moral loss to a sum of money to be agreed upon by the ICPR.
   b. Each claimant with proven immovable property shall be compensated as per the adjudication of the ICPR.
   c. The ICPR shall provide financial and economic support, enabling the resettlement and rehabilitation of Palestinians residing in refugee camps.

d. The refugees shall be entitled to financial and economic support from the ICPR for resettlement and rehabilitation.

5. The State of Israel undertakes to participate actively in implementing the program for the resolution of the refugee problem. Israel will continue to enable family reunification and will absorb Palestinian refugees in special defined cases, to be agreed upon with the ICPR.
6. The Palestinian side undertakes to participate actively in implementing the program for the resolution of the refugee problem. The Palestinian side shall enact a program to encourage the rehabilitation and resettlement of Palestinian refugees presently resident in the West Bank and Gaza Strip, within these areas.
7. The PLO considers the implementation of the above a full and final settlement of the refugee issue in all its dimensions. It further undertakes that no additional claims or demands arising from this issue will be made upon the full implementation of this Framework Agreement.

Article VIII: Israeli–Palestinian Standing Committee

1. The Parties shall establish an Israeli–Palestinian Standing Committee (hereafter: 'IPSC'), which will commence activities upon the signing of this Framework Agreement.
2. This IPSC shall be authorized to deal with all matters related to the smooth transition between the Interim Agreement and Final Status Agreement.
3. The IPSC shall also coordinate activities related to the implementation of the Final Status Agreement.

Article IX: Water Resources

1. The Parties agree that they possess the same natural water resources essential for each nations livelihood and survival.
2. Water rights and issues are laid out in Annex Five to the Final Status Agreement.
3. With a view to achieving a comprehensive and lasting settlement of all water problems between them, the Parties jointly undertake to ensure that the management and development of their water

resources should not in any way harm or imperil the water resources of the other.

4. The Parties further agree to the following:
   a. The development of existing and new water resources to increase availability and minimize wastage.
   b. The prevention of contamination of water resources.
   c. The transfer of information and joint research and the review of the potential for water enhancement.
5. The Parties agree to prepare as soon as possible, but not later than May 5, 1999, an agreed upon coordinated separate and joint water management plan for the joint aquifers that will guarantee optimal use and development of water resources for the benefit of the Israeli and Palestinian nations.
6. The Parties agree to seek to extend their joint co-operation to the Hashemite Kingdom of Jordan, in particular with regard to the waters of the Jordan River and the Dead Sea and to seek to promote wider regional understanding on the exploitation and management of water resources in the Middle East.

Article X: Time Frame and Implementation

A. The Preparatory Period: May 5th 1996 to May 4th 1999

1. With the signing of this Framework Agreement and its entry into force not later than May 5th 1996, the Preparatory Period for Final Status shall commence. Immediately thereafter, the Parties shall:
   a. Establish the IPSC (Israeli–Palestinian Standing Committee) along the lines laid down in Article VIII.
   b. Extend invitations to donor countries to join the Government of Sweden and themselves in formation of the ICPR (International Commission for Palestinian Refugees).

   The Preparatory Period shall end not later than May 4th 1999.
2. During this period it is agreed that the following shall be implemented:
   a. The Final Status Agreement with all Annexes will be prepared, based on the agreements and principles laid down in this Framework Agreement.
   b. Consequently, and based on the mechanisms for border delineation set out in Annex One to the Final Status

Agreement, the joint delineation of borders and official extra-territorial and other passages shall be finalized.

c. The Israeli–Palestinian Coordinating Security Commission (CSC) shall be established and commence its deliberation, not later than May 5th 1998. The CSC shall establish the mechanism for dealing with security issues relating to Israeli citizens in the State of Palestine, and Palestinian citizens in the State of Israel.
d. The Parties shall invite the co-sponsors to the Peace Process and other agreed upon third parties, to establish an International Observer Force (IOF) as agreed upon in Annex two to the Final Status Agreement.
e. The Government of Israel shall establish a program to encourage Israeli settlers to resettle within Israel's sovereign territory. Settlers wishing to take part in this program shall be compensated by the Israeli government before January 1st, 1999, according to guidelines to be announced within three months of the entry into force of this Framework Agreement.
f. The agreed upon reformed Jerusalem Municipal System shall be inaugurated not later than May 5th 1999.
g. Both sides shall prepare and agree on a Jerusalem Master Plan as described in Article VI.
h. In accordance with Article VII of this Framework Agreement, the PLO shall establish a program to encourage the rehabilitation and resettlement of Palestinian refugees presently residing in the West Bank and Gaza Strip, within these areas.
i. The Parties shall promote the work of the ICPR as stipulated in Article VII to this Agreement.
j. The Parties shall prepare an agreed upon coordinated, separate and joint water management plan for the joint aquifers.
k. As soon as possible, but not later than May 4th 1999, the interim period shall come to an end and a full Final Status Agreement shall be signed and a Peace Treaty shall be initiated.

B. The Implementation Period: May 5th 1999 to May 4th 2000

1. With the signing and entry into force of the Israeli–Palestinian Final Status Agreement, the implementation of the Final Status settlement will commence. The creation of the Independent State

of Palestine within secure and recognized borders shall be promulgated by the PLO and its relevant agencies. Immediately thereafter, but not later than within two months, the Peace Treaty shall be signed.

2. The Government of the State of Israel shall extend immediate and full diplomatic recognition to the State of Palestine and to al-Quds as its capital, as described in Article VI and Annex Three to the Final Status Agreement.
3. The Government of the State of Palestine shall extend immediate and full diplomatic recognition to the State of Israel and to Yerushalayim as its capital, as described in Article VI and Annex Three to the Final Status Agreement.
4. Provisions relating to the normalization of Israeli–Palestinian relations shall be implemented as described in Article III.
5. Upon entry into force of the Israeli–Palestinian Final Status Agreement, the withdrawal of Israeli Military and Security Forces shall commence and the agreed security provisions shall be implemented according to the schedule described in Article II and Annex Two to the Final Status Agreement.
6. Within the 'City of Jerusalem' elections for the two sub-municipalities will be held. The two sub-municipalities shall appoint a Joint Parity Committee for the Old City Area (as outlined in Article VI paragraph 12 to this agreement), and a proportional (2:1) Joint Higher Municipal Council which will elect the Mayor of the 'City of Jerusalem'.
7. The parties agree to continue to work jointly and separatly within the framework of the multilateral working groups and other relevant fora towards:
   a. The establishment of a Middle East free from hostile coalitions and alliances;
   b. The creation of a Middle East free from weapons of mass destruction both conventional and non-conventional within the context of a comprehensive, lasting and stable settlement.

C. The Post-Implementation Period: May 5th 2000 to May 4th 2007

1. Israeli residual forces shall remain on Palestinian territory. The CSC shall continue to coordinate Israeli and Palestinian security needs.

2. Responsibility for the security of Israeli citizens residents in the State of Palestine, shall remain with the CSC.

D. The Post-November 5th 2007 Period

Remaining Israeli residual forces shall withdraw from the Palestinian State contingent on the attainment of peace treaties and security arrangements between Israel and the relevant Arab parties.

NOTES

Introduction

1. Segev (2001), pp. 311–12.
2. As Shindler observes, 'a central issue in terms of Jewish response was that the Zionist leadership, including Jabotinsky, had already left the country for the 16th Zionist Congress in Zurich . . . The political vacuum created thus allowed *Doar Hayom* and the Pro-Wailing Wall Committees to pursue a more radical agenda . . .' Joseph Klausner, one of the Zionist representatives, had established the 'Pro-Wailing Wall Committee' and his sympathies generally lay with the more activist Revisionist movement. Luke described him as 'someone who would not listen to reason and preferred emotional rather than intellectual arguments' (Shindler (2006), pp. 96–104).
3. Segev (2001). See Chapters 13 – 'The Nerves of Jerusalem' – and 14 – 'Hebron, 1929' – for a fuller account of the events which preceded and followed Luke's mediation.
4. Bercovitch and Langley (1993), p. 675.
5. *Ibid.*
6. Bercovitch (1994), p. 7; Bercovitch (2002), p. 8.
7. Malley and Agha (2009).
8. Interviews with Aaron Miller and Ron Pundak.
9. *Ibid*, Jan Eliasson; Eliasson (2002), p. 175.
10. Touval (1982), pp. 11–14.
11. Young (1967), p. 81; Princen (1992).
12. Zartman and Rubin (2000).
13. Salacuse (2000), pp. 258–9.
14. Touval (2000), pp. 168–9.
15. Bercovitch and Gartner (2009), p. 26.
16. Bercovitch (2002), p. 15.

17. Sheppard (1984); Beardsley *et al.* (2006); Bercovitch (1994) and (2002); Bercovitch and Gartner (2009); Bercovitch and Houston (2000); Touval and Zartman (1985); Wilkenfeld *et al.* (2003).
18. Beardsley *et al.* (2006), p. 66; Bercovitch (1994), p. 17.
19. *Ibid*, pp. 78–81.
20. *Ibid.*
21. Stein (1989).
22. Agha *et al.* (2003), p. 1.
23. Klein and Malki (2006), p. 113.
24. Agha *et al.* (2003), pp. 4–5.
25. Bercovitch (1994), p. 7.
26. Kleiboer (1996), p. 362.
27. Bjereld (1989); Bjereld and Carmesund (2008).
28. Palme (1993); Bergh (2001).

Chapter 1 The Israeli–Palestinian Conflict: Competing National Narratives and the Eternal 'Rashomon Effect'

1. Kacowicz (2005).
2. Bernadotte (1948), p. 278.
3. Antonius (1945), p. 386.
4. Bramstedt (1945), p. 34.
5. Oz (2006), p. 4.
6. Lowenthal (1996), p. 41.
7. Interview with Ehud Barak. LHCMA – Elusive Peace catalogue: Vol. 2/2.
8. *Ibid*; 'Israel, the Conflict, and Peace: Answers to frequently asked questions.' http://www.mfa.gov.il/MFA/Terrorism+Obstacle + to + Peace/Palestinian + terror + since + 2000/Israel-+ the + Conflict + and + Peace + Answers + to + Frequen.htm;.
9. Pressman (2003), pp. 36–7.
10. Nora (1989), pp. 8–9.
11. Halbwachs quoted in Litvak (2009), p. 12.
12. *Ibid* (1992), p. 40.
13. Litvak (2009), p. 17.
14. Nora (1989), p. 9.
15. Lowenthal (1996), p. 49.
16. Khalili (2007), p. 4.
17. Zerubavel (1995) and (1996).
18. Litvak (2009), pp. 17–18.
19. Halbwachs (1992), pp. 38, 50; Tossavainen (2006), pp. 24–7. Shriver quotes Niebuhr to make precisely this same point: 'Where common memory is lacking, where [people] do not share in the same past, there can be no real community, and where community is to be formed common memory must be created.' (Shriver (1999), p. 210).

20. Gillis (1996), p. 3.
21. Lowenthal (1996), p. 43.
22. Zertal (2005), p. 23.
23. Schwartz *et al.* (1986), p. 150.
24. Lassner and Troen (2007), p. 8.
25. Lowenthal (1996), p. 53.
26. Kacowicz (2005), p. 344; Tossavainen (2006), p. 26.
27. Kriesberg (2001), p. 374.
28. Kelman (1999), p. 588.
29. Bar-Tal and Salomon (2006), p. 21.
30. Kelman (1987). p. 355.
31. Ayissi (2001), p. 49.
32. Wendt (1992).
33. Snyder and Jervis (1999), p. 16.
34. Bar-Tal and Salomon (2006); Bar-Tal (2000).
35. For more on the relationship between 'ingroup love' and 'outgroup hate', see Brewer (1999).
36. Lonni (2001/2).
37. Ben-Gurion referred to the Bible as the 'Jews' sacrosanct title-deed to Palestine ... with a genealogy of 3,500 years.' (Wetherell (2005), p. 81).
38. The term 'myth' is used here and throughout this book without intending any disrespect.
39. Lassner and Troen (2007), p. 202. See also Kimmerling (2008), pp. 86–7.
40. *Ibid*, p. 210.
41. See Leviticus 23:42–3.
42. Tossavainen (2006), p. 43; Smith (1999), pp. 208–9.
43. Pinsker (1975), p. 75.
44. *Ibid*, p. 81.
45. *Ibid*, pp. 81, 84.
46. *Ibid*, pp. 74, 77.
47. Herzl (1936), pp. 14–15.
48. Kornberg (1993), p. 173.
49. Khalidi (2006), p. 36; Mayer (2008), p. 101.
50. Hirst (2003), pp. 135–7. Ha'am had in fact alerted Zionists to this reality already in 1891, and together with Yitzhak Epstein and others continued to raise concerns about the Arab presence in Palestine and the problems this would pose for a Jewish state there. See Mayer (2008), pp. 100–13.
51. Antonius (1945), p. 393.
52. Litvak (2009), pp. 100; 106–17.
53. Lassner and Troen (2007) pp. 90 and 245.
54. Sway (2002), p. 83.
55. Porath (1974), pp. 2–4.
56. Kimmerling (2008), p. 61.
57. Sayigh (1979), quoted in Matar (2011), p. 26. See also Ze'evi (2008).

58. Kimmerling (2008), p. 62.
59. For different takes on the existence of Palestinian nationalism around the turn of the 20th century, see Gerber (2003) and (2008); Khalidi (1997); Kimmerling (2008); Litvak (2009); Muslih (1988); Porath (1974) and (1977).
60. Rouhana (2006), p. 118.
61. Khalidi (1997), p. 153.
62. Gerber (2008), pp. 45–7.
63. Porath (1974), p. 24; Schulz (1999), p. 24.
64. Kimmerling (2008), p. 87.
65. Pinsker (1975), p. 87.
66. Zerubavel (2006), p. 75.
67. Smith (1999), p. 215. Smith notes that the heroes of the Davidic and Solomonic kingdom were magnified, 'their exploits continually recounted, its temple held up as the religious ideal, its literature treated as canonical', while 'the religious interpretation and popular imagination have excised the hardships, corruption and exploitation of the united Israelite kingdom ...'
68. Kimmerling (2005), pp. 102–3; 190–1.
69. Lassner and Troen (2007), pp. 215, 219, 261.
70. Schwartz *et al.* (1986), pp. 151–9.
71. See Zerubavel (1991) and (1996) for analyses of how the traditional heroic Trumpeldor narrative, including his last words, has been used by Israeli politicians and modified to fit the dominant ideology of contemporary Israeli society.
72. Zerubavel (2006), p. 73.
73. Zertal (2005), p. 21; Segev (2001), p. 125.
74. *Ibid*, p. 23.
75. Avraham Stern, founder of the militant group *Lehi*, espoused a 'philosophy of blood sacrifice' in the struggle against the British. His poetry 'spoke of self-sacrifice and martyrdom, of blood and fire'. See Shindler (2006), pp. 145–6, 189–90.
76. Zerubavel (2006), p. 77.
77. Zertal (2005), p. 23.
78. Segev (2001), pp. 318–27.
79. Halbwachs (1992), pp. 64–5.
80. Zertal and Eldar (2007), p. 249.
81. *Ibid*, pp. 262–4.
82. Gerber (2008), pp. 61–9.
83. *Ibid*, pp. 180–1.
84. Khalidi (1997), pp. 106–10; Lassner and Troen (2007), p. 75.
85. Porath (1974), p. 6.
86. Segev (2001), p. 127.
87. Gerber (2008), pp. 71–5; Segev (2001), p. 127.
88. Segev (2001), Chapter 6: 'Nebi Musa, 1920', pp. 127–44.
89. Hirst (2003), pp. 199–200.

90. Segev (2001), p. 362.
91. Gerber (2008), p. 141; Hirst (2003), pp. 215–16.
92. Matar (2011), p. 39. Matar notes that these men were executed for their role in the Hebron massacres of 1929 and were not part of the revolt, as some Palestinians believe.
93. Khalili (2007), pp. 131–2.
94. *Ibid*, pp. 117–22; Wilkinson (2006). See also Fisk (2005), pp. 584–8, 619–22.
95. Zertal (2005), p. 2.
96. *Maariv*, 16/04/1996, quoted in foreword of Tossavainen (2006).
97. Arendt (1985), p. 19.
98. Gorenberg (2006), pp. 32–3.
99. Zertal (2005), pp. 105–7.
100. Arendt (1985), p. 10.
101. Segev (2010).
102. Cesarani (2004), p. 332.
103. Zertal (2005), pp. 3–4; 114.
104. *Ibid*, p. 110.
105. *Ibid*, p. 97–8. To *The New York Times* he added the further comment, 'I have no doubt that the Egyptian dictatorship is being instructed by the large number of Nazis who are there.'
106. Segev (2007), p. 284.
107. *Ibid*, pp. 283–4.
108. Bregman (2002), p. 61.
109. Segev (2007), p. 285.
110. Aggestam (1999), p. 81. Begin referred to the PLO as 'the Arab SS'.
111. Zertal (2005), p. 175. Zertal observes that in his book 'A Place Among the Nations', Netanyahu draws a systematic analogy between al-Husseini, Hitler, and Arafat.
112. Peri (2000), pp. 4–6.
113. Savir (1998), p. 248.
114. Shindler (2008), pp. 260–1. Though Netanyahu and other Likud leaders formally opposed the labelling of Rabin and Peres as 'murderers' and 'traitors' following the Oslo Agreement, their language was nonetheless highly incendiary, and described them, among many other things, as 'shrinking Israel into Auschwitz borders'.
115. Interview with Saeb Erekat.
116. Antonius (1945).
117. Khalidi (1997) and (2006). This view is substantiated by Segev (2001) whose research on the British, Jewish and Arab attitudes during the Mandatory period is extremely illuminating.
118. Khalidi (1997), p. 174; Gordon (2008), pp. 55–6.
119. Gerber (2008), pp. 136, 98.
120. *Ibid* (2003), p. 37.

121. Antonius (1945), pp. 410–12.
122. For more detailed reasoning behind the Palestinian rejection, see Antonius (1945), pp. 399–409.
123. According to Segev, Ben-Gurion reasoned that the promise of forced transfer outweighed all the drawbacks of the Peel Commission. The proposal was of 'huge consequence' because for the first time a 'really Jewish' state was on the verge of becoming a reality. A small Jewish state was only the beginning, a springboard from which to redeem the land in its entirety. See Segev (2001), pp. 403–8 for more on this and Masalha (1992) on the concept of transfer in Zionist thought.
124. Khalidi (2006), p. 1.
125. Morris (2004); Esber (2005).
126. Persson (1979), p. 184 (see footnote).
127. Flapan (1987), p. 228.
128. Sayigh (1997a), p. 666; Sayigh (1997b), p. 19; Webman (2009), pp. 29–30; Hassassian (2001/2), pp. 55–7.
129. Milshtein (2009b), pp. 71–3, 79–83.
130. Sayigh (1997a), p. 668.
131. Milshtein (2009a), pp. 51–3.
132. *Ibid* (2009b), p. 60.
133. Pappé (2001), p. 7.
134. Segev (2007), p. 526. See Jamal (2000), pp. 39–42 for a discussion of how this was reflected in Israeli peace discourse during the Oslo process.
135. Shriver (1999), p. 215.
136. Bar-On (2006), pp. 154–6.
137. Pappé (1997), pp. 38–9.
138. Shriver (1999), p. 214.
139. Pappé (2001), p. 7.
140. Antonius (1945), p. 411.
141. Said (1994), p. 167. This point is also made by Arendt (2004), p. 368.
142. Rynhold (2007).
143. Bar-On (2006), p. 168.
144. See Gordon (2008), pp. 55–62 for a more detailed discussion on the negative effects of the occupation on Palestinian education and the development of nationalism.
145. Brown (2006), pp. 240–1.
146. Bar-On and Adwan (2006), pp. 206–7.
147. Steinberg (2002).
148. Webman (2009), pp. 32–3.
149. Sayigh (2001), p. 54.
150. Interview with Amnon Lipkin-Shahak.
151. Normalisation with Israel is viewed by Islamists as a threat to Arab-Muslim identity, based on theological edicts pertaining to foreign sovereignty over part of *dar al-Islam*, and the spread and influence of iniquitous Western culture and ideas (Sela (2005), pp. 39; 49–51).

152. Sayigh (1997b), p. 25.
153. Gunning (2004).
154. Stedman (1997).
155. Rouhana (2006), p. 119.
156. Kelman (2001), p. 197.
157. Sprinzak (1991), pp. 39–43. Though dominated by the right-wing, the Land of Israel Movement also brought a number of prominent left-wing figures into its fold, indicating a wider ideological popularity. See also Shindler (1995), pp. 71–2.
158. Ma'oz (1999), p. 70.
159. Pappé (2003), p. 44.
160. Sprinzak (1991) pp. 43–51; Zertal and Eldar (2007), p. 5. See Wetherell (2005) and Tamarin (1973) for further analysis of the consequences and implications of the political use of religious language. While these use the Bible and Zionism as their case study, it is important to emphasise that their conclusions and lessons are equally applicable to the politicisation of any religion.
161. Zertal and Eldar (2007); Gorenberg (2006).
162. Interview with Geoffrey Aronson.
163. Gazit (2003), p. 18; Gordon (2008), p. 26; Quigley (2005), pp. 177–8; Gorenberg (2006), pp. 99–102, 358.
164. See Shindler (1995) and (2006) for an in-depth analysis of the origins and development of military Zionism and the Israeli political right, from Ze'ev Jabotinsky and the Revisionist movement to Begin, Netanyahu and Likud. See also Kaplan (2005).
165. Zertal and Eldar (2007), p. 55.
166. Shindler (1995), p. 85.
167. Zertal and Eldar (2007), pp. 73–4.
168. Sprinzak (1991), pp. 124–38.
169. *Ibid* (1991).
170. Peled (2001/2), p. 18.
171. Efron (2003), p. 54.
172. 'Comprehensive Settlement Population, 1972–2009', The Foundation for Middle East Peace (FMEP). http://www.fmep.org/settlement_info/settlement-info-and-tables/stats-data/comprehensive-settlement-population-1972–2006.
173. Sprinzak (2000).
174. Barak (2005), p. 727.
175. Kriesberg (2002), pp. 558–9.
176. Abbas (1995), p. 111.
177. Fisk (2005), pp. 494–5.
178. LeBor (2007), p. 51.
179. Kriesberg (2002) and (2004).
180. Pappé (2006); Bar-On and Adwan (2006). Rothstein appears to lean towards Pappé's view when he acknowledges that 'stable peace may thus require a

concerted effort to revise the historical canon, to begin teaching a new version of history, and to marginalise and contain the extremists who reject this effort.' (Shriver (1999), p. 211).

181. Bar-On (2006), p. 167.
182. Interview with Saeb Erekat.

Chapter 2 The Evolution of Swedish Relations with Israel and the Palestinians: From a Labour Love Affair to the Two-State Solution

1. *Ibid.*
2. *The Jerusalem Post*, 11/02/1996. SAA – Series 4.2: Vol. 9.
3. *The New York Times*, 16/12/1988. SAA – Series 4.2: Vol. 1.
4. Yegar (1993), pp. 23–5; Abadi (2001), p. 23.
5. This use was regulated very precisely by the government to a few limited occasions, on certain lines, and under supervision of the Swedish army. Moreover, the government made it clear to Hitler that this was not to set a regular precedent, but was an isolated arrangement.
6. Abadi (2001), p. 25.
7. Bernadotte (1948), pp. 276–7.
8. UN General Assembly Resolution 186. Available at: http://unispal.un.org/UNISPAL.NSF/0/A9A8DA193BD46C54852560E50060C6FD.
9. Touval (1982). See Chapter 2 entitled 'Bernadotte' for an analysis of his efforts.
10. Persson (1979), p. 112. Ben-Gurion was referring to the British Foreign Secretary Ernest Bevin who was an anti-Zionist. See also Shamir (1994), p. 75.
11. Touval (1982), p. 36.
12. Shamir (1994), p. 75. Shamir writes that 'Lehi took no responsibility for the deed; the idea was conceived in Jerusalem by Lehi members operating more or less independently. Our opinion was asked and we offered no opposition.'.
13. Yegar (1993), p. 35.
14. Bjereld (1989), p. 42.
15. Abadi (2001), p. 27.
16. Yegar (1993), p. 36.
17. 'Memorial for Folke Bernadotte', 08/05/1995. SAA – Series 4.2: Vol. 7.
18. Interview with Anders Lidén; Interview with Ulf Hjertonsson; Schori (2008), p. 154.
19. Holmberg (2008), p. 81.
20. Yegar (1993), p. 32.
21. Carmesund (2005), p. 51; Svensson (2008), p. 22.
22. *Ibid*, p. 52; Morris (2004), pp. 436–7.
23. *Ibid*, pp. 54–5, 58, 65–8; Svensson (2008), p. 22.
24. Persson (1979), p. 184.
25. Bernadotte (1948), p. 5.
26. Yegar (1993), pp. 45–6.

27. Abadi (2001), pp. 31–2.
28. Yegar (1993), p. 41.
29. Bjereld (1989), pp. 48–9.
30. Östberg (2009), p. 122.
31. 'SSU Kongressen, 1958.' OPA – Series 2.4.0: Vol. 003.
32. Interview with Ulf Hjertonsson.
33. Bjereld (1989), p. 56.
34. Interview with Ulf Hjertonsson. In a personal professional capacity, this stance evoked a fair amount of criticism among Swedish diplomats, for example at the annual meeting of Swedish ambassadors in August 1967.
35. Letter from Palme to Rydén, 13/11/1969. SAA – Series 4.2: Vol. 1.
36. Bjereld and Carmesund (2008), p. 11. Years later, Jarring told fellow Swedish diplomat Stig Elvemar that he would in fact have found an official Swedish position helpful in his dealings with the Arabs and Israelis (Interview with Stig Elvemar).
37. Östberg (2008), pp. 161–2.
38. Dalsjö (2006).
39. Andrén and Möller (1990), p. 74.
40. Speech, 02/02/1970. OPA – Series 2.4.0: Vol. 018.
41. Yegar (1993), p. 49.
42. Viklund (1989), pp. 58–9.
43. Ekengren (2005), pp. 202–3.
44. Johannesson (2002), pp. 147–8.
45. Speech, 12/05/1964. OPA – Series 2.4.0: Vol. 004; Palme (1968), pp. 9–22.
46. Eliasson (2002), p. 170; Interview with Jan Eliasson.
47. Speech, 19/04/1975. OPA – Series 2.4.0: Vol. 065.
48. *Ibid*, 30/07/1965. OPA – Series 2.4.0: Vol. 005.
49. Palme (1968), pp. 212–18.
50. Interview with Pierre Schori; Peterson (2002), p. 23.
51. Antman and Schori (1996), p. 124; Ekengren (2005), p. 153.
52. Peterson (2002), p. 388.
53. Speech, 07/04/2001 – SAA – Series 4.2: Vol. 40.
54. Ekengren (2005), p. 202; Antman and Schori (1996), pp. 161–2.
55. *Ibid*, pp. 157–67.
56. In the mid-1960s, the Minister of Development Cooperation Ulla Lindström was forced to resign when her demand for the rapid expansion of foreign aid clashed with those of the Minister of Finance, Gunnar Sträng.
57. Östberg (2008), p. 106.
58. Speech, 30/07/1965. OPA – Series 2.4.0: Vol. 005. The specification – 'for it is after all Vietnam that I have spoken about' – was not included in the original speech which Prime Minister Erlander and Foreign Minister Nilsson had approved. The words were added to the original manuscript in pencil (Östberg (2008), p. 273).
59. *Ibid*. OPA – Series 2.4.0: Vol. 005.

60. Peterson (2002), p. 391.
61. Speech, 21/02/1968. OPA – Series 2.4.0: Vol. 012.
62. *Ibid.* Already in September 1965, a poll showed that 42 per cent of the population were against American actions in Vietnam, with only 12 per cent in favour (Östberg (2008), pp. 279–81). Indeed, Sweden developed an anti-war movement second only to the American in scope and organisation. A petition against the war circulated by the Social Democrats collected a remarkable 2,688,782 signatures (Antman and Schori (1996), p. 127).
63. Östberg (2009), pp. 108–10.
64. Statement made by Palme, 23/12/1972. OPA – Series 2.4.0: Vol. 044.
65. *Time* magazine, 'Sweden's Olof Palme: Neutral But Not Silent', 29/01/1973. Accessible at: http://www.time.com/time/magazine/article/0,9171,903763,00.html?promoid=googlep/.
66. Interview with Pierre Schori.
67. Eliasson (2002), pp. 170–1.
68. American president Richard Nixon reportedly referred to Palme as 'that Swedish asshole' (Östberg (2008), p. 296).
69. Speech, 02/02/1970. OPA – Series 2.4.0: Vol. 018. Palme noted that 'it has now been generally admitted in Europe that our policy of neutrality is one of the factors which has served to keep Northern Europe relatively calm and stable.' A press release (OPA – Series 2.4.0: Vol. 047) issued during a visit to Stockholm by Soviet Minister Alexei Kosygin in April, 1973, showed that the Soviets too shared this view.
70. As articulated in Sweden's statements in the UN General Assembly's general debate and the annual Government Declaration on foreign policy issues in the Riksdag.
71. Bjereld (1995), pp. 28–9.
72. Ehnmark (2002), p. 29.
73. Speech, 19/04/1975. OPA – Series 2.4.0: Vol. 065.
74. Antman and Schori (1996), p. 174.
75. Speech, 12/01/1980. OPA – Series 2.4.0: Vol. 090.
76. *Ibid.*
77. Speech, 13/03/82. OPA – Series 2.4.0: Vol. 100.
78. Arvidsson (2006), p. 325–6.
79. Ekengren (2005), p. 181–6.
80. Eliasson (2002), p. 172; Antman and Schori (1996), p. 132–3.
81. Yegar (1993), p. 52.
82. Palme (1968), pp. 212–8.
83. Yegar (1993), p. 49–50.
84. Östberg (2009), p. 124.
85. Interview with Pierre Schori.
86. Report from the delegation's trip to Israel, 25–30 January 1970. SAPA # 1889 – F-02-H, Vol. 1B.
87. *Ibid.*

88. Östberg (2009), p. 123. At that same conference, the decision was taken to send a fact-finding mission to report on the prospects for a peaceful resolution of the conflict. Completed in 1977, the report by SI Middle East co-ordinator and Austrian Chancellor, Bruno Kreisky, found that from an Arab perspective a Palestinian state was 'an obvious precondition for any peaceful solution' ('Mission of the Socialist International to the Middle East.' SAA – Series 4.2: Vol. 1).
89. Peterson (2002), pp. 400–1; Östberg (2009), p. 124.
90. Eliasson (2002), p. 172.
91. Wistrich (2007), pp. 13–4. Wistrich uses even stronger, vociferous language to describe Kreisky, of whom Palme is considered a disciple. Kreisky, a Jewish anti-Zionist and the first European leader to officially receive Arafat, undoubtedly influenced Palme's thinking on the matter. The two worked closely with German Chancellor Willy Brandt in an attempt to expand the foreign policy role of the SI.
92. Speech, 15/05/1967. OPA – Series 2.4.0: Vol. 011.
93. Östberg (2009), p. 122.
94. Speech, 15/05/1967. OPA – Series 2.4.0: Vol. 011.
95. Interview with Ulf Hjertonsson.
96. Yegar (1993), pp. 69–71.
97. Interview with Pierre Schori; Östberg (2009), p. 123.
98. Östberg (2009), pp. 124–5.
99. Speech, 22/11/1974. OPA – Series 2.4.0: Vol. 062.
100. *Ibid*, 11/11/1975. SAPA # 1889 – F-02-I, Vol. 10.
101. *Ibid*, 22/11/1974. OPA – Series 2.4.0: Vol. 062.
102. Östberg (2009), p. 124.
103. Interview with Pierre Schori.
104. Speech, 01/07/1982. OPA – Series 2.4.0: Vol. 102.
105. *Ibid*, 07/08/1982. SAPA # 1889 – F-02-I, Vol. 11.
106. *Svenska Dagbladet*, 13/04/1983. SAA – Series 4.2: Vol. 1.
107. Speech, 13/04/1983. OPA – Series 2.4.0: Vol. 104.
108. Holmberg (2008), p. 88.
109. Yegar (1993), pp. 78–9.
110. *ibid*, p. 125.
111. *Svenska Dagbladet*, 13/04/1983. SAA – Series 4.2: Vol. 1.
112. Yegar (1993), pp. 102–3.
113. Bjereld (1989), p. 191.
114. Yegar (1993), p. 85.
115. *Ibid*, p. xiii.
116. Speech, 02/02/1970. OPA – Series 2.4.0: Vol. 018; Östberg (2009), pp. 110–12.

Chapter 3 'Quiet Diplomacy'

1. *The Independent*, 17/12/1988. SAA – Series 4.2: Vol. 1.
2. Savir (1998), p. 15.

3. Rothstein (2002), p. 3.
4. Åström (1992), p. 141.
5. Palme (1993), p. 37.
6. Exchange of letters between Makhlouf and Toresson. SAPA # 1889 – F – 02 – I: Vol. 9.
7. Interview with Mathias Mossberg.
8. *Ibid*, Stig Elvemar.
9. Address to the UN General Assembly by Ambassador Ferm, 01/12/1987. SAA – Series 4.2: Vol. 1.
10. Interview with Mathias Mossberg.
11. Riksdag statement, 09/02/1988. SAA – Series 4.2: Vol. 1.
12. See Chapter 2, 'Olof Palme and "active neutrality".'
13. Riksdag statement, 09/02/1988. SAA – Series 4.2: Vol. 1.
14. Interview with Mathias Mossberg.
15. Palme (1993), pp. 43–8.
16. Sten Andersson interview notes, 02/04/1990. SAA – Series 4.2: Vol. 2.
17. A clause in the 1975 ceasefire agreement between Israel and Egypt, which the Americans mediated, stipulated an American–Israeli understanding that US officials would not recognise or negotiate with the PLO.
18. Sten Andersson interview notes, 02/04/1990. SAA – Series 4.2: Vol. 2.
19. *The New York Times*, 16/12/1988. SAA – Series 4.2: Vol. 1.
20. See Rabie (1995) for a personal account of these efforts. Arafat later told Rabie that his work represented 'at least 90% of all efforts to facilitate the dialogue' (p. 96).
21. Sten Andersson interview notes, 02/04/1990. SAA – Series 4.2: Vol. 2.
22. Interview with Ulf Hjertonsson.
23. Rabie (1995), pp. 70–1.
24. Letter from Erell to Andersson, 18/11/1988. SAA – Series 4.2: Vol. 1.
25. Foreign Ministry memo, 14/03/1989. SAA – Series 4.2: Vol. 2. See Appendix I for the full text of the document.
26. *Ibid.*
27. See Appendix III. Letter from Arafat to Andersson, 07/12/1988. SAA – Series 4.2: Vol. 1.
28. Interview with Ulf Hjertonsson.
29. It was originally supposed to be held in New York, but Arafat had been denied a visa to enter the United States, a decision Swedish and other foreign diplomats objected to, but to no avail.
30. *The Washington Post*, 16/12/1988. SAA – Series 4.2: Vol. 1.
31. *Ibid*; Palme (1993), pp. 143–8.
32. Interview with Ulf Hjertonsson.
33. Andersson (1993), p. 379.
34. Interview with Mathias Mossberg.
35. *Ibid*, Ulf Hjertonsson.
36. Palme (1993), p. 143.

37. Rabie (1995), pp. 86–7.
38. Andersson (1993), p. 380.
39. *Ibid.*
40. Interview with Mathias Mossberg.
41. *The Independent*, 17/12/1988. SAA – Series 4.2: Vol. 1; Andersson (1993), p. 378.
42. Palme (1993), p. 149.
43. Interview with Mathias Mossberg.
44. *Ibid.*
45. Interview with Anders Lidén.
46. Yitzhak Rabin, for example, could reportedly not stand Andersson and refused to travel to Stockholm following the Nobel Peace Prize ceremony in Oslo in 1994, which is customary for Nobel Peace laureates.
47. *The Washington Post*, 16/12/1988. SAA – Series 4.2: Vol. 1.
48. Palme (1993), p. 150.
49. *Ibid*, pp. 180–1.
50. Interview with Mathias Mossberg; Interview with Ulf Hjertonsson.
51. Wallensteen (2011).
52. Miller (2008), p. 72.
53. Zartman (1997), p. 197.
54. Aly (1994); Ben-Ami (2004); Kelman (2007).
55. Fisk (2005), p. 472.
56. Rynhold (2007), p. 424.
57. Miller (2008), p. 58.
58. Corbin (1994), p. 17.
59. For a collection of diplomatic communiqués documenting the fall of the Soviet Union and Swedish concerns stemming from it, see 'Ett Imperium Imploderar' ('An Empire Implodes'), in Swedish. Available at: http://issuu.com/utrikesdepartementet/docs/ett_imperium_imploderar_skrift/1.
60. Palme (1993), pp. 239–42; Interview with Mathias Mossberg.
61. *Svenska Dagbladet*, 13/04/1983. SAA – Series 4.2: Vol. 1.
62. Waage (2005), p. 7. See also Waage (2002) for further analysis of Norwegian Middle East policy.
63. Interview with Mathias Mossberg.
64. Jones (1999), pp. 108–9.
65. Interview with Mathias Mossberg.
66. See Waage (2000) and (2004).
67. Waage (2005), p. 7.
68. Jones (1999), p. 109.
69. Interview with Terje Rød-Larsen.
70. *Ibid.*
71. Interview with Dan Kurtzer.
72. Jones (1999), p. 111.
73. Interview with Terje Rød-Larsen.

74. Interview with Ron Pundak.
75. Pundak has described other attempts by Hirschfeld and himself to court support for a channel from the British and the Danish governments, among others, but to no avail. As far as Pundak was concerned, Norway 'was one of the options, it wasn't *the* option' (Interview with Ron Pundak).
76. Jones (1999), p. 112.
77. Corbin (1994), p. 34.
78. Jones (1999), p. 110.
79. Waage (2008), p. 60.
80. *Ibid*, p. 59.
81. Interview with Terje Rød-Larsen.
82. On 2 December, two days before Hirschfeld met Abu Ala in London, a bill sponsored by Beilin and others within the Labour party to revoke the law prohibiting contacts with the PLO had its first reading in the Knesset. It was passed soon after on 19 January 1993.
83. Interview with Terje Rød-Larsen.
84. *Ibid.*
85. Waage (2005), p. 9.
86. Holst's wife Marianne was a researcher at FAFO, and was working on the living conditions study. She was present at the first meeting at Borregard to present some initial findings of the study in order to give real credibility to the smokescreen, but only learned of the secret channel around this time.
87. Interview with Terje Rød-Larsen.
88. *Ibid.*
89. Qurie (2006), p. 139.
90. Waage (2004), p. 108; Waage (2005), p. 12.
91. Abbas (1995), pp. 106–8; Beilin (1999), pp. 105–13; Waage (2005), pp. 12–13.
92. Beilin (1999), p. 113.
93. Interview with Terje Rød-Larsen.
94. Qurie (2006), pp. 239–40
95. Interview with Terje Rød-Larsen.
96. Waage (2005), p. 14.
97. Abbas (1995), p. 104.
98. Waage (2004), p. 107.
99. Interview with Terje Rød-Larsen.
100. *Ibid.*
101. Aggestam (2002), pp. 67–8.
102. Waage (2005), p. 16.
103. Beilin (1999), p. 127.
104. Waage (2005), p. 17.
105. Interview with Yossi Beilin.
106. Abbas (1995), p. 104.
107. Corbin (1994), pp. 179–80.

108. Interview with Mathias Mossberg. Throughout this period, communication between the Norwegian and Swedish Foreign Ministries about the Middle East was sporadic and not to the standard the Swedes desired. Whether due to the maintenance of secrecy, the fact that a Conservative government was in office in Sweden, or neighbourly rivalry, Holst insisted that the Swedes were to be kept completely out of the loop.
109. Butenschøn (1997), pp. 7–8.
110. Waage (2005), p. 20.
111. Ashrawi (2000); Behrendt (2007); Ben-Ami (2004), (2005) and (2006); Ma'oz (1999); Rothstein (1999), (2002b), and (2006); Rothstein, Ma'oz, and Shikaki (2002); Rynhold (2008); Said (2001); Shikaki (1999); Steinberg (2006b).
112. Interview with Terje Rød-Larsen. This position, though caveated, is also echoed in Rothstein (2002a), p. 18.
113. Kelman (2001), p. 190. Nonetheless, Kelman caveats this by noting that 'the mutual recognition of the Oslo agreement ... did not go beyond a pragmatic acceptance of the fact that the other exists and must be accommodated in order to achieve a mutually satisfactory solution of the conflict' (Jamal (2000), p. 49).
114. For many Palestinians and Arab nationalists, the Oslo Agreement 'shook the fundamental premises of collective identity and interests underpinning pan-Arab nationalism' in a conflict perceived not only as a 'conflict of borders' but a 'conflict of survival.' To them, Oslo represented an Israeli concept of a settlement based on a *fait accompli* without addressing the fundamental causes of the conflict to ensure a 'just and comprehensive' peace (Sela (1995), pp. 40–4). See Jamal (2000) for an analysis of the asymmetry of recognition inherent in the Oslo agreement, and Said (2001) for a wider Palestinian nationalist critique.
115. Interview with Saeb Erekat.
116. Waage (2004), pp. 229–36; Waage (2005), p. 20.
117. Interview with Terje Rød-Larsen.
118. Waage (2004), p. 244.
119. Interview with Terje Rød-Larsen.
120. *Ibid*, Dan Kurtzer.
121. Waage (2004), pp. 109–11; Beilin (1999), p. 88.
122. Kurzter *et al.* (2013), p. 42.
123. Interview with Dan Kurtzer; Quandt (2001); Indyk (2009). Describing the Israeli–Syrian peace process under Clinton, Miller notes that 'never has so much time and energy been expended on a process that produced so little in the end' (Miller (2008), p. 254).
124. Indyk (2009), p. 85.
125. *Ibid*, Chapters 1 ('Syria First') and 5 ('The Anatomy of Rabin's Oslo Decision').
126. Interview with Dan Kurtzer; Kurtzer *et al.* (2013), p. 38.
127. *Ibid*.

128. 'Starstruck with both Rabin and the Oslo breakthrough, Bill Clinton and the rest of us on his team never thought about imposing ourselves on a process we hadn't negotiated.' Clinton said that Oslo 'felt like a gift', something which fell into their lap. 'Under these circumstances no one was going to ask tough questions or challenge concepts. Why spoil the party?' (Miller (2008), pp. 262–3).
129. See Quandt (2001), Chapter 11, 'Clinton the Facilitator'.
130. Miller (2008), p. 249.
131. Following the massacre, the Jordanians, Palestinians, and Syrians all broke off negotiations with Israel, and a Security Council Resolution critical of Israel was put on the table. An understanding was engineered which involved US abstention on the Resolution while the Arabs returned to the negotiations. Indyk reasons that the lesson the Americans learned here was that 'encouraging multiple Arab–Israeli negotiations is preferable to concentrating on only one because that gives the US the ability to take advantage of the rivalries and differing interests of the Arab players to overcome the obstacles to progress.' (Indyk (2009), p. 117) Although undoubtedly an accurate observation, this one positive aspect cannot excuse the wider neglect of the Oslo breakthrough.
132. Involved again in the interim negotiations, Larsen had in fact offered to move beyond facilitation, but Savir refused: '... I asked him [Larsen] to refrain from any further attempts at mediation. From day one in Oslo, we had been firmly against any third-party intervention in the substantive side of the negotiations. We welcomed outside involvement in creating a conducive atmosphere, persuading the sides to be flexible, and tempering their highs or lows. But the two parties had to arrive at the actual formulas of the agreements on their own. Thus Terje, who always honoured the wishes of the sides, abandoned his attempt to compose a "Larsen 3" document [exploring settler withdrawal from Hebron and the institution of an international force with additional Palestinian police] as a compromise' (Savir (1998), p. 129).
133. Savir (1998), p. 41.
134. Ross (2004), p. 200.
135. *Ibid*, p. 202.
136. *Ibid*, p. 195.
137. Meital (2006), pp. 69–70; Kurtzer and Lasensky (2008), p. 44; Miller (2008), pp. 241–2.
138. Kurtzer and Lasensky (2008), pp. 43–6, 'Lesson #5.' In the study group's consultations and interviews, the lack of accountability was highlighted more than any other issue.
139. Indyk (2009), p. 143.
140. Interview with Dan Kurtzer.
141. Pruitt (1997), p. 243; Zayyad (2002), p. 151; Ben-Ami (2004), pp. 2–3.
142. Ben-Ami (2004), pp. 2–3.
143. Rynhold (2008), pp. 119–22.

Chapter 4 The 'Beilin–Abu Mazen Understandings' or the 'Stockholm Document': a Trying Time for Track II

1. Interview with Yossi Beilin.
2. 'Palestinian-Israeli final status project – June 1996 report.' SAA – Series 4.2: Vol. 41.
3. Fisk (2005), p. 554.
4. Savir (1998), p. 80.
5. Shikaki (2002), pp. 40–6.
6. Rothstein (2002), p. 18.
7. Savir (1998), p. 157.
8. Interview with Yair Hirschfeld.
9. *Ibid*, Ron Pundak. This point is also made in Rothstein (1999), pp. 223–5, and Miller (2002), p. 32.
10. *Ibid*, Yossi Beilin.
11. *Ibid*, Ahmad Khalidi.
12. *Ibid*, Hussein Agha.
13. *Ibid*, Ann Dismorr.
14. *Ibid*, Ahmad Khalidi.
15. *Ibid*, Hussein Agha.
16. *Ibid*, Mathias Mossberg.
17. *Ibid*, Sven-Eric Söder.
18. Schori was a veteran of the Palme era, and an outspoken critic of Israeli occupation.
19. Memo from Schori to Carlsson and Andersson, 25/08/1994, SAA – Series 4.2: Vol. 4.
20. Interview with Yossi Beilin; Interview with Pierre Schori.
21. Foreign Ministry press release, 27/10/1994. SAA – Series 4.2: Vol. 4.
22. *Ibid*, 01/12/1994. SAA – Series 4.2: Vol. 4.
23. Interview with Sven-Eric Söder.
24. *Ibid*, Ahmad Khalidi.
25. Agha *et al.* (2003), p. 89; Interview with Ann Dismorr.
26. Qurie (2006), pp. 114–20, 135–42.
27. Interview with Ron Pundak.
28. *Ibid*, Yair Hirschfeld.
29. *Ibid*, Ron Pundak.
30. *Ibid*, Yair Hirschfeld.
31. *Ibid*, Ahmad Khalidi; Agha *et al.* (2003), p. 72.
32. *Ibid*, Yair Hirschfeld.
33. Agha *et al.* (2003), p. 89; Interview with Ahmad Khalidi.
34. Interview with Ahmad Khalidi.
35. *Ibid*, Hussein Agha.
36. *Ibid*, Ann Dismorr.
37. *Ibid*, Sven-Eric Söder.

38. *Ibid*, Ann Dismorr.
39. *Ibid*, Yair Hirschfeld.
40. *Ibid*, Yossi Beilin.
41. *Ibid*, Ann Dismorr.
42. Agha *et al.* (2003), p. 81.
43. Letter from Schori to Andersson, 'Breakfast with Beilin in Jerusalem, 11/04/1995'. SAA – Series 4.2: Vol. 6.
44. Memo from Jerusalem to Stockholm, 27/02/1995. SAA – Series 4.2: Vol. 6.
45. Letter from Schori to Andersson, 'Breakfast with Beilin in Jerusalem, 11/04/1995'. SAA – Series 4.2: Vol. 6.
46. Interview with Ahmad Khalidi.
47. *Ibid*, Hussein Agha.
48. *Ibid*, Hussein Agha.
49. *Ibid*, Yossi Beilin.
50. Agha *et al.* (2003), p. 82.
51. Interview with Hussein Agha.
52. *Ibid.*
53. Interview with Ahmad Khalidi.
54. *Ibid*, Ahmad Khalidi.
55. Email correspondence with Yossi Beilin, 16 August 2014.
56. Agha is critical of Beilin's 'theatrical' account of the final session on 31 October. Beilin writes that 'Abu Mazen was very emotional; when we embraced I saw tears in his eyes'; Agha dismisses this as 'bullshit'. He also recalled that Beilin 'asked to have a meeting "between four eyes" with Abu Mazen, and afterwards Abu Mazen said, "I don't understand why he wanted to have a four eyes, he didn't say anything"' (Beilin (1999), p. 177; Interview with Hussein Agha). See Appendix IV for the text of the document as it stood at the end of this meeting.
57. Interview with Ahmad Khalidi; Interview with Hussein Agha.
58. Agha *et al.* (2003), pp. 82–3; Interview with Ann Dismorr.
59. Interview with Ron Pundak; Interview with Yair Hirschfeld; Agha *et al.* (2003), pp. 72, 82–3.
60. *Ibid*, Yossi Beilin.
61. *Ibid*, Ron Pundak.
62. *Ibid*, Yossi Beilin.
63. *Ibid*, Hussein Agha.
64. *Ibid*, Yossi Beilin; Interview with Ahmad Khalidi.
65. *Ibid*, Yossi Beilin.
66. *Ibid*, Hussein Agha.
67. Beilin (1999), p. 186.
68. Interview with Ahmad Khalidi.
69. Beilin (1999), p. 178.
70. Interview with Yair Hirschfeld.
71. *Ibid.*
72. Interview with Hussein Agha.

73. See Chapter V, 'The failure of American and Swedish mediators'.
74. Interview with Yossi Beilin.
75. Although some suggest that Israel accepted them and the Palestinians did not, this orthodoxy is being revised. Both sides replied to the understandings with a 'Yes, but . . .' Dan Kurtzer has explained that 'they both kind of accepted, and they both had lots of reservations . . . The Israelis were more systematic about it, and they said, "We accept this, here are 18 reservations." The Palestinians said, "Well, we don't like part A, we don't like Part B. . .", so stylistically, it came off probably a little more negative, but at the end of the day they both didn't like parts of it . . .' (Interview with Dan Kurtzer).
76. The new government also sought to intensify Swedish efforts in the wider realm of international conflict prevention beyond the Middle East. Hjelm-Wallén produced reports on the matter in 1996 and 1997, identifying and outlining objectives and principles for future Swedish preventive efforts. (Björkdahl (2007), pp. 178–9).
77. This avenue was later explored in theory, but did not produce any results worth mentioning. (Memo from Damascus to Stockholm, 'Re: Israel–Syria', 18/01/1995. SAA – Series 4.2: Vol. 5).
78. Memo from Schori to Carlsson and Andersson, 25/08/1994. SAA – Series 4.2: Vol. 4.
79. Foreign Ministry memo, 'Discussions with deputy Foreign Minister Beilin', 30/01/1995. SAA – Series 4.2: Vol. 11.
80. Foreign Ministry document, 'Swedish Middle East policy, Dec. 1994', 19/12/1994. SAA – Series 4.2: Vol. 4.
81. *Ibid.*
82. As noted in Chapter III, Rabin did not take Carlsson up on his invitation, largely due to his distaste for Sten Andersson.
83. Foreign Ministry memo, 'The Prime Minister's discussions with Shimon Peres and Yasser Arafat, 12/12/94', 28/11/1994. SAA – Series 4.2: Vol. 5.
84. *Ibid*, 'Discussions between Schori and Peres', 05/12/1994, and Foreign Ministry memo, 'Sten Andersson's visit to Jerusalem, Gaza, and Tel Aviv, 2–5 December', 06/12/1994. SAA – Series 4.2: Vol. 4.
85. Confidential Foreign Ministry memo, 'The Prime Minister's discussions with Israeli Foreign Minister Peres, 12/12/94', 14/12/1994. SAA – Series 4.2: Vol. 5.
86. *Ibid*, 'The Prime Minister's discussions with PLO Chairman Yasser Arafat, 12/12/94', 14/12/1994. SAA – Series 4.2: Vol. 5.
87. Press release on aid to the West Bank and Gaza (no date). SAA – Series 4.2: Vol. 5.
88. On 29 November 1994, Schori laid out five brief ambitions to the Riksdag in response to questions on the subject from other members (SAA – Series 4.2: Vol. 4). These points mirror the content of a Foreign Ministry memo on aid to the West Bank and Gaza from November 11, a brief to prepare for the visit of Nabil Shaath (SAA – Series 4.2: Vol. 4).

89. Letter from Abdel Meguid of the Arab League to Andersson, 22/12/1994. SAA – Series 4.2: Vol. 4.
90. Press release on aid to the West Bank and Gaza (no date). SAA – Series 4.2: Vol. 5.
91. Letter from Larsen to Schori, 17/01/1995. SAA – Series 4.2: Vol. 5.
92. On the eve of the Social Democratic election victory, Larsen was having a drink with Peres. Schori received a phone call from Larsen, not only to congratulate him on their victory, but also to reaffirm Swedish commitment to the Israeli–Palestinian peace process. Larsen's message went along the lines of, 'Now you are back in again, that's great. We want you to be seriously involved, not like the previous government which was quite restrained. We propose, Shimon and I, that you commit 10 million SEK to industrial parks and other infrastructure in Gaza.' Schori replied positively that he could indeed imagine sponsoring such a project. After a brief silence, Larsen replied, 'What?!' and said aside to Peres, 'Shimon, he said yes!' (Interview with Pierre Schori).
93. Interview with Pierre Schori.
94. 'Sweden's role as "shepherd" for children in the Middle East within the framework of the Madrid process: the next step', 04/10/1994. SAA – Series 4.2: Vol. 4.
95. Riksdag statement by Schori, 31/10/1996. SAA – Series 4.2: Vol. 41.
96. Foreign Ministry memo, 'Aid to the West Bank and Gaza', 11/11/1994. SAA – Series 4.2: Vol. 4; Foreign Ministry memo, 'Aid to the West Bank and Gaza', 22/02/1995. SAA – Series 4.2: Vol. 6.
97. *Ibid.*
98. During his first term in office, Netanyahu referred to this as Arafat's 'revolving door policy'.
99. Confidential Foreign Ministry memo, 'Conversation with Nabil Shaath in Gaza, 25 and 26/01', 28/01/1995. SAA – Series 4.2: Vol. 5.
100. *Israel Today*, March 1995. SAA – Series 4.2: Vol. 6
101. Confidential Foreign Ministry memo, 'Schori and Eliasson's discussion with Peres, 24/01/95', 30/01/1995. SAA – Series 4.2: Vol. 11.
102. *Haaretz*, 06/08/1995. SAA – Series 4.2: Vol. 9.
103. Letter from Roxman to Schori, 09/10/1995. SAA – Series 4.2: Vol. 9.
104. Foreign Ministry memo, 'The Prime Minister's conversation with President Yasser Arafat, 30/01/96', 02/02/1996. SAA – Series 4.2: Vol. 8.
105. *Ibid*, 'Ministerial visit to Israel and the Palestinian Territories', 13/02/1996. SAA – Series 4.2: Vol. 8.
106. *Ibid*, 'Ministerial visit to Israel and the Palestinian Territories', 13/02/1996. SAA – Series 4.2: Vol. 8; *Dagens Nyheter*, 11/02/1996. SAA – Series 4.2: Vol. 9.
107. *Haaretz*, 11/02/1996. SAA – Series 4.2: Vol. 8.
108. OPIC draft Palestine strategy, 17/04/1996. SAA – Series 4.2: Vol. 9.
109. Funding proposal, 28/08/1995. SAA – Series 4.2: Vol. 8.
110. *Svenska Dagbladet*, 11/02/1996. SAA – Series 4.2: Vol. 9.

111. *The Jerusalem Post*, 11/02/1996. SAA – Series 4.2: Vol. 9.
112. Foreign Ministry memo, 'Ministerial visit to Israel and the Palestinian Territories', 13/02/1996. SAA – Series 4.2: Vol. 8.
113. http://www.mfa.gov.il/MFA/Terrorism+Obstacle + to + Peace/Palestinian + terror + since + 2000/Suicide + and + Other + Bombing + Attacks + in + Israel + Since.htm.
114. Despite being approved, however, the text of the Charter was not actually re-drafted.
115. As Rothstein has observed with regard to Oslo, terrorism exerts a disproportionately negative effect on the context of a peace process. (Rothstein (1999), pp. 231–2).
116. Rabinovich (1999), p. 71; Ben Aharon (2004), p. 65.
117. Savir (1998), p. 87.
118. 'What does the Israeli election mean for Swedish Middle East policy?', 01/06/1996. SAA – Series 4.2: Vol. 41.
119. Interview with Hussein Agha; Interview with Ahmad Khalidi.
120. 'Palestinian–Israeli final status project – June 1996 report.' SAA – Series 4.2: Vol. 41.
121. *The Jerusalem Post*, 11/02/1996. SAA – Series 4.2: Vol. 9.
122. 'What does the Israeli election mean for Swedish Middle East policy?', 01/06/1996. SAA – Series 4.2: Vol. 41.
123. 'Some thoughts on the peace process after Hebron and the Swedish role', 26/01/1997. SAA – Series 4.2: Vol. 41.
124. Ma'oz (2002), p. 138. Palestinian casualty figures differ in various sources: Abu Ala, for example, writes that 'at least 62 Palestinians died and some 1,300 were injured' (Qurie (2008), p. 22).
125. *Riksdag* statements by Hjelm-Wallén, 23/10/1996 and 31/10/1996; *Riksdag* statements by Schori, 25/10/1996 and 31/10/1996. SAA – Series 4.2: Vol. 41.
126. Swedish statement in the Security Council, 05/03/1997 http://www.swedenabroad.com/Page____13229.aspx.
127. Swedish statement in the Security Council, 21/03/1997 http://www.swedenabroad.com/Page____13230.aspx.
128. A Security Council statement condemning the 20 March terrorist attack in Tel Aviv which killed three Israeli women was prepared and supported by Sweden, but American diplomats expressed the desire that no statements whatsoever be issued by the Council (Transcript of radio interview with Jan Eliasson, 24/03/1997. SAA – Series 4.2: Vol. 41).
129. Swedish Embassy in Tel Aviv to Stockholm, 'Israeli demarche about Swedish statements', 24/03/1997. SAA – Series 4.2: Vol. 41.
130. Memo from Jerusalem to Stockholm, 'The Israeli–Palestinian conflict: a few reflections on Sweden's role and Sten Andersson's mission', 19/04/1997. SAA – Series 4.2: Vol. 41.
131. *Ibid.*
132. See Appendix II.

133. See Appendix III.
134. Interview with Yair Hirschfeld.
135. Pundak (2005/2006).
136. Rothstein (2002), p. 10.
137. Savir (1998), p. 311.
138. Interview with Hanna Siniora. Indeed, a fund existed at the disposal of the Swedish consulate in Jerusalem for this purpose.
139. *Ibid*, Yair Hirschfeld.
140. *Ibid*, Gerald Steinberg.
141. Liel (2005/2006).
142. Interview with Yair Hirschfeld.
143. *Ibid*, Walid Salem. See also Mi'ari (1999), p. 342.
144. *Ibid*, Gerald Steinberg.
145. Nasser-Najab (2005/2006).
146. Rynhold (2008), pp. 118–20; Steinberg (2002).
147. Herzog and Hai (2004).
148. Foreign Ministry memo, 'The Stockholm group II meet in London, 19–20 July'. SAA – Series 4.2: Vol. 41.
149. Interview with Hussein Agha.
150. 'Stockholm group Phase II – Progress report July 1997'. SAA – Series 4.2: Vol. 41.
151. Interview with Yossi Beilin.
152. Foreign Ministry memo, 'Sweden in the Middle East: room for a more active policy?', 11/09/1997. SAA – Series 4.2: Vol. 41.
153. Riksdag debate, 29/01/1998. Available at: http://www.riksdagen.se/webbnav/index.aspx?nid=101&bet=1997/98:58.
154. Indyk (2008), pp. 177–8.
155. Miller (2008), p. 273.
156. Ross (2004), p. 268.
157. Miller (2008), pp. 263–4.
158. Indyk (2009), p. 116.
159. 'Sten Andersson's meeting with Arafat in London', 04/06/1996. SAA – Series 4.2: Vol. 41.
160. Quandt (2001), pp. 345–6; Memo from Jerusalem to Stockholm, 'Some thoughts on the peace process after Hebron and the Swedish role', 26/01/1997. SAA – Series 4.2: Vol. 41.
161. Albright address on the Middle East to the National Press Club, 06/08/1997. http://usembassy-israel.org.il/publish/press/visits/september97/albright305.html.
162. Ross (2004), p. 356.
163. 'Notes from a meeting between Andersson and Shaath in New York, 28/09/97', 05/10/1997. SAA – Series 4.2: Vol. 41.
164. Quandt (2001), p. 351.
165. 'Minutes from Schori's breakfast meeting with Beilin, Hirschfeld, Pundak and Levy in Jerusalem, 28/01/98.' SAA – Series 4.2: Vol. 39.

166. Ross (2004), p. 387.
167. Quandt (2001), p. 352.
168. Miller (2008), pp. 273–5.
169. Ross (2004), pp. 376–7, 385.
170. Fisk (2005), p. 535.
171. Qurie (2008), pp. 65–8.
172. Miller (2008), pp. 275–6.
173. *Ibid*, pp. 269–70.
174. Memo from Jerusalem to Stockholm, 'Conversation with Arafat', 28/02/1999. SAA – Series 4.2: Vol. 39.
175. The Jordanians were particularly infuriated by a botched Israeli assassination attempt against Hamas leader Khaled Meshaal in Amman in September 1997. Consequently, King Hussein insisted upon the release of Sheikh Ahmad Yassin, the head of Hamas, from Israeli prison. This episode had the unfortunate effect of strengthening Palestinian rejectionists.

Chapter 5 The 'Stockholm Channel' and Beyond: 'a Bit of a Con' and a 'Tragedy of Errors'

1. Interview with Aaron Miller.
2. Malley and Agha (2001).
3. Interview with Anonymous.
4. *Ibid*, Aaron Miller.
5. *Ibid*, Mathias Mossberg.
6. Svenning (2005), pp. 308–9. In these pages, Svenning also recounts an awkward statement by Persson at the annual summit of Swedish ambassadors in 2003, where he referred to Vietnam, Palme's cause célèbre, as a 'fucking communist dictatorship'.
7. Fichtelius (2007), p. 339; Persson (2007), p. 258.
8. Persson (2007), p. 261.
9. Fichtelius (2007), pp. 345, 349.
10. *Ibid*, p. 338.
11. *Dagens Nyheter*, 12/06/97. Persson writes in his autobiography that the figures were apparently later shown to be inflated, but nevertheless makes the unassailable point that any doubt over this historical event, no matter how statistically small, must strive to be corrected (Persson (2007), p. 246).
12. Svenning (2005), pp. 288–9.
13. The book is also available online in PDF format, and can be found at: http://www.levandehistoria.se/forintelsen.
14. 'Speech at Israel's 50th anniversary, 26/04/1998'. SAA – Series 4.2: Vol. 39.
15. Svenning (2005), p. 294.
16. 'Regarding the Prime Minister's speech on Israel's 50th anniversary', 29/04/1998. SAA – Series 4.2: Vol. 39.

17. 'Questions and Answers on the Middle East', 05/05/1998. SAA – Series 4.2: Vol. 8.
18. Interview with Ann Dismorr.
19. Fichtelius (2007), p. 283.
20. Holocaust survivor and Nobel prize winner Elie Wiesel told Persson that he would be remembered as an honourable figure in Jewish history (Svenning (1995), p. 290).
21. Nuder (2008), pp. 187–91.
22. Interview with Pär Nuder.
23. *Ibid.*
24. Persson (2007), p. 258.
25. Wiel-Berggren (1999).
26. *Aftonbladet*, 07/10/1999.
27. Fichtelius (2007), pp. 339–40.
28. Miller (2008), p. 278.
29. Interview with Terje Rød-Larsen; Miller (2008), p. 279. Barak does not appear to have been impressed with Oslo. He abstained on the Knesset vote over the acceptance of Oslo II, and had serious reservations about its security aspects.
30. See Indyk (2008), Chapters 1 and 12, 'Syria First' and 'Syria Redux'.
31. Ross (2004), p. 507.
32. Sher (2006), p. 15.
33. Ross (2004), pp. 593–4.
34. Email correspondence with Gilead Sher, 16 August 2014.
35. Miller (2008), pp. 283–4.
36. Malley and Agha (2001), p. 65; Bregman (2005), p. 33.
37. Ross (2004), p. 603.
38. Interview with Aaron Miller.
39. *Ibid*, Amnon Lipkin Shahak.
40. Miller (2008), p. 279.
41. Ross (2004), pp. 595–8.
42. Interview with Anonymous.
43. Letter from Andersson to the Party executive, 11/07/2001. SAA – Series 4.2: Vol. 40.
44. Interview with Ahmad Khalidi.
45. *Ibid*, Rob Malley.
46. Telephone interview with Gilead Sher.
47. Interview with Ahmad Khalidi.
48. Telephone interview with Gilead Sher.
49. Interview with Hussein Agha.
50. *Ibid*, Ahmad Khalidi.
51. 'Visit by Areikat to Bjurner', 04/11/1999. SAA – Series 4.2: Vol. 40.
52. *Ibid.*
53. Interviews with Hussein Agha and Ahmad Khalidi.
54. *Ibid*, Mathias Mossberg.

55. Letter from Andersson to the Party executive, 11/07/2001. SAA – Series 4.2: Vol. 40.
56. Interviews with Aaron Miller and Amnon Lipkin Shahak; Ross (2004), p. 604.
57. Qurie (2008), pp. 101, 110.
58. Interview with Amnon Lipkin Shahak.
59. 'Draft itinerary for the visit of Abu Mazen, 6–8 March', 02/03/2000. SAA – Series 4.2: Vol. 35.
60. Interview with Sven-Eric Söder.
61. *Ibid*, Mathias Mossberg; Letter from Andersson to the Party executive, 11/07/2001. SAA – Series 4.2: Vol. 40.
62. Interview with Pär Nuder.
63. Sher (2006), p. 21.
64. Interview with Pär Nuder.
65. *Ibid*, Ahmad Khalidi.
66. Ross (2004), pp. 604–5.
67. Bregman (2005), pp. 64–5.
68. Ross (2004), pp. 604–9.
69. Interview with Amnon Lipkin-Shahak.
70. *Ibid*, Saeb Erekat.
71. Qurie (2008), p. 110.
72. Ross (2004), p. 611.
73. Interview with Hussein Agha.
74. *Ibid*, Ahmad Khalidi.
75. Sher (2006), p. 26; Qurie (2008), p. 114.
76. Interview with Pär Nuder.
77. Ross (2004), p. 612.
78. Sher (2006), p. 27.
79. Qurie (2008), p. 115; Ross (2004), p. 613.
80. Interview with Pär Nuder.
81. Qurie (2008), p. 115.
82. Sher (2006), p. 28.
83. Qurie (2008), p. 118.
84. Bregman (2005), p. 69. This description is echoed by Sher in Swisher (2004), p. 209.
85. Qurie (2008), p. 91; Ben-Ami (2006), p. 252.
86. Interview with Gilead Sher. LHCMA – Elusive Peace catalogue: Vol. 2/20.
87. Sher (2006), pp. 27–8.
88. Interview with Pär Nuder.
89. Swisher (2004), p. 210.
90. Miller (2008), pp. 292–3.
91. Swisher (2004), p. 210–11.
92. Fichtelius (2007), pp. 342–3.
93. Interview with Aaron Miller.

94. Qurie (2008), p. 120.
95. Interview with Ehud Barak. LHCMA – Elusive Peace catalogue: Vol. 2/2.
96. This view is presented in Beilin (2004), p. 144, Ben-Ami (2006), p. 252, Miller (2008), p. 292, Sher (2006), p. 27, Swisher (2004), p. 209, and was suggested in interviews with Yossi Beilin and Mathias Mossberg.
97. Interview with Ahmad Khalidi; Swisher (2004), p. 205. Ross has admitted that the Americans were largely at fault for the misunderstanding which led to this. When Netanyahu was creating problems in the twelfth hour of Wye, he wanted to change the type of prisoners released in the third phase of release. The Americans never made it clear to the Palestinians exactly what this meant, and, with time running out before the signing ceremony, did not want to cause any complications (Ross (2004), p. 458). When Netanyahu released criminals rather than political prisoners, maintaining that this was in accordance with their agreement, Asfour and Dahlan blamed Abu Mazen since he was seen to have negotiated it with the Israelis.
98. Ross (2004), p. 613; Interview with Ahmad Khalidi.
99. Interview with Amnon Lipkin-Shahak.
100. Qurie (2008), p. 116.
101. *Ibid*, anonymous.
102. *Ibid*, Hussein Agha.
103. *Ibid*, Saeb Erekat.
104. *Ibid*.
105. Interview with Ahmad Khalidi.
106. Ross (2004), pp. 617–18. See also Pressman (2001); Pundak (2001); Sayigh (2001).
107. Sontag (2001), p. 80.
108. See Heller (2000), pp. 72–4.
109. Ross (2004), pp. 601–2.
110. Miller (2008), p. 291; Ross (2004), pp. 602–3.
111. Interview with Ahmad Khalidi.
112. Qurie (2008), pp. 152–3.
113. Interview with Ehud Barak. LHCMA – Elusive Peace catalogue: Vol. 2/2.
114. *Ibid*, Saeb Erekat. LHCMA – Elusive Peace catalogue: Vol. 3/6.
115. *Ibid*, Ehud Barak. LHCMA – Elusive Peace catalogue: Vol. 2/2.
116. *Ibid*, Amnon Lipkin-Shahak.
117. *Ibid*, Aaron Miller.
118. *Ibid*, Dan Kurtzer; Kurtzer and Lasensky (2008), p. 37.
119. Miller (2008), p. 280.
120. *Ibid*, p. 292–3.
121. Interview with Rob Malley.
122. Beilin (2004), pp. 153–4.
123. Interview with Yossi Beilin.
124. *Ibid*, anonymous.
125. *Ibid*, Yair Hirschfeld.

126. Indyk (2008), p. 251. As Indyk describes, this problem also plagued Barak at a key moment in his negotiations with the Syrians.
127. Ben-Ami (2006), p. 256.
128. Interview with Rob Malley.
129. *Ibid*, Yossi Beilin. For further analysis of the failure of Camp David, see Ben-Ami (2006); Bregman (2005); Enderlin (2003); Finkelstein (2007); Freedman (2008); Indyk (2008); Kurtzer and Lasensky (2008); Malley and Agha (2001) and (2002b); Meital (2006); Miller (2008); Morris (2002); Morris *et al.* (2002); Pressman (2003); Pundak (2001); Qurie (2008); Ross (2004); Sher (2006); Sontag (2001); Swisher (2004); Zunes (2001).
130. Pressman (2003), p. 41.
131. Interview with anonymous.
132. *Ibid.*
133. Qurie (2008), p. 122.
134. Interview with Pär Nuder.
135. *Ibid.*
136. Fichtelius (2007), p. 345; Persson (2007), p. 261.
137. Interview with Pär Nuder.
138. *Ibid*, Anders Lidén.
139. *Ibid*, Hussein Agha.
140. *Ibid*, Ahmad Khalidi.
141. *Ibid*, Hussein Agha.
142. *Ibid*, Mathias Mossberg; Ross (2004), pp. 611 and 613.
143. As it happens, Abu Mazen did know, so this would not have had a great deal of impact, but it reflects the divergence between the two.
144. Interview with Pär Nuder.
145. *Ibid*, Mathias Mossberg.
146. *Ibid*, Ahmad Khalidi.
147. *Ibid*, Mathias Mossberg.
148. *Ibid*, Hussein Agha.
149. 'Moratinos in Jerusalem', 21/09/2000. SAA – Series 4.2: Vol. 37; Interviews with Hussein Agha, Yossi Beilin and Ahmad Khalidi.
150. Interview with Ahmad Khalidi.
151. *Ibid*, Mathias Mossberg.
152. Nuder (2008), pp. 99, 214.
153. Interview with Ahmad Khalidi.
154. 'Meeting with the Stockholm group, 20–21 Dec. 2000', SAA – Series 4.2: Vol. 38.
155. Interview with Hussein Agha.
156. *Ibid*, Hussein Agha, Ahmad Khalidi, Catharina Kipp, Mathias Mossberg and Pierre Schori.
157. *Ibid*, Anders Lidén.
158. *Ibid*, Catharina Kipp.

159. Schori (2008), pp. 161–2.
160. 'Prime Minister Persson's meeting with Arafat 07/09', 08/09/2000. SAA – Series 4.2: Vol. 37.
161. 'Foreign Minister Lindh's meeting with Shaath, 12/08/00', 12/08/2000. SAA – Series 4.2: Vol. 37.
162. 'Prime Minister Persson's meeting with Prime Minister Barak 08/09', 08/09/2000. SAA – Series 4.2: Vol. 37.
163. Letter from Andersson to Arafat, 09/08/2000. SAA – Series 4.2: Vol. 37.
164. Interview with Ahmad Khalidi.
165. *Ibid*, Mathias Mossberg.
166. Letter from Andersson to the Party executive, 11/07/2001. SAA – Series 4.2: Vol. 40.
167. Schori (2008), p. 162.
168. Letter from Stanley Sheinbaum to Clinton on conversation with Shaath, 15/08/2000. SAA – Series 4.2: Vol. 37.
169. Interview with Madeleine Albright. LHCMA – Elusive Peace catalogue: Vol. 4/1 (formerly 2/49).
170. *Ibid.*
171. 'EU lunch with Minister Ben-Ami', 03/08/2000. SAA – Series 4.2: Vol. 37.
172. *Aftonbladet*, 21/10/2000; Svenning (2005), pp. 293–4.
173. Fichtelius (2007), p. 339.
174. Interview with Pär Nuder.
175. Sher (2006), p. 222.
176. Interview with Saeb Erekat.
177. Speech by Arafat in Davos, Switzerland, 28/01/2001. Available at: http://www.mfa.gov.il/MFA/MFAArchive/2000_2009/2001/3/Sharm%20el Sheikh%20Fact-Finding%20Committee%20-%20Second%20St#appendix.
178. Interviews with Anders Lidén and Pär Nuder.
179. Fichtelius (2007), p. 349.
180. Letter from Andersson to Arafat, 14/12/2000. SAA – Series 4.2: Vol. 38.
181. Interview with Mathias Mossberg.
182. Speech at the OPIC, 08/11/2000. SAA – Series 4.2: Vol. 38.
183. Letter from Andersson to the Party executive, 11/07/2001. SAA – Series 4.2: Vol. 40.
184. *Ibid.*
185. Svenning (2005), p. 300.
186. Nuder (2008), p. 212.
187. Pundak (2001), pp. 39, 42.
188. Interview with Aaron Miller.
189. *Ibid*, Ahmad Khalidi.
190. *Ibid.*
191. Fichtelius (2007), p. 345.
192. Speeches by Abu Ala and Shimon Peres, 08/11/2001. SAA – Series 4.2: Vol. 42.

Conclusions

1. *The New Yorker*, 05/10/2009 http://www.newyorker.com/talk/2009/10/05/091005ta_talk_collins An alternative formulation is quoted in Klieman (2000), p. 18.
2. Fichtelius (2007), p. 345.
3. Persson (2007), pp. 257–8.
4. For a more detailed account of Peres' reasoning, see Eriksson (2013), pp. 216–8.
5. Shai Feldman, speaking at the International Institute for Strategic Studies (IISS), 06/11/2007.
6. Eriksson (2013), pp. 222–3.
7. Hassassian (2002), p. 114.
8. Bar-Siman-Tov (2004), pp. 64–6.
9. Ross (2004), p. 589.
10. Kelman (1999a), p. 598.
11. Kriesberg (2001), p. 389.
12. Herzog and Hai (2004).
13. Corbin (1994), pp. 17–18.
14. Kleiboer (1996), p. 372.
15. Hopmann (2001), p. 459.
16. Haass (1990), p. 4.
17. Princen (1992), p. 22.
18. Savir (1998), p. 280.
19. Miller (2008), p. 263.
20. Interview with Yossi Beilin.
21. Crocker *et al.* (2002); Kriesberg (2001); Saunders (2001). 'The issue is not whether a bilateral initiative or a third party role is the correct approach, but rather what mix of involvement is the most appropriate at a particular time in a particular situation' (Saunders (2001), p. 489).
22. Halim (2002); Bronson (2002); Joffe (2002); Hirschfeld (2004), pp. 264–5; Miller (2002), p. 36.
23. Dan Kurtzer, US Ambassador to Egypt at the time, recalls that there 'was no outreach to the Arabs almost at all.' Mubarak felt that he was invited to events 'for show' without being afforded an important role, and Camp David served as his 'payback': 'we needed the Arabs to be supportive of what we were doing with Arafat, and I know Mubarak – because I was there at the time – he wouldn't deal with us because we had kept him out of the show .... It was an awful, awful situation. And we never brought them into the picture' (Interview with Dan Kurtzer). See also Kurtzer and Lasensky (2008).
24. Crocker *et al.* (2002), p. 250.
25. *Ibid*, p. 249.
26. Interview with Rob Malley.
27. *Ibid*, Dan Kurtzer.

Appendices

1. Rabie (1995), pp. 175–6.
2. Available at: http://www.jewishvirtuallibrary.org/jsource/Peace/beilinmazen.html.

BIBLIOGRAPHY

PRIMARY SOURCES

Interviews

Hussein Agha – London – 13 September 2010
Geoffrey Aronson – Washington, D.C. – 29 January 2009
Yossi Beilin – Tel Aviv – 12 May 2009
Ann Dismorr – Stockholm – 17 April 2009
Jan Eliasson – Stockholm – 2 September 2009
Stig Elvemar – Stockholm – 22 April 2010
Saeb Erekat – Jericho – 12 June 2009
Gabriel Fahel – Ramallah – 11 June 2009
Yair Hirschfeld – Tel Aviv – 17 May 2009
Ulf Hjertonsson – New York – 13 January 2009
Hiba Husseini – Ramallah – 9 June 2009
Ahmad Khalidi – London – 9 September 2010
Catharina Kipp – Stockholm – 30 July 2010
Dan Kurtzer – Princeton – 13 February 2009
Anders Lidén – New York – 14 February 2009
Amnon Lipkin-Shahak – Tel Aviv – 1 June 2009
Rob Malley – Washington, D.C. – 23 February 2009
Aaron Miller – Washington, D.C. – 4 February 2009
Mathias Mossberg – Lund – 18 August 2009
Pär Nuder – Stockholm – 28 April 2009
Ron Pundak – Tel Aviv – 7 May 2009
Terje Rød-Larsen – New York – 11 February 2009
Jonathan Rynhold – Modi'in – 13 May 2009
Walid Salem – Jerusalem – 14 June 2009
Pierre Schori – Stockholm – 28 August 2009
Gilead Sher (Telephone interview) – Tel Aviv – 9 July 2013
Hanna Siniora – Tantur – 8 June 2009

Sven-Eric Söder – Stockholm – 21 August 2009
Gerald Steinberg – Jerusalem – 24 May 2009

Archives

Arbetarrörelsens arkiv och bibliotek (*Swedish Labour Movement Archives and Library*)

- Olof Palmes Arkiv (OPA) (www.olofpalme.org)
- Sten Anderssons Arkiv (SAA)
- *Svenska Arbetarpartiets Arkiv* (SAPA) (Swedish Labour Party Archives)

Liddell Hart Centre for Military Archives (LHCMA), King's College London

SECONDARY SOURCES

Abadi, J., 'Sweden's Policy toward Israel: Constraints and Adjustments', *Middle Eastern Studies*, Vol. 37, No. 2, April 2001

Abbas, M. (1995), *Through Secret Channels* (Reading: Garnet Publishing Ltd)

Aggestam, K. (1999), *Reframing and Resolving Conflict: Israeli–Palestinian Negotiations 1988–1998* (Lund, Sweden: Lund Uni. Press)

———, 'Quasi-Informal Mediation in the Oslo Channel: Larsen and Holst as Individual Mediators', in Bercovitch, J. ed. (2002), *Studies in International Mediation* (Basingstoke: Palgrave Macmillan)

Agha, H., Feldman, S., Khalidi, A., and Schiff, Z. (2003), *Track II Diplomacy: Lessons from the Middle East* (Cambridge, MA: MIT Press)

Aly, Abdel Monem Said, 'The Road to Oslo and Beyond: Prospects for an Arab–Israeli Peace', *Security Dialogue*, Vol. 25, No. 1, 1994, pp. 37–51

Andersson, S. (1993), *I de lugnaste vatten* [*In the calmest waters*, Swedish] (Stockholm: Tiden)

Andrén, N. and Möller, Y. (1990), *Från Undén till Palme: Svensk Utrikespolitik Efter Andra Världskriget* [*From Undén to Palme: Swedish Foreign Policy After the Second World War*, Swedish] (Stockholm: Norstedt)

Antman, P. and Schori, P. (1996), Olof *Palme: Den Gränslöse Reformisten* [*Olof Palme: The Limitless Reformist*, Swedish] (Stockholm: Tidens Förlag)

Antonius, G. (1945), *The Arab Awakening: The Story of the Arab National Movement* (London: Hamish Hamilton)

Arendt, H. (1985), *Eichmann in Jerusalem: A Report on the Banality of Evil* (London: Penguin Books)

——— (2004), *The Origins of Totalitarianism* (New York: Schocken Books)

Arvidsson, C. (2006), *Olof Palme: Med Verkligheten som Fiende* [*Olof Palme: Reality as the Enemy*, Swedish] (Stockholm: Timbro)

Ashrawi, H. 'The Failure of Oslo: Charting a New Course' 2000 http://www.thejerusalemfund.org/carryover/pubs/20001116pb.html (accessed on 24 July 2006)

Åström, S. (1992), *Ögonblick: Från Ett Halvsekel i UD-tjänst* [*Moments: From half a century serving the Foreign Ministry*, Swedish] (Stockholm: Bonnier Alba)

Ayissi, A., 'Territorial Conflicts: Claiming the Land', in Zartman, I.W. ed. (2001), *Preventive Negotiation: Avoiding Conflict Escalation* (Lanham, M.D.: Rowman & Littlefield Publishers Inc.)

Bar-On, D. and Adwan, S., 'The Psychology of Better Dialogue between Two Separate but Interdependent Narratives' in Rotberg, R.I. ed. (2006), *Israeli and Palestinian Narratives of Conflict: History's Double Helix* (Bloomington, Indiana: Indiana University Press)

Bar-On, M., 'Conflicting Narratives or Narratives of a Conflict: Can the Zionist and Palestinian Narratives of the 1948 War Be Bridged?' in Rotberg, R.I. ed. (2006), *Israeli and Palestinian Narratives of Conflict: History's Double Helix* (Bloomington, Indiana: Indiana University Press)

Bar-Siman-Tov, Y., 'Peace Policy as Domestic and Foreign Policy: The Israeli Case', in Sofer, S. ed. (2001), *Peacemaking in a Divided Society: Israel After Rabin* (London: Frank Cass)

———, 'Dialectics Between Stable Peace and Reconciliation' in Bar-Siman-Tov, Y. ed. (2004), *From Conflict Resolution to Reconciliation* (Oxford: Oxford University Press)

Bar-Tal, D., 'From Intractable Conflict Through Conflict Resolution to Reconciliation: Psychological Analysis', *Political Psychology*, Vol. 21, No. 2, 2000

——— and Salomon, G., 'Israeli–Jewish Narratives of the Israeli–Palestinian Conflict: Evolution, Contents, Functions and Consequences' in Rotberg, R.I. ed. (2006), *Israeli and Palestinian Narratives of Conflict: History's Double Helix* (Bloomington, Indiana: Indiana University Press)

Barak, O., 'The Failure of the Israeli–Palestinian Peace Process, 1993–2000', *Journal of Peace Research*, Vol. 42, No. 6, 2005, pp. 719–36

Beardsley, K.C., Quinn, D., Biswas, B. & Wilkenfeld, J., 'Mediation Style and Crisis Outcomes', *Journal of Conflict Resolution*, Vol. 50, No. 1, February 2006, pp. 58–86

Behrendt, S. (2007), *The Secret Israeli–Palestinian Negotiations in Oslo: Their success and why the process ultimately failed* (London: Routledge)

Beilin, Y. (1999), *Touching Peace: From the Oslo Accord to a Final Agreement* (London: Weidenfeld & Nicolson)

——— (2004), *The Path to Geneva: The Quest for a Permanent Agreement, 1996–2004* (New York: RDV Books)

Ben-Aharon, Y., 'Foundering Illusions: The Demise of the Oslo Process' in Rothstein, R.L., Ma'oz, M. & Shikaki, K. eds (2002), *The Israeli–Palestinian Peace Process: Oslo and the Lessons of Failure* (Brighton: Sussex Academic Press)

Ben-Ami, S. 'The Rise and Fall of the Oslo Process.' Speech at the University of Utah Middle East Centre, 2 March 2004. Available at: http://www.mec.utah.edu/Lectures/2004%20lecture%20pages/ben-ami.html

———, 'So Close and Yet So Far: Lessons from the Israeli–Palestinian Peace Process', *Israel Studies*, Vol. 10, No. 2, Summer 2005

——— (2006), *Scars of War, Wounds of Peace: The Israeli-Arab Tragedy* (New York: Oxford University Press)

Bercovitch, J., 'The Structure and Diversity of Mediation in International Relations' in Bercovitch, J. & Rubin, J.Z. eds (1994), *Mediation in International Relations: Multiple Approaches to Conflict Management* (London: Macmillan Press Ltd)

———, 'Introduction: Putting Mediation in Context' in Bercovitch, J. ed. (2002), *Studies in International Mediation* (Basingstoke: Palgrave Macmillan)

——— and Gartner, S.S., 'Is there method in the madness of mediation? Some lessons for mediators from quantitative studies of mediation' in Bercovitch, J. & Gartner, S.S. eds (2009), *International Conflict Mediation: New Approaches and Findings* (London: Routledge)

——— and Houston, A., 'Why Do They Do It Like This? An analysis of the factors influencing mediation behaviour in international conflicts', *Journal of Conflict Resolution*, Vol. 44, No. 2, April 2000, pp. 170–202

——— and Langley, J., 'The Nature of the Dispute and the Effectiveness of International Mediation', *Journal of Conflict Resolution*, Vol. 37, No. 4, December 1993, pp. 670–91

Berggren, H. (2010), *Underbara dagar framför oss: En biografi över Olof Palme* [*Wonderful days ahead of us: A biography of Olof Palme*, Swedish] (Stockholm: Norstedts)

Bergh, S.I. 'Sweden and the Middle East Peace Process: The 1988 U.S.–PLO Dialogue and the 1995 "Stockholm Agreement"' Unpublished M.Phil thesis, Oxford University, 2001

Bernadotte, F. (1948), *Istället för Vapen* [*Instead of Weapons*, Swedish] (Stockholm: Nordstedts)

Bjereld, U., 'Critic or Mediator? Sweden in World Politics 1945–1990', *Journal of Peace Research*, Vol. 32, No. 1, 1995

——— (1989), *Svensk Mellanösternpolitik* [*Swedish Middle East policy*, Swedish] (Stockholm: Carlssons)

——— and Carmesund, U. eds (2008), Israel *och Palestina: 60 år i våra röda hjärtan* [*Israel and Palestine: 60 years in our red hearts*, Swedish] (Stockholm: Hjalmarson & Högberg)

Björkdahl, A., 'Constructing a Swedish Conflict Prevention Policy Based on a Powerful Idea and Successful Practice', *Cooperation and Conflict*, Vol. 42, No. 2, 2007, pp. 169–85

Bramstedt, E.K. (1945), *Dictatorship and Political Police: The Technique of Control by Fear* (London: Routledge)

Bregman, A. (2002), *Israel's Wars: A History since 1947* (London: Routledge)

——— (2005), *Elusive Peace* (London: Penguin Books)

Brewer, M.B., 'The Psychology of Prejudice: Ingroup Love or Outgroup Hate?', *Journal of Social Issues*, Vol. 55, No. 3, 1999

Bronson, R., 'The Reluctant Mediator', *The Washington Quarterly*, Vol. 25, No. 4, Autumn 2002, pp. 177–86

Brown, N.J., 'Contesting National Identity in Palestinian Education' in Rotberg, R.I. ed. (2006), *Israeli and Palestinian Narratives of Conflict: History's Double Helix* (Bloomington, Indiana: Indiana University Press)

Browning, C.S., 'Branding Nordicity: Models, Identity and the Decline of Exceptionalism', *Cooperation and Conflict*, Vol. 42, No. 1, 2007, pp. 27–51

Butenschøn, N., 'The Oslo Agreement in Norwegian Foreign Policy', University of Durham, Centre for Middle Eastern and Islamic Studies, Occasional Paper #56, January 1997

Carmesund, U., 'Swedish Support for Zionism and the Palestinian Refugees: The "Swedish–Israel aid" and Kfar Achim/Qastina', *Holy Land Studies*, Vol. 4, No. 2, 2005

Carnevale, P.J., 'Mediating From Strength', in Bercovitch, J. ed. (2002), *Studies in International Mediation* (Basingstoke: Palgrave Macmillan)

Cesarani, D. (2004), *Eichmann: His Life and Crimes* (London: William Heinemann)

Corbin, J. (1994), *Gaza First: The Secret Norway Channel to Peace Between Israel and the PLO* (London: Bloomsbury Publishing Ltd)

Crocker, C., Hampson, F.O. & Aall, P., 'Two's Company But Is Three a Crowd? Some Hypotheses about Multiparty Mediation' in Bercovitch, J. ed. (2002), *Studies in International Mediation* (Basingstoke: Palgrave Macmillan)

——— (2004), *Taming Intractable Conflicts: Mediation in the Hardest Cases* (Washington D.C.: USIP Press)

Dalsjö, R. (2006), *Life-Line Lost: The Rise and Fall of 'Neutral' Sweden's Secret Reserve Option of Wartime Help From the West* (Stockholm: Santérus Academic Press Sweden)

Efron, N.J. (2003), *Real Jews: Secular vs. Ultra-Orthodox and the Struggle for Jewish Identity in Israel* (New York: Basic Books)

Ehnmark, A., '1789 Års Man', in Åsard, E. ed. (2002), *Politikern Olof Palme* [*Olof Palme the Politician*, Swedish] (Stockholm: Hjalmarson & Högberg)

Ekengren, A-M. (2005), *Olof Palme och Utrikespolitiken: Europa och Tredje Världen* [*Olof Palme and Foreign Policy: Europe and the Third World*, Swedish] (Umeå: Boréa)

Eliasson, J., 'Olof Palme och Utrikespolitiken' in Åsard, E. ed. (2002), *Politikern Olof Palme* [*Olof Palme the Politician*, Swedish] (Stockholm: Hjalmarson & Högberg)

Enderlin, C. (2003), *Shattered Dreams: the Failure of the Peace Process in the Middle East, 1995–2002* (New York: Other Press)

Eriksson, J. (2013), 'Israeli Track II Diplomacy: The Beilin–Abu Mazen Understandings' in Jones, C. & Petersen, T. eds (2013), *Israel's Clandestine Diplomacies* (London: Hurst)

Esber, R.M., 'Rewriting the History of 1948: The Birth of the Palestinian Refugee Question Revisited', *Holy Land Studies*, Vol. 4, No. 1, 2005

Fichtelius, E. (2007), *Aldrig ensam alltid ensam: samtalen med Göran Persson, 1996–2006* [*Never alone always alone: the conversations with Göran Persson, 1996–2006*, Swedish] (Stockholm: Norstedts)

Finkelstein, N.G., 'The Camp David II Negotiations: How Dennis Ross Proved the Palestinians Aborted the Peace Process', *Journal of Palestine Studies*, Vol. 36, No. 2, 2007

Fisk, R. (2005), *The Great War For Civilisation: The Conquest of the Middle East* (London: Fourth Estate)

Flapan, S. (1987), *The Birth of Israel: Myths and Realities* (New York: Pantheon Books)

Freedman, L. (2008), *A Choice of Enemies: America Confronts the Middle East* (London: Weidenfeld & Nicolson)

Gazit, S. (2003), *Trapped Fools: Thirty Years of Israeli Policy in the Territories* (London: Frank Cass)

Gerber, H., 'Zionism, Orientalism, and the Palestinians', *Journal of Palestine Studies*, Vol. 33, No. 1, Fall 2003

———, 'Foreign Occupiers and Step Children: Zionist Discourse and the Palestinians, 1882–1948' in Podeh, E. & Kaufman, A. eds (2006), *Arab-Jewish Relations: From Conflict to Resolution?* (Brighton: Sussex Academic Press)

——— (2008), *Remembering and Imagining Palestine: Identity and Nationalism from the Crusades to the Present* (Basingstoke: Palgrave Macmillan)

Gillis, J.R. ed. (1996), *Commemorations: The Politics of National Identity* (Princeton, N. J.: Princeton University Press)

Gordon, N. (2008), *Israel's Occupation* (Berkeley, California: University of California Press)

Gorenberg, G. (2006), *The Accidental Empire: Israel and the Birth of the Settlements, 1967–1977* (New York: Times Books)

Gunning, J., 'Peace with Hamas? The transforming potential of political participation', *International Affairs*, Vol. 80, No. 2, (2004), pp. 233–55

Haass, R. (1990), *Conflicts Unending* (New Haven, CT: Yale University Press)

Halbwachs, M. (1992), *On Collective Memory* [edited and translated by Lewis A. Coser] (Chicago, Illinois: University of Chicago Press)

Halim, Ahmed Abdel, 'The Unique Role of Moderate Arab States', *The Washington Quarterly*, Vol. 25, No. 4, Autumn 2002, pp. 187–97

Halperin, E., 'Group-based Hatred in Intractable Conflict in Israel', *Journal of Conflict Resolution*, Vol. 52, No. 5, 2008, pp. 713–36

Hassassian, M., 'Historical Dynamics Shaping Palestinian National Identity', *Palestine–Israel Journal of Politics, Economics, and Culture*, Vol. 8, No. 4, 2001 and Vol. 9, No. 1, 2002

———, 'Why Did Oslo Fail? Lessons for the Future' in Rothstein, R.L., Ma'oz, M. & Shikaki, K. eds (2002), *The Israeli–Palestinian Peace Process: Oslo and the Lessons of Failure* (Brighton: Sussex Academic Press)

Heller, M. (2000), Continuity and Change in Israeli Security Policy, Adelphi Paper 335, IISS Publications (Oxford & New York: Oxford University Press)

Herzl, T. (1936), *The Jewish State*, 3rd edn (London: Central Office of the Zionist Organisation)

Herzog, S. and Hai, A. (2004), *The Power of Possibility: The Role of People-to-People Programs in the Current Israeli–Palestinian Reality* (Tel Aviv: ECF/Friedrich Ebert Stiftung)

Hirschfeld, Y., 'The Case for a Combined Grand Strategy for Peace: An Israeli View', *Brown Journal of World Affairs*, Vol. 10, No. 2, Winter/Spring 2004

Hirst, D. (2003), *The Gun and the Olive Branch*, 3rd edn (New York: Nation Books)

Holmberg, G., 'Hur Israel fick en plats i mitt röda hjärta' in Bjereld, U. & Carmesund, U. eds (2008), *Israel och Palestina: 60 år i våra röda hjärtan* [*Israel and Palestine: 60 years in our red hearts*, Swedish] (Stockholm: Hjalmarson & Högberg)

Hopmann, P.T., 'Bargaining and Problem Solving: Two Perspectives on International Negotiation', in Crocker, C. & Hampson, F.O. & Aall, P. eds (2001), *Turbulent Peace: The Challenges of Managing International Conflict* (Washington D.C.: The United States Institute of Peace Press)

Indyk, M. (2009), *Innocent Abroad: An Intimate Account of American Peace Diplomacy in the Middle East* (New York: Simon & Schuster)

Jamal, A., 'The Palestinians in the Israeli Peace Discourse: A Conditional Partnership', *Journal of Palestine Studies*, Vol. 30, No. 1, Autumn 2000

Jawad, S.A., 'The Arab and Palestinian Narratives of the 1948 War' in Rotberg, R.I. ed. (2006), *Israeli and Palestinian Narratives of Conflict: History's Double Helix* (Bloomington, Indiana: Indiana University Press)

Joffe, J., 'Mediation in the Middle East', *The Washington Quarterly*, Vol. 25, No. 4, Autumn 2002, pp. 171–5

Johannesson, K., 'Olof Palmes Retorik' in Åsard, E. ed. (2002), *Politikern Olof Palme* [*Olof Palme the Politician*, Swedish] (Stockholm: Hjalmarson & Högberg)

Jones, D. (1999), *Cosmopolitan Mediation?: Conflict Resolution and the Oslo Accords* (Manchester: Manchester University Press)

Kacowicz, A., 'Rashomon in the Middle East: Clashing Narratives, Images, and Frames in the Israeli–Palestinian Conflict', *Cooperation and Conflict*, Vol. 40, No. 3, 2005

Kaplan, E. (2005), *The Jewish Radical Right: Revisionist Zionism and its Ideological Legacy* (Madison, Wisconsin: University of Wisconsin Press)

Kelman, H.C., 'The political psychology of the Israeli–Palestinian conflict: How can we overcome the barriers to a negotiated solution?', *Political Psychology*, Vol. 8, No. 3, 1987, pp. 347–63.

———, 'The interdependence of Israeli and Palestinian national identities: The role of the other in existential conflicts', *Journal of Social Issues*, Vol. 55, No. 3, 1999, pp. 581–600

———, 'The role of national identity in conflict resolution: Experiences from Israeli–Palestinian problem-solving workshops', in Ashmore, R.D., Jussim, L. & Wilder, D. eds (2001), *Social identity, intergroup conflict, and conflict reduction* (Oxford and New York: Oxford University Press)

———, 'Israeli–Palestinian Peace: Inching Toward and Looking Beyond Negotiations', *Middle East Policy*, Vol. 14, No. 3, 2007

Khalidi, R. (1997), *Palestinian Identity: The Construction of Modern National Consciousness* (New York: Columbia University Press)

——— (2006), *The Iron Cage: The Story of the Palestinian Struggle for Statehood* (Boston, MA: Beacon Press)

Khalili, L. (2007), *Heroes and Martyrs of Palestine: The Politics of National Commemoration* (Cambridge: Cambridge University Press)

Kimmerling, B. (2005), *The Invention and Decline of Israeliness: State, Society and the Military* (Berkeley: University of California Press)

——— (2008), *Clash of Identities: Explorations in Israeli and Palestinian Societies* (New York: Columbia University Press)

Kleiboer, M., 'Understanding Success and Failure of International Mediation', *Journal of Conflict Resolution*, Vol. 40, No. 2, June 1996, pp. 360–89

Klein, M. and Malki, R., 'Israeli–Palestinian Track II Diplomacy' in Kaufman, E., Salem, W. & Verhoeven, J. eds (2006), Bridging the Divide: Peacebuilding in the Israeli–Palestinian Conflict (London: Rienner)

Klieman, A. (2000), *Israeli Diplomacy in the Back-channel, Davis Occasional Papers*, No. 80 (Jerusalem: The Leonard Davis Institute for International Relations)

Kornberg, J. (1993), *Theodor Herzl: From Assimilation to Zionism* (Indianapolis: Indiana University Press)

Kriesberg, L., 'Mediation and the Transformation of the Israeli–Palestinian Conflict', *Journal of Peace Research*, Vol. 38, No. 3, 2001, pp. 373–92

———, 'The Relevance of Reconciliation Actions in the Breakdown of Israeli–Palestinian Negotiations, 2000', *Peace & Change*, Vol. 27, No. 4, October 2002

———, 'Comparing Reconciliation Actions Within and Between Countries' in Bar-Siman-Tov, Y. ed. (2004), *From Conflict Resolution to Reconciliation* (Oxford: Oxford University Press)

Kurtzer, D. and Lasensky, S. (2008), *Negotiating Arab-Israeli Peace: American Leadership in the Middle East* (Washington D.C.: USIP Press)

———, Quandt, W., Spiegel, S., and Telhami, S. (2013), *The Peace Puzzle: America's Quest for Arab-Israeli Peace, 1989–2011* (Ithaca, NY: Cornell University Press)

Lassner, J. and Troen, S.I. (2007), *Jews and Muslims in the Arab World: Haunted By Pasts Real and Imagined* (Plymouth: Rowman & Littlefield)

LeBor, A. (2007), *City of Oranges: Arabs and Jews in Jaffa* (London: Bloomsbury)

Liel, A., 'People-to-People: Telling the Truth about the Israeli–Palestinian Case', *Palestine–Israel Journal of Politics, Economics and Culture*, Vol. 12, No. 4 & Vol. 13, No. 1, 2005/2006

Litvak, M. ed. (2009), *Palestinian Collective Memory and National Identity* (New York: Palgrave Macmillan)

Lonni, A., 'Parallel Strategies in Israeli and Palestinian Experience', *Palestine–Israel Journal of Politics, Economics, and Culture*, Vol. 8, No. 4, 2001 and Vol. 9, No. 1, 2002

Lowenthal, D., 'Identity, Heritage, and History', in Gillis, J.R. ed. (1996), *Commemorations: The Politics of National Identity* (Princeton, N.J.: Princeton University Press)

Malley, R. and Agha, H., 'Camp David: Tragedy of Errors', *New York Review of Books*, Vol. 48, No. 13, 9 August, 2001

———, 'The Last Negotiation: How to End the Middle East Peace Process', *Foreign Affairs*, Vol. 81, No. 3, May 2002

———, 'Camp David and After: An Exchange (2. A Reply to Ehud Barak)', *New York Review of Books*, Vol. 49, No. 10, 13 June 2002

———, 'How Not to Make Peace in the Middle East', *New York Review of Books*, Vol. 56, No. 1, January 2009

Ma'oz, M., 'The Oslo Agreements: Toward Arab-Jewish Reconciliation', in Rothstein, R.L. ed. (1999), *After the Peace: Resistance and Reconciliation* (Boulder, CO: Lynne Rienner Publishers)

———, 'The Oslo Peace Process: From Breakthrough to Breakdown' in Rothstein, R.L., Ma'oz, M. & Shikaki, K. eds (2002), *The Israeli–Palestinian Peace Process: Oslo and the Lessons of Failure* (Brighton: Sussex Academic Press)

Masalha, N. (1992), *Expulsion of the Palestinians: The Concept of 'Transfer' in Zionist Political Thought, 1882–1948* (Washington DC: Institute for Palestine Studies)

Matar, D. (2011), *What It Means to be Palestinian: Stories of Palestinian Peoplehood* (London: I.B.Tauris)

Mayer, A.J. (2008), *Plowshares Into Swords: From Zionism to Israel* (London: Verso)

Meital, Y. (2006), *Peace in Tatters* (London: Lynne Rienner)

Mi'ari, M., 'Attitudes of Palestinians Toward Normalization with Israel', *Journal of Peace Research*, Vol. 36, No. 3, 1999

Miller, A.D., 'The Pursuit of Israeli–Palestinian Peace: A Retrospective', in Rothstein, R.L., Ma'oz, M. & Shikaki, K. eds (2002), *The Israeli–Palestinian Peace Process: Oslo and the Lessons of Failure* (Brighton: Sussex Academic Press)

——— (2008), *The Much Too Promised Land* (New York: Bantam Books)

Milshtein, M., 'The Memory that Never Dies: The Nakba Memory and the Palestinian National Movement' in Litvak, M. ed. (2009), *Palestinian Collective Memory and National Identity* (New York: Palgrave Macmillan)

———, 'Memory "from Below": Palestinian Society and the Nakba Memory' in Litvak, M. ed. (2009), *Palestinian Collective Memory and National Identity* (New York: Palgrave Macmillan)

Morris, B., 'Camp David and After: An Exchange (1. An Interview with Ehud Barak)', *New York Review of Books*, Vol. 49, No. 10, 13 June 2002

——— (2004), *The Birth of the Palestinian Refugee Problem Revisited* (Cambridge: Cambridge University Press)

——— Malley, R. and Agha, H., 'Camp David and After – Continued', New *York Review of Books*, Vol. 49, No. 11, 27 June 2002

Muslih, M. (1988), The Origins of Palestinian Nationalism (New York: Columbia University Press)

Nasser-Najjab, N., 'Post-Oslo Dialogue: An Evaluation', *Palestine–Israel Journal of Politics, Economics and Culture*, Vol. 12, No. 4 & Vol. 13, No. 1, 2005/2006

Nora, P., 'Between Memory and History: Les Lieux de Memoire', *Representations*, Vol. 26, Spring, 1989

Nuder, P. (2008), *Stolt men inte nöjd* [*Proud but not satisfied*, Swedish] (Stockholm: Norstedts)

Östberg, K. (2008), *I Takt Med Tiden: Olof Palme 1927–1969* [*In Time with Time*, Swedish] (Stockholm: Leopard)

——— (2009), *När Vinden Vände: Olof Palme 1969–1986* [*When the Wind Changed*, Swedish] (Stockholm: Leopard)

Oz, A. (2006), *How to Cure a Fanatic* (Princeton: Princeton University Press)

Palme, O. (1968), *Politik Är Att Vilja* [*Politics Is To Aspire*, Swedish] (Stockholm: Prisma)

Palme, S. (1993), *Tyst Diplomati* [*Quiet Diplomacy*, Swedish] (Stockholm: Norstedts)

Pappé, I., 'Post-Zionist Critique on Israel and the Palestinians', parts 1–3, *Journal of Palestine Studies*, Vol. 26, No. 2; Vol. 26, No. 3; Vol. 26, No. 4, 1997

———, 'Fear, Victimhood, Self, and Other', *The MIT Electronic Journal of Middle East Studies*, Vol. 1, 2001

———, 'The Square Circle: The Struggle for Survival of Traditional Zionism' in Nimni, E. ed. (2003), *The Challenge of Post-Zionism: Alternatives to Israeli Fundamentalist Politics* (London: Zed Books)

———, 'The Bridging Narrative Concept' in Rotberg, R.I. ed. (2006), *Israeli and Palestinian Narratives of Conflict: History's Double Helix* (Bloomington, Indiana: Indiana University Press)

Peled, Y., 'Inter-Jewish Challenges to Israeli Identity', *Palestine–Israel Journal of Politics, Economics, and Culture*, Vol. 8, No. 4, 2001 and Vol. 9, No. 1, 2002

Peri, Y. ed. (2000), *The Assassination of Yitzhak Rabin* (Stanford, California: Stanford University Press)

Persson, G. (2007), *Min Väg, Mina Val* [*My Path, My Choices*, Swedish] (Stockholm: Bonniers)

Persson, S. (1979), *Mediation & Assassination: Count Bernadotte's Mission to Palestine 1948* (London: Ithaca Press)

Peterson, T.G. (2002), *Olof Palme som jag minns honom* [*Olof Palme as I remember him*, Swedish] (Stockholm: Bonniers)

Pinsker, L. (1975), *Road to Freedom: Writings and addresses* (Westport, Connecticut: Greenwood Press)

Porath, Y. (1974), *The Emergence of the Palestinian Arab National Movement, Vol. I 1918–1929* (London: Frank Cass)

——— (1977), *The Palestinian Arab National Movement: From Riots to Rebellion, Vol. II 1929–1939* (London: Frank Cass)

Pressman, J., 'Visions in Collision: What Happened at Camp David and Taba?', *International Security*, Vol. 28, No. 2, Autumn 2003

Princen, T. (1992), *Intermediaries in International Conflict* (Princeton, N.J.: Princeton Uni. Press)

Pruitt, D., 'Ripeness Theory and the Oslo Talks', *International Negotiation*, No. 2, 1997, pp. 237–50

Pundak, R., 'From Oslo to Taba: What Went Wrong?', *Survival*, Vol. 43, No. 3, Autumn 2001

———, 'Looking Back: An Evaluation of People-to-People', *Palestine–Israel Journal of Politics, Economics and Culture*, Vol. 12, No. 4 & Vol. 13, No. 1, 2005/2006

Quandt, W.B. (2001), *Peace Process: American Diplomacy and the Arab-Israeli Conflict since 1967* (Washington D.C. & Berkeley: Brookings Institution Press & University of California Press)

Quigley, J.B. (2005), *The Case for Palestine: An International Law Perspective* (Durham, North Carolina: Duke University Press)

Qurie, A. (2006), *From Oslo to Jerusalem: The Palestinian Story of the Secret Negotiations* (London: I.B.Tauris)

——— (2008), Beyond *Oslo, the Struggle For Palestine: Inside the Middle East Peace Process from Rabin's Death to Camp David* (London: I.B.Tauris)

Rabie, M. (1995), *U.S.–PLO Dialogue: Secret Diplomacy and Conflict Resolution* (Gainesville: University Press of Florida)

Rabinovitch, I. (1999), *Waging Peace: Israel and the Arabs at the End of the Century* (New York: Farrar, Straus and Giroux)

Ross, D. (2004), *The Missing Peace* (New York: Farrar, Straus and Giroux)

Rotberg, R.I. ed. (2006), *Israeli and Palestinian Narratives of Conflict: History's Double Helix* (Bloomington, Indiana: Indiana University Press)

Rothstein, R.L., 'Fragile Peace and Its Aftermath', in Rothstein, R.L. ed. (1999), *After the Peace: Resistance and Reconciliation* (Boulder, CO: Lynne Rienner Publishers)

———, 'A Fragile Peace: Are There Only Lessons of Failure?' in Rothstein, R.L., Ma'oz, M. & Shikaki, K. eds (2002), *The Israeli–Palestinian Peace Process: Oslo and the Lessons of Failure* (Brighton: Sussex Academic Press)

———, 'Breaking the Genetic Code of Conflict: Or, Why Oslo Failed' in Podeh, E. & Kaufman, A. eds (2006), *Arab–Jewish Relations: From Conflict to Resolution?* (Brighton: Sussex Academic Press)

Rouhana, N., 'Zionism's Encounter with the Palestinians: The Dynamics of Force, Fear, and Extremism' in Rotberg, R.I. ed. (2006), *Israeli and Palestinian Narratives of Conflict: History's Double Helix* (Bloomington, Indiana: Indiana University Press)

Rynhold, J., 'Cultural Shift & Foreign Policy Change: Israel and the Making of the Oslo Accords', *Cooperation and Conflict*, Vol. 42, No. 4, 2007

———, 'Realism, Liberalism, and the Collapse of the Oslo Process: Inherently Flawed or Flawed Implementation?', in Ben-Porat, G. ed. (2008), *The Failure of the Middle East Peace Process?: A Comparative Analysis of Peace Implementation in Israel/Palestine, Northern Ireland, and South Africa* (Basingstoke: Palgrave Macmillan)

Said, E.W. (1994), *The Politics of Dispossession: The Struggle for Palestinian Self-Determination, 1969–1994* (London: Chatto & Windus)

———, *The End of the Peace Process: Oslo and After* (New York: Vintage Books)

Saunders, H.H., 'Pre-negotiation and Circum-negotiation: Arenas of Multi-level Peace Processes' in Crocker, C., Hampson, F.O., & Aall, P. eds (2001), *Turbulent Peace: The Challenges of Managing International Conflict* (Washington D.C.: USIP Press)

Savir, U. (1998), *The Process: 1100 days that changed the Middle East* (New York: Random House)

Sayigh, R. (1979), *Palestinians: From Peasants to Revolutionaries* (London: Zed Books)

Sayigh, Y. (1997), *Armed Struggle and the Search for State: the Palestinian National Movement, 1949–1993* (Oxford: Oxford University Press)

———, 'Armed Struggle and State Formation', *Journal of Palestine Studies*, Vol. 26, No. 4, 1997

———, 'Arafat and the Anatomy of a Revolt', *Survival*, Vol. 43, Autumn 2001

Schori, P., 'Israel 60 år och Mellanösterns framtid' in Bjereld, U. & Carmesund, U. eds. (2008), *Israel och Palestina: 60 år i våra röda hjärtan* [*Israel and Palestine: 60 years in our red hearts*, Swedish] (Stockholm: Hjalmarson & Högberg)

Schulz, H. (1999), *The Reconstruction of Palestinian Nationalism: Between Revolution and Statehood* (Manchester: Manchester University Press)

Schwartz, B., Zerubavel, Y., and Barnett, B., 'The Recovery of Masada: A Study in Collective Memory', *Sociological Quarterly*, Vol. 27, No. 2, 1986

Segev, T. (2001), *One Palestine, Complete: Jews and Arabs Under the British Mandate* (New York: Owl Books, Henry Holt & Co.)

——— (2007), *1967: Israel, the War, and the Year That Transformed the Middle East* (London: Little, Brown)

———, 'Eichmann united the Jewish people', *Haaretz*, 4 February, 2010. http://www.haaretz.com/print-edition/news/eichmann-united-the-jewish-people-1.262725

Sela, A., 'Politics, Identity and Peacemaking: The Arab Discourse on Peace with Israel in the 1990s', Israel Studies, Vol. 10, No. 2, Summer 2005

Shamir, Y. (1994), *Summing Up: An Autobiography* (London: Weidenfeld and Nicolson)

Sher, G. (2006), *The Israeli–Palestinian Peace Negotiations, 1999–2001: Within Reach* (London: Routledge)

Shikaki, K., 'The Internal Consequences of Unstable Peace: Psychological and Political Responses of the Palestinians', in Rothstein, R.L. ed. (1999), *After the Peace: Resistance and Reconciliation* (Boulder, CO: Lynne Rienner Publishers)

———, 'Ending the Conflict: Can the Parties Afford It?' in Rothstein, R.L., Ma'oz, M. & Shikaki, K. eds (2002), *The Israeli–Palestinian Peace Process: Oslo and the Lessons of Failure* (Brighton: Sussex Academic Press)

Shindler, C. (1995), *Israel, Likud and the Zionist Dream: Power, Politics and Ideology from Begin to Netanyahu* (London: I.B.Tauris)

——— (2006), *The Triumph of Military Zionism: Nationalism and the Origins of the Israeli Right* (London: I.B.Tauris)

——— (2008), *A History of Modern Israel* (Cambridge: Cambridge University Press)

Shlaim, A. (2001), *The Iron Wall: Israel and the Arab World* (London: Penguin)

Shriver Jr., D.W., 'The Long Road to Reconciliation: Some Moral Stepping-Stones' in Rothstein, R.L. ed. (1999), *After the Peace: Resistance and Reconciliation* (Boulder, CO: Lynne Rienner Publishers)

Smith, A.D. (1999), *Myths and Memories of the Nation* (Oxford: Oxford University Press)
Snyder, J. and Jervis, R., 'Civil War and the Security Dilemma', in Walter, B. & Snyder, J. eds (1999), *Civil Wars, Insecurity and Intervention* (New York: Columbia Uni. Press)
Sontag, D., 'Quest for Middle East Peace: How and Why it Failed', The *New York Times*, 26 July 2001
Sprinzak, E. (1991), The *Ascendance of Israel's Radical Right* (Oxford: Oxford University Press)
———, 'Israel's Radical Right and the Countdown to the Rabin Assassination' in Peri, Y. ed. (2000), *The Assassination of Yitzhak Rabin* (Stanford, California: Stanford University Press)
Stedman, S.J., 'Spoiler Problems in Peace Processes', *International Security*, Vol. 22, No. 2, Fall 1997, pp. 5–53
Stein, J.G., 'Pre-negotiation in the Arab–Israeli Conflict: the Paradoxes of Success and Failure', in Stein, J.G. (1989), *Getting to the Table: The Processes of International Prenegotiation* (Baltimore: Johns Hopkins University Press)
Steinberg, G.M., 'Unripeness and Conflict Management: Re-Examining the Oslo Process and its Lessons', Occasional Paper #4, Bar Ilan University, 18 June 2002. Available at: http://faculty.biu.ac.il/~steing/conflict/Papers/re-examiningoslo.pdf (accessed on 24 July 2006)
———, 'Starting Over After Oslo', *Jerusalem Issue Brief*, Vol. 2, No. 6, 22 August 2002. Available at: http://faculty.biu.ac.il/~steing/election%20PDFs/startingoverafteroslo.pdf
Svenning, O. (2005), *Göran Persson och hans värld* [*Göran Persson and his world*, Swedish], (Stockholm: Norstedts)
Svensson, E., 'Fact Finding-resor i österled' in Bjereld, U. & Carmesund, U. eds (2008), *Israel och Palestina: 60 år i våra röda hjärtan* [*Israel and Palestine: 60 years in our red hearts*, Swedish] (Stockholm: Hjalmarson & Högberg)
Sway, Mustafa Abu, 'Islamic Perspectives on the Oslo Process' in Rothstein, R.L., Ma'oz, M., & Shikaki, K. eds (2002), *The Israeli–Palestinian Peace Process: Oslo and the Lessons of Failure* (Brighton: Sussex Academic Press)
Swisher, C.E. (2004), *The Truth About Camp David* (New York: Nation Books)
Tamarin, G.R., 'The Influence of Ethnic and Religious Prejudice on Moral Judgement' in Tamarin, G.R. ed. (1973), *The Israeli Dilemma: Essays on a Welfare State* (Rotterdam: Rotterdam University Press)
Tossavainen, M. (2006), *Heroes and victims: the Holocaust in Israeli historical consciousness* (Lund: Lund University Press)
Touval, S. (1982), *The Peace Brokers: Mediators in the Arab-Israeli Conflict, 1948–1979* (Princeton, NJ: Princeton University Press)
——— and Zartman, I.W. eds (1985), *International Mediation in Theory and Practice* (Boulder, Colorado: Westview Press)
Viklund, D. (1989), *Neutralitetsdebatten: Tro, Vetande och Illusioner* [*The Neutrality Debate: Belief, Knowledge and Illusions*, Swedish] (Stockholm: Norstedts)
Waage, H.H., 'How Norway Became One of Israel's Best Friends', *Journal of Peace Research*, Vol. 37, No. 2, 2000
———, 'Explaining the Oslo Back-channel: Norway's Political Past in the Middle East', Middle East Journal Vol. 56, No. 4, 2002

——— (2004), *Peacemaking Is a Risky Business: Norway's Role in the Peace Process in the Middle East, 1993–96*, PRIO Report 1/2004 (Oslo: International Peace Research Institute)

———, 'Norway's Role in the Middle East Peace Talks: Between a Strong State and a Weak Belligerent', *Journal of Palestine Studies*, Vol. 34, No. 4, 2005

———, 'Postscript to Oslo: the Missing Files', Journal *of Palestine Studies*, Vol. 38, No. 1, 2008

Wallensteen, P., 'An Experiment in Academic Diplomacy', in Johansen, J. & Jones, J.Y. eds (2011), *Experiments with Peace: Celebrating Peace on Johan Galtung's 80th Birthday* (Cape Town: Pambazuka Press)

Webman, E., 'The Evolution of a Founding Myth: The Nakba and Its Fluctuating Meaning', in Litvak, M. ed. (2009), *Palestinian Collective Memory and National Identity* (New York: Palgrave Macmillan)

Wendt, A., 'Anarchy is what states make of it: the social construction of power politics', *International Organization*, Vol. 46, No. 2, Spring 1992

Wetherell, D., 'The Use and Misuse of Religious Language: Zionism and the Palestinians', *Holy Land Studies*, Vol. 4, No. 1, 2005

Wiel-Berggren, N., 'En glädjens dag för Per Ahlmark och alla Israelvänner' ['A happy day for Per Ahlmark and all friends of Israel', Swedish], 1999. Available at: http://www.menorah-sweden.com/artiklar/politik.99-nr4s12.html (accessed on 15 July 2006)

Wilkenfeld, J., Young, K., Asal, V., & Quinn, D., 'Mediating International Crises: Cross-national and experimental perspectives', Journal of Conflict Resolution, Vol. 47, No. 3, June 2003, pp. 279–301

Wilkinson, H., 'The Israeli Government's Counter-Terrorism Policy of Assassination During the al-Aqsa Intifada of 2000 to 2005', Unpublished Dissertation, King's College London, 2006

Wistrich, R.S., 'Anti-Zionism and Antisemitism: The Case of Bruno Kreisky', ACTA Paper no. 30, The Vidal Sassoon International Center for the Study of Antisemitism, December 2007

Yegar, M. (1993), *Neutral Policy – Theory vs. Practice: Swedish–Israeli Relations* (Jerusalem: Israel Council on Foreign Relations)

Young, O. (1967), *The Intermediaries: Third Parties in International Crises* (Princeton, New Jersey: Princeton University Press)

Zartman, I.W., 'Explaining Oslo', *International Negotiation*, No. 2, 1997, pp. 195–215

Zayyad, Ziad Abu, 'The Middle East Peace Process – Where to Next?' in Rothstein, R.L., Ma'oz, M. & Shikaki, K. eds (2002), *The Israeli–Palestinian Peace Process: Oslo and the Lessons of Failure* (Brighton: Sussex Academic Press)

Ze'evi, D., 'Clans and Militias in Palestinian Politics', Middle East Brief, Crown Centre for Middle East Studies, Brandeis University, No. 26, February 2008. Available at: http://www.brandeis.edu/crown/publications/meb/MEB26a.pdf

Zertal, I. (2005), *Israel's Holocaust and the Politics of Nationhood* (Cambridge: Cambridge University Press)

Zertal, I. and Eldar, A. (2007), *Lords of the Land: the war over Israel's settlements in the occupied territories, 1967–2007* (New York: Nation Books)

Zerubavel, Y., 'The Politics of Interpretation: Tel Hai in Israel's Collective Memory', *AJS Review*, Vol. 16, No. 1/2, 1991

——— (1995), *Recovered Roots: Collective Memory and the Making of Israeli National Tradition* (Chicago, Illinois: University of Chicago Press)

———, 'The Historic, the Legendary, and the Incredible: Invented Tradition and Collective Memory in Israel', in Gillis, J.R. ed. (1996), *Commemorations: The Politics of National Identity* (Princeton, N.J.: Princeton University Press)

———, 'Patriotic Sacrifice and the Burden of Memory in Israeli Secular National Hebrew Culture' in Makdisi, U. & Silverstein, P. eds (2006), *Memory and Violence in the Middle East and North Africa* (Bloomington, Indiana: Indiana University Press)

Zunes, S., 'The United States and the Breakdown of the Israeli–Palestinian Peace Process', *Middle East Policy*, Vol. 8, No. 4, 2001

INDEX

www.ingramcontent.com/pod-product-compliance
Ingram Content Group UK Ltd.
Pitfield, Milton Keynes, MK11 3LW, UK
UKHW020205290926
15470UKWH00001B/18

9 781784 532291